The Chinese Kitchen

Deh-Ta Hsiung

Deh-ta Hsiung was born in Beijing and travelled widely throughout China as a teenager. Coming from a family of gourmets and scholars, his interest in food and wine was encouraged as part of his traditional Chinese upbringing.

Deh-ta came to England in 1950 to complete his education at Oxford and in London, where he now lives. He is an acknowledged expert on Chinese food and cookery and besides being the author of several best-selling books and a food and wine consultant for Chinese restaurants and food manufacturers, he is also a tutor of international renown. He was a regular teacher at the late Ken Lo's Chinese Cookery School in London, and has taught at the Ballymaloe Cookery School in Co. Cork, Ireland on several occasions, as well as in France, Italy, Finland and as far afield as India, where he was sent by the UN.

Several of Deh-ta's books have been translated into all the major European languages, and the German edition of *The Chinese Kitchen* was awarded a silver medal by the Gastronomische Akademie Deutschlands in 2001.

The Chinese Kitchen

Deh-Ta Hsiung

with a foreword by Ken Hom

Kyle Cathie Limited

In loving memory of THELMA LAMBERT HSIUNG 1937–1994
sometimes my severe critic
sometimes my enthusiastic collaborator
and my devoted wife of 35 years

This edition printed in 2008 for
Bookmart Ltd
Blaby Road
Wigston
Leicester LE18 4SE

First published in Great Britain 1999 by
Kyle Cathie Limited
122 Arlington Road
London NW1 7HP
general.enquiries@kyle-cathie.com

First published in paperback 2001

This revised edition published 2006

10 9 8 7 6 5 4 3 2

ISBN (13-digit) 978 1 85626 895 0

For additional photographic acknowledgements see page 240

Title page photograph of rice paddy by Chris Caldicott (Royal Geographical Society)

Edited by Sophie Bessemer and Kate Oldfield
Copy-edited by Robina Pelham-Burn
Home economy by Kathy Man
Chinese calligraphy by Xing Liü
Designed by Geoff Hayes
Production by Lorraine Baird

Deh-Ta Hsiung is hereby identified as the author of this work in accordance with Section 77 of the Copyright, Designs and Patents Act 1988

A Cataloguing In Publication record for this title is available from the British Library.

Colour separation by Chroma Graphics Pte Ltd, Singapore
Printed in Singapore by Craftprint International, Ltd

Note to Australian and New Zealand readers

Tablespoons: The Australian tablespoon equals 4 teaspoons, whereas the British and New Zealand tablespoon equals 3 teaspoons. This difference is insignificant in the recipes in this book.

Brand names: Not all brands named are available in Australia and New Zealand, but similar products will be available. Ask at your Asian supermarket.

Spring onions (p 108): Spring onions (green onions) are also known as shallots in some parts of Australia and in New Zealand.

Fish and seafood: Substitute the following:
Fillets: Use any firm, white fish fillets or cutlets.
Whole fish: Suitable fish include snapper, bream, flounder, barramundi, terakihi.
Prawns (p 178): Raw (green) prawns are usually sold fresh, not frozen.
Crabs: Use any salt-water crab.

Growing seasons: Wherever mentioned, these refer to the northern hemisphere; readers will easily be able to substitute southern hemisphere seasons.

Author's acknowledgements

A great number of friends and colleagues gave me unfailing encouragement and advice while I was engaged upon this book, and it is quite impossible to name them all here, but I would just like to record my special gratitude to the following:

Ken Hom for offering to write the glowing foreword; Chef Kam-po But of Ken Lo's Memories of China, London SW1 for advice and test-cooking a number of recipes; Mr Sai-ming Lee of the Green Cottage, London NW3 (my family's favourite local Chinese restaurant) for providing special ingredients (shark's fin, birds' nest, dried scallops and oysters etc); and Mr Wing Yip (the addresses of his stores can be found on page 235) for his generosity in providing materials and utensils used for photography.

I also wish to thank my publisher Kyle Cathie for her unwavering support and encouragement, and my heartfelt thanks to her diligent editors Kate Oldfield and Sophie Bessemer, whose dedication deserves a medal of the highest order.

Publishers' acknowledgements

The publishers wish to thank Wing Yip for generously supplying much of the food and cooking utensils used in the photographs and Liberty, Neal Street East, David Mellor and Thomas Goode for the china and glassware. They would also like to express a particular debt to Xing Liü, whose dedication and skill in the art of calligraphy shine through on almost every page.

CONTENTS

FOREWORD

BY KEN HOM

As more and more people cook with Chinese ingredients and as Chinese flavours have become increasingly popular, much confusion has arisen about what ingredients to buy, how one should look for them, and which brands are the best. Thanks to Deh-Ta Hsiung's encyclopaedic survey of Chinese ingredients and their use in the Chinese kitchen all will now become clear.

Whenever I travel to Chinatowns throughout the world or to Hong Kong, Taiwan or China themselves, whether in markets, restaurants or private homes, I always encounter Chinese cuisine in all of its variety and pungency and in an atmosphere redolent with taste and flavours. Despite regional variations, one senses a unity of style which comes from shared techniques, flavours, ingredients and philosophy which are unique to Chinese cuisine. This style cannot just be ascribed to the emphatic use of ginger, spring onions and garlic, the basic trinity of Chinese seasoning, nor the unique application of soy sauce. The matter is at once more complex and quite straightforward.

Most apparent in the Chinese philosophy of food is an accent on the freshness of ingredients and the balance of tastes. The food markets of China have some of the best fresh produce in the world. They are full of exotic fruits and vegetables – longans, water chestnuts, wild rice shoots, fresh straw mushrooms, fresh bamboo shoots, smoked garlic, sprouts, yellow cucumbers – the range of which is difficult to imagine in the West. To such fresh ingredients the Chinese cook then adds the spices, flavourings and seasonings that are clearly, although not obtrusively, present in every dish. Here too the variety is staggering – sometimes in the best Chinese markets, the number of condiments is impossible to count and there may be dozens of different sorts of chilli bean paste or soy sauce. This masterful combination of freshness and variety produces the endless assortment of dishes I am lucky enough to witness and taste again and again on many visits to every region of China.

The good news, however, is that most ingredients, seasonings and vegetables in one form or another are available in the West and becoming increasingly so with expanding trade and the spread of an international style of cuisine. Many of the ingredients called for in the recipes in this book can now be obtained from ordinary supermarkets, and Chinese grocers and supermarkets worldwide will stock the rest.

Using the ingredients as his starting point, Deh-Ta Hsiung demystifies the Chinese culinary art and its traditions and in the process he brings to us recipes renowned for their accessibility and irresistible deliciousness. Under his skilful instructions and guidance, you will be rewarded in your search for the most authentic Chinese ingredients. You will find helpful advice on what to look for when shopping for these exotic ingredients, how to use them, and how to store them, as well as which particular brands you should look for and why.

Whether you take it with you shopping or savour it at home, this bold and unique cookbook with its great wealth of information and photographs will guide you clearly and simply through the thicket of ingredients readily available in supermarkets and Chinese grocers today. Then, suitably informed, you will be able to achieve the same results as good Chinese cooks everywhere.

It is my hope that with this book you will be tempted to try some of the more complex Chinese recipes. And, with the knowledge of good ingredients, you will understand the flavours and tastes of this fascinating cuisine and enjoy it as much as the Chinese do. I personally look forward to tasting every single delicious recipe, as I know you will. I trust this major culinary work from the masterchef himself will be a proud companion to your Chinese cookery books as well as becoming a standard reference.

Luscious chilli peppers hanging out to dry

INTRODUCTION

At the end of the nineteenth century Rudyard Kipling was famously moved to declare 'East is East, and West is West, and never the twain shall meet'. Today, at the turn of another century, we see the situation quite differently.

Cultural exchanges between China and the outside world have taken place ever since the time of the Roman Empire and for hundreds of years many aspects of Chinese civilisation have been admired in the West and have influenced its cultural development. However, until very recent times, one of China's greatest traditions, its culinary art, has been comparatively unknown. A gulf between Western and Eastern cultures has given rise to certain misunderstandings and confusions about exactly what Chinese food and cooking actually means. My aim in writing this book is to try to bridge this gulf for I believe that, armed with the right materials, everyone can appreciate and re-create the true essence of Chinese food.

The Chinese Kitchen God depicted on a calendar of 1895

In the early days of exchange between the East and the West, the few linguists there were could not be expected to be specialists in all the different fields, least of all in food and cooking. Given the advance and sophisticated development of the Chinese language over many years the vocabulary of the West soon proved to be inadequate. Once a definition had been struck and passed into common usage it very quickly became established as fact, however misconceived its origin may have been.

Take, for instance, the very basic Chinese condiment known in English as 'soy sauce'. I am afraid that this is a big misnomer. It must have been a real puzzle for whoever was given the task of translating the Chinese term *jiang* into English, for there is no equivalent in any European language; to confuse the issue yet further, nor is there an equivalent term for 'sauce' in the Chinese language! Thus we have a series of misinterpreted terms from soy sauce right through to oyster sauce, shrimp sauce, mushroom sauce and so on.

In fact the history of *jiang* or soy sauce can be traced back more than two thousand years. For centuries, it was considered one of the seven basic daily necessities for any household – the other six being fuel, rice, oil, salt, vinegar and tea. For the slightly better off the indispensable daily items would also include wine, sugar and spices.

Measuring and selling cooking oil

If you substitute bread for rice on the list, you will see immediately how closely it resembles the contents of the store cupboard in a modern Western kitchen. But you may claim that you don't always have a bottle of soy sauce at home – at any rate, you do not look upon it as an indispensable item. To this, I would suggest that, if you substitute tomato ketchup, Worcestershire Sauce or brown sauce, all of which have an oriental origin, then you do use *jiang* as one of your daily necessities.

The translation of cooking techniques is another linguistic minefield. Already the English language has to borrow foreign terms from the French, such as 'sauté' and 'blanche', to describe various cooking methods. Now when confronted with the unique Chinese cooking method *chao*, generally rendered as 'stir-fry', most cookery books give only the basic technique without going into the finer points. However there are at least half a dozen different methods of stir-frying in China, each requiring a particular process of preparation and par-cooking beforehand, and the same is true for deep-frying, shallow-frying, braising and steaming.

All these potential pitfalls, linguistic and otherwise, are easy to overcome as you will quickly discover. So, before progressing to the essential ingredients and recipes within the book, I urge you to take a moment to familiarize yourself with some of the principles of Chinese cooking.

The Chinese Meal

What distinguishes Chinese cooking from other food cultures lies not only in the preparation and cooking, but also in the serving and eating of the food. A Chinese meal does not follow the conventional Western sequence of soup, fish, meat, dessert and cheese course. An everyday Chinese meal, whether served at home or in a restaurant, is like a buffet, with all the dishes (including soup) placed in the centre of the table together. Everyone just helps themselves to whatever they like, not from every dish on the table, but from one or two dishes at a time and each person will be given a bowl of rice to accompany these dishes. Only on a formal occasion are the dishes served course by course, but even then they will appear in groups rather singly, and, with the exception of the soup course, never is an individual dish served to one person.

The serving sequence for a formal dinner or banquet will run something like this:

Assorted cold starters
4–6 hot starters
Soup
4–6 main dishes
Rice or noodles
Desserts (both sweet and savoury)

Thin-skinned oranges

The reason for serving Chinese food this way is the Chinese division between *fan*, grains and other starch foods known as staples, and *cai*, cooked meat and vegetable dishes. Grains in the various forms of rice or wheaten flour (bread, pancakes, noodles or dumplings), make up the *fan* part of the meal; vegetables and meats, cut up and mixed in various combinations into individual dishes constitute the *cai* part. It is in the successful combining of various ingredients and the blending of different flavours for the preparation of the *cai* that the fine art and skill of Chinese cookery, its haute cuisine, lie.

While an everyday meal must be equally balanced between *fan* and simply prepared *cai* dishes, for a formal banquet the emphasis is shifted very much on to the *cai* dishes which are mostly lavish and elaborate. The rice at a formal banquet is only served at the end of the meal as a token offering, for by then, everyone is too full to want any starchy food.

To achieve the perfect balance in a Chinese meal requires the harmonious blending of four elements – colour, aroma, flavour and shape, – a principle which applies to the making of each individual dish as much as to the meal as a whole.

Colour Each ingredient has its own natural colour and certain items change their colour after cooking. The cook should bear this in mind when selecting the ingredients – is the dish to have contrasting or complementary colours? And what are the colours of other dishes that are being served at the same time?

Aroma Every ingredient has its own aroma or fragrance, some sharp, some subtle. Most meats and fish have a rather strong smell and require an agent to suppress it, and enhance the cooked aroma. The Chinese use rice wine for this purpose and seasonings such as spring onions, ginger and garlic.

Flavour Flavour is closely related to aroma and colour – the different ingredients must not be mixed indiscriminately; the matching of flavours should be controlled rather than casual. Some cooks like to mix contrasting flavours and unrelated textures, others prefer to match similar flavours and colours. Some wish the flavour of each ingredient to be preserved, others believe in the fusion of flavours. This blending of different flavours is the central principle of harmony.

Shape The shape of an ingredient and how it is cut is crucial in achieving the proper effect. Slices are matched with slices, shreds with shreds, cubes with cubes, chunks with chunks and so on. This is not just for the sake of appearance, which is an important element of Chinese cooking, but also because ingredients of the same size and shape require about the same amount of time in cooking.

There is also a fifth element to take into consideration when creating your meal:

Texture A dish may have just one, or several contrasting textures such as tenderness, crispness, crunchiness, smoothness, and softness. The textures to be avoided are sogginess, stringiness and hardness. To achieve the right texture it is essential to observe the rules of heat and timing, what the Chinese refer to as *huohou*. You may have the right ingredients and seasonings, have prepared the food correctly and may even be using a proper wok, but unless you can master the degree of heat and the duration of the cooking needed, you will, I'm afraid, fail miserably each time! Most Chinese ingredients are cut into small pieces before cooking and require only a very short cooking time, thus retaining their natural flavours, texture and of course nutritional value. If the degree of heat is not hot enough the food will need to be cooked for longer, so instead of a dish of shiny, crisp and delicate food, you will end up with a dull-looking soggy mess with little texture to speak of.

The Chinese Philosophy of Food – Achieving the Right Balance

One of the long-standing Chinese beliefs about food is the close relationship it has with the state of one's health. The Taoist school of philosophy (which has run side by side with Confucianism for many years) developed an entire nutritional science of food, which was based on familiar yin-yang principles.

This Taoist approach classifies all foods into those that possess the 'yin', meaning cool quality, and those that possess the 'yang', or hot quality. When the yin-yang forces in the body are not balanced, illness results. To combat this disorder, it is necessary to eat the foods that will redress the balance. This belief was documented in the third century BC at the inception of herbal medicine and the links between nutrition and health, and it is still a dominant concept in Chinese culture today.

The yin-yang principle can also be seen in the basic dualism of nature: yin is feminine, dark, cool and passive; yang in contrast is masculine, bright, hot and active. But unlike the dualism of the Western world in which good and evil are in perpetual conflict, yin and yang complement each other and form a harmonious pair, as symbolized by the interlocking figures within a perfect circle.

Over the years, as the yin-yang concept developed along dualistic lines, it was combined with the 'five elements' concept of the Naturalism school of thought which held that all nature is made up in varying combinations of five elements or powers of nature: metal, wood, water, fire and earth. (The parallel to the four elements of the ancient Greeks: earth, fire, air and water is striking.)

The number five has always played an important part in Chinese food culture. The

Yin-yang symbol on a wall in the Forbidden City

earliest book on medicine, *Neijing* (Internal Channels), written over two thousand years ago proposed that the body needed 'five flavours' to live: five grains for nourishment, five fruits for support, five animals for benefit, and five vegetables for energy.

This idea is perpetuated not just in the famous Chinese five-spice powder , but also in the traditional flavours seen as fundamental to Chinese cooking: sweet, sour, bitter, hot and salty. Originally, the flavouring agents were all natural products such as honey, fruit jam, unripe fruit, nuts, herbs, chillies, peppers, and salt. Later, processed seasonings such as sugar, vinegar and that unique *jiang* (soy) were produced and then the Chinese created two additional flavours: *xiang* which translates as 'fragrant' or 'aromatic', a taste associated with wine, garlic, spring onions, sesame seeds, Sichuan pepper and other such spices; and *xian* which broadly means 'delicious' or 'savoury', a flavour originally produced by a good chicken and meat stock, and later by items such as oyster sauce, mushroom sauce, shrimp sauce and monosodium glutamate. Not content with such a tapestry of flavours, the Chinese went on to create several 'new' flavours – of which the most famous example is probably sweet and sour; others include combinations such as hot and sour or aromatic and hot.

Whether amateur or professional, every cook works to the yin-yang principle – a dish must have a harmonious balance and/or contrast of colours, aromas, flavours and textures. So we find one of the best manifestations of the yin-yang principle in Chinese cooking in the way we blend seasonings in complementary pairs: salt (yin) with pepper (yang); sugar (yin) with vinegar (yang); spring onion (yin) with ginger (yang); soy (yin) with wine (yang) and so on. No rules can be set for the exact yin-yang combination, since it is all done by subtle intuition and a feel for the whole process – an experienced cook knows by instinct what does and does not go together to achieve a balance.

Stir-frying in a giant built-in wok

Wheat terraces of northern China

Chinese Regional Cooking

For a country so vast, it is surprising how little the various cooking styles of China differ. Despite the diversity of their climates and natural resources, from the Peking cuisine in the North to the Cantonese cooking of the South, the food is still prepared and served according to the basic *fan-cai* principles. However a keen observer will notice that there are subtle regional differences. While the Southerners eat rice as their staple, in the North this part of the meal is usually provided by wheaten flour products such as pancakes and wheat noodles. The preferred seasonings also differ – the northerners tend to use a lot of vinegar in their cooking, easterners use more sugar, westerners like chillies and peppers and southern food is supposed to have a greater amount of the 'delicious' flavouring known as *xian* which is one of the reasons why Cantonese cooking is held in such high regard throughout China.

There are also of course various regional specialities – both in cooked dishes and in processed foods – as well as a range of special condiments, all of which I have explained throughout the book. With modern methods of transportation and refrigeration, as well as a constant exchange of ideas (and cooks) between different regions, the dishes and special products need no longer be confined to their place of origin. To take just one example, the famous dish of Peking Duck can be eaten as easily in Shanghai as in Hong Kong, or even further afield still in London or New York. For the essence of Chinese food is not so much what you cook, but how it is prepared and cooked. Wherever he or she may be abroad, the Chinese cook can be relied upon to produce a good and delicious meal using only the ingredients available locally.

Techniques Involved in Chinese Cooking

It is common knowledge that in Chinese cooking, 85–90 percent of the time is spent in preparation; the actual cooking time is very quick, usually no more than a few minutes, or even seconds in the case of stir-frying. Of course, there are dishes that require longer cooking time, but these are rather rare.

The Chinese cooking process involves the following: selection of ingredients, preliminary preparation, cutting, marinating or coating, cooking, seasoning, presentation and serving.

Selection of ingredients This is possibly the single most important factor for, if an ingredient is of poor quality, then even a master chef could not make it into a palatable dish. This point was stressed in an eighteenth-century cookery book written by Yuan Mei, one of China's foremost scholar-gourmets. A professed hedonist, Yuan Mei wrote that the fundamental concept was to understand the natural properties or qualities of a food. The search for ideal ingredients meant that the credit for any fine meal must be shared between the cook (6 points out of 10), and the purveyor (4 points).

Cabbages being unloaded for the market

Preliminary preparation This process affects the colour, aroma, flavour and nutritional value of the final results. Fresh ingredients need to be cleaned, and dried items have to be soaked and rinsed. Always wash vegetables before cutting them up, so they don't lose so many vitamins in the water. Other tasks include trimming off excess fat from meat, cleaning or skinning fish, peeling and de-veining prawns and rinsing certain canned ingredients in fresh water.

Cutting Ensuring that the raw ingredients are cut into the correct sizes, thickness and shapes is important in Chinese cooking. First of all, the size and shape of the cut ingredient must be suitable for the particular method of cooking. For instance, ingredients for quick stir-frying should be small thin slices or shreds, not large thick chunks. Secondly, it is necessary to understand the character of the ingredients, their likely change in texture and colour when cooked. Tender ingredients can be cut thicker than tougher ones that require longer cooking time. Finally, do not mix different shapes and sizes in the same dish, but do vary them in different dishes for a meal. Most ingredients are either sliced, shredded or cubed to different sizes as necessary. They can also be coarsely chopped or even finely minced.

In addition it may be necessary to use the techniques of flower-cutting when cutting squid and kidney and vegetable carving for decorative garnishes. Sometimes, of course, a more rigorous method is called for, namely that of chopping through the bone of a whole chicken or duck after it is cooked. Greater details for all these methods are given in the recipes.

A very effective traditional way of transporting tomatoes

Marinating and coating Most vegetables are ready for cooking after cutting, but items such as fish, poultry and meat are usually marinated with sugar, soy, rice wine, and cornflour, or coated with egg white and cornflour paste, or dipped in an egg-and-flour batter, before being cooked. Marinating helps to intensify the flavour of the ingredients, and tenderize the meat at the same time. Coating delicate items such as fish, prawns and white meats helps to preserve their colour and texture during cooking.

Cooking There are more than 50 different cooking methods in China, but they can be divided into four main categories: water-cooking (boiling, poaching, blanching, and stewing), oil-cooking (frying and braising), steam-cooking, and fire-cooking (roasting and barbecuing). A single dish may require one, or two or even more cooking methods and each will produce a different result. All the different cooking methods will be explained in detail for each recipe – just remember that for whichever method is used, the degree of heat and the cooking time are crucial, particularly for stir-frying, quick-braising and steaming.

Seasoning The principle of seasoning is to enhance the natural flavour of the ingredients, not to overpower it. The Chinese term for cooking is *peng-tiao*, which actually means 'to cook and to blend', indicating that cooking and seasoning (blending of flavours) are closely linked to each other. There are three stages at which seasonings are applied: before, during, and after cooking. Seasoning before cooking usually refers to marinating, which is fairly simple and easy to accomplish. Seasoning after cooking is in the form of dips or sauces and is also used for certain cooking methods such as deep-frying, steaming, blanching and poaching, in which the food cannot be seasoned while it is being cooked. However it is in seasoning during cooking that the fine art of Chinese cuisine lies; its application may appear simple, but the precise quantity of each seasoning used and the order and timing for its use have to be exact, especially for stir-fried and quick-braised dishes, when a fraction of a second could make all the difference. For this reason, it is advisable to mix together beforehand any seasonings that are to be added at the same time so that they can be added to the wok at speed.

Presentation As described earlier, the visual appeal of a dish is very important in Chinese cooking. A true gourmet should be able to judge the success of a dish purely by its appearance – if it doesn't look right, then it won't taste right. This is why colour and shape are two of the main characteristics of Chinese cuisine.

The presentation I am talking about has to do with the way the food is cut and cooked, and the receptacles in which it is served. In ancient China, there used to be strict rules for different utensils to be used for different food on different occasions – these rules are no longer in practice, but one should bear in mind that the colour of the dishes or plates should be in shades of pale blue, green, yellow, red or white, never dark brown, purple or black, so that the natural colour of the cooked food can stand out. Also the shape of the serving dish should always be round or oval, never square or rectangular.

The garnish, if there is one, should be simple, such as sprigs of fresh coriander leaves, or chopped or shredded spring onions. Garnishes in the form of decoratively carved vegetables may seem impressive, but sometimes they can be a distraction from the true quality of the food itself. At any rate, they require a special set of carving knives and the skill of a gifted chef, so should only be used for lavish banquets as an exhibition of prowess. There is also a special dish called a *pinpan*, served as an hors d'oeuvre in a restaurant on formal occasions, which consists of assorted cold cuts all beautifully arranged on a large plate or shallow platter. These dishes require long preparation and as a result it is always necessary to place your order well in advance – usually at least 24 hours' notice is required!

Serving A Chinese meal is served absolutely ready to eat – there is no last-minute carving on the table, no dishing out separate items such as vegetables or sauce. At a Chinese table, when everyone is seated, the host will raise his chopsticks and say *'chin-chin'* ('please-please') – and then everyone picks up their chopsticks and tucks in. In very polite society, the host and hostess constantly serve the guests, helping them to more food from the centre of the table, so that the guests do not have to stretch at all to help themselves.

Obviously there is no need for you to serve a Chinese meal in this manner – by all means use a spoon and fork if you prefer. However, I believe most people find it enormously satisfying to be able to use chopsticks for a Chinese meal, because almost all Chinese food is prepared in such a way that it is easily picked up by chopsticks. Since you can only pick up one morsel at a time, eating with chopsticks encourages you to savour the flavour of the food and eat more slowly, which is much better for digestion.

AUTHOR'S NOTES ON THE INGREDIENTS

Within the pages of this book you will find all the essential ingredients needed for Chinese cooking, many of which crop up more than once in the recipes. I have not cross-referenced for each occurrence for lack of space. If an ingredient in a recipe looks unfamiliar, look in the index.

One of the problems researching Chinese ingredients is that so many of them have several different names in China, depending on where they are eaten. Please note that I have not included every one when transliterating – this applies particularly to vegetables and fruits, but the scientific Latin name should be a sufficient identification tool in any case.

For each recipe I have listed the ingredients in the order in which they are used and have given both metric and imperial measurements. Please make sure when preparing and weighing the food that you stick to one measuring system only.

ESSENTIAL EQUIPMENT

Very little special equipment is required for Chinese cooking, since most Western kitchens will have adequate equivalent utensils. Traditional Chinese cooking utensils and equipment are of an ancient design, and are normally made of basic and inexpensive materials. The main items needed are listed below, but the two unique necessities are the wok and the Chinese kitchen knife commonly known as the Chinese cleaver. Unfortunately any Western counterparts to these will prove expensive and ineffective.

Wok
A most versatile cooking pan, the wok can be used not just for stir-frying, but also for shallow-frying, deep-frying, steaming, braising, soup-making, and even smoking. In other words, the whole spectrum of Chinese cooking methods can be executed from one single utensil. There are two basic types of wok on the market, and I would advise you to have one of each, since neither is very expensive. The most common one is the double-handled wok, made of lightweight carbonized steel, often sold as a set with the lid, ladle, spatula, rack and other accessories. This type is ideal for braising, deep-frying and steaming. For stir-frying you need the other type, the single-handled wok. Both versions have either a rounded bottom for a gas cooker, or a slightly flattened base for electric hobs. Do not make the mistake of purchasing a wok made from stainless steel or another material apart from steel or iron. Such woks are no good for cooking since they get damaged easily when used over a high heat.

Note: Before you can use a new wok it must be seasoned. To do this, put the empty pan over a high heat to burn off the coating until it is blackened inside. Then, once the wok has cooled, clean it in soapy hot water with a stiff brush and rinse well. Dry the wok over a moderate heat and coat the entire surface with cooking oil using a soaked pad of kitchen paper – now the wok is ready for use. After each use, clean the wok with hot water, but do not use any detergents, since these will strip away the seasoning with the result that food will stick to the wok. After cleaning, dry the wok well over a moderate heat, and apply a thin coat of oil over the surface before putting it away, this will prevent it getting rusty if it is not used frequently. After you have used the wok several times, it will acquire a beautiful, glossy finish, and it should last you a lifetime. If it does become rusty, don't throw it away, but start by burning off the rust and re-season it as before.

Chinese cleaver
The name is misleading since a cleaver is a hefty stainless steel or carbonized steel blade used primarily for chopping. The Chinese cleaver on the other hand is an all-purpose knife used not just for chopping but also for cutting and slicing.

There are three basic sizes of Chinese cleavers. No. 1 is the heaviest and is mainly used as a chopper; No. 3 is the lightest and is really a slicer; in between these is the dual-purpose No. 2 which is an ideal kitchen knife to have. Its versatility is such that you can use the front, lighter half of the blade for gentle cutting such as slicing, shredding, filleting and scoring; the rear, heavier half of the blade for chopping (with force) through the bone; the back of the blade for pounding; and the flat side of the blade for crushing and transporting cut ingredients into the cooking pan or onto a serving plate.

Single-handled wok with round base

Double-handled wok with flat base

Chinese steamer
The traditional Chinese steamers made of bamboo come in various sizes – the larger one, about 32cm (12in) in diameter, is most useful, as it will take a whole fish or duck for steaming. The smaller ones are for cooking dim sum and for warming pancakes, so they have a limited use at home. The food to be steamed is usually placed in a bowl or plate uncovered, then the dish is placed inside the rack of a steamer, the lid is put on and the steamer is placed inside a wok with plenty of boiling water in it. Thus the cooking is done by intense hot steam under and around the food, and the bamboo steamer imparts a subtle fragrance to the food, something lacking if the food is cooked in a modern aluminium steamer.

Note: A wok can also be used as a steamer on its own – fill the wok about one-third full with water, bring to the boil, place the food in a bowl or dish on a rack or trivet inside the wok and cover the wok with the dome-shaped lid. There you have an improvised steamer!

Chinese casseroles (sand or clay pots)

Bamboo steamers

Chinese casserole (sand or clay pot)
Earthenware – hence the name sand or clay pot – casseroles used as cooking utensils must have preceded metal ones by many thousands of years in China. There are two basic shapes with several sizes: the most common shape is a squat pot with sloping sides, glazed on the inside, with a flared, hollow handle and lid; the other type is also squat but it has two handles and a smoother-textured exterior. In China, clay pots are always used for stove-top cooking, and since they retain an overall even heat they are used for slow cooking such as braising. Most clay pots are rather fragile, and they do crack easily, so make sure the base is dry before you place it on the cooker, and that the inside has some water or stock to start with.

Chinese strainer
Two types are used in the Chinese kitchen: one is made of copper or steel wire with a long bamboo handle; the other is made of perforated stainless steel. Both are useful for scooping food out of hot oil or liquid, and because of their shape and size a large quantity of food can be scooped out at one go when you need to avoid over-cooking certain ingredients.

Chinese strainer (stainless steel)

Chinese strainers

Chinese ladle

The ladle performs several functions and is indispensable in the professional kitchen. It is really a miniature wok with a long handle and is used not only for stirring, but also for adding ingredients and seasonings to the wok during cooking, and then transferring cooked food from the wok to a serving dish or bowl. You can also use it as a measurer – a standard-sized ladle will hold about 175ml (6 fl oz) liquid, just enough to fill a rice bowl.

Chinese spatula

This should have a rounded end to match the contours of the wok, so it can be used for scraping and lifting food from the bottom of the wok.

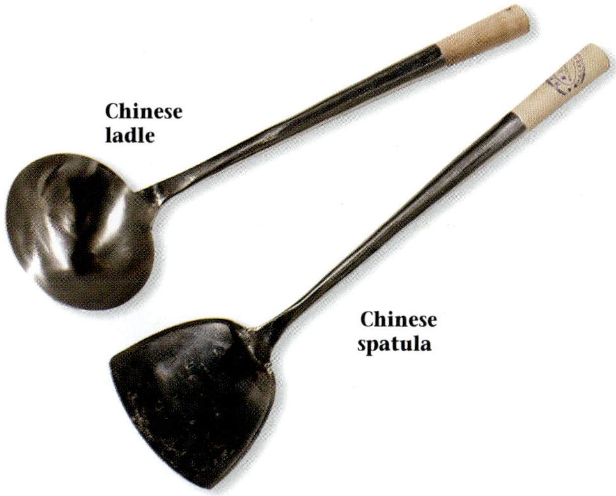

Chinese ladle

Chinese spatula

Chopping block and cooking chopsticks

Cooking chopsticks

A Chinese cook will not generally use a fork in the kitchen – in its place he or she will use chopsticks. Chopsticks can be used for tasks such as mixing, tasting, stirring and even beating. They also make very good tongs.

Chopping block

The traditional Chinese chopping block is a cross-section of a tree trunk, which must be properly maintained to avoid it splitting. It makes an ideal base when cutting meat and poultry through the bone. Of course it is possible to obtain split-free wood blocks as well as plastic ones made of acrylic. But these lack the aesthetic appeal of the traditional tree trunk with its beautiful pattern of grains. To prevent a wood block from splitting, season a new one with a liberal dose of vegetable oil on both side. Let the wood absorb as much oil as it will take, then sponge the block with salt and water and dry thoroughly. Never soak the block in water nor wash it with any detergent. After each use, just scrape it clean with the blade of your knife, then wipe the surface with a sponge or cloth wrung out in plain hot water. Always stand the block on its side when not in use to prevent it from warping.

To serve Chinese food truly authentically you may want to invest in porcelain place settings which should include chopsticks, rice bowl, spoon and plate and a tea set of a standard-sized teapot with cups and saucers.

Chinese place setting

Chinese tea set

FEED FOR

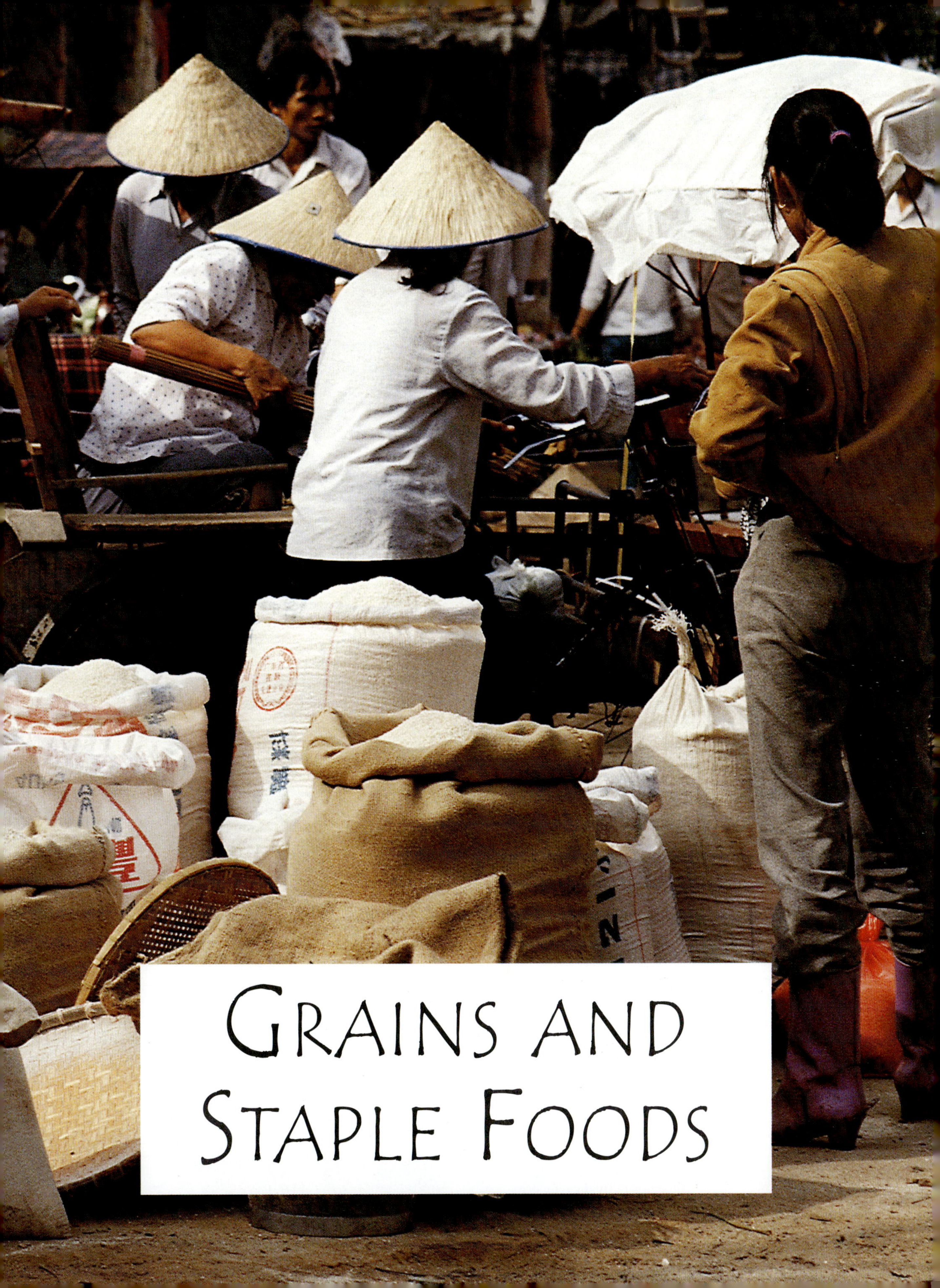

GRAINS AND STAPLE FOODS

米

RICE

(MI) *Oryza sativa*

One cannot imagine Chinese food without rice. In English 'rice' can mean raw or cooked rice, or even the unhusked rice also known as paddy, while in China there is a different word for each of them: unhusked rice is *dao*, husked but uncooked rice is *mi*, and cooked rice then becomes the *fan*.

Rice in Chinese is synonymous with 'meal'. It is so central to everyday Chinese life that when we greet friends we ask them not how they are but 'Have you eaten any *fan* yet?'

Short-grain rice

Long-grain rice

HOW IT GROWS

Rice has been cultivated in China since the Shang dynasty (18th–12th century BC) and there are more than 40,000 different strains of rice grown in China, which fall into the four basic categories listed above. Some types of rice are more suited to being grown on wet land, others prefer dry land. The colder climate of northern China permits only a single crop of rice to be harvested each year (the northern Chinese traditionally eat more wheat and less rice than their southern compatriots), while there are usually two crops (early and late) in the temperate South. The early crops are planted in February/March and harvested in July, the late crops are planted in May/June and harvested in November.

APPEARANCE AND TASTE

There are four main groups of rice: long-grain, short-grain, sticky and glutinous. The most widely grown type is the long-grain rice known in Chinese as *xiandao*, which is similar to Indian patna rice. The short-grain rice known as *jingdao* is not to be confused with the round-grain sticky rice *zhandao*, which in turn is different from glutinous rice (*ruodao*). As oenologists at blind tastings can tell the origin and vintage of a particular wine, I remember a distant relation (a rice broker) who had a legendary reputation for distinguishing different strains of rice. By simply chewing a raw grain, he would be able to say where it had been grown and even estimate the yield of a crop.

BUYING AND STORING

In China, one used to be able to buy rice loose from a rice merchant in a shop

Autumn harvest of the late crops in Guangdong province

which sold nothing except polished rice (with at least half a dozen varieties) ready for cooking. Now the choice is rather limited. Back in the sixties, China used to export rice for foreign consumption, but now, partly because of the growing population, and partly owing to the failed agricultural policy, China has to import rice (and wheat) from abroad. Perhaps the nearest one can get in the West to the distinctive flavour of Chinese-grown rice is Thai fragrant rice, which is widely available from Oriental stores and supermarkets. Keep the rice in an air-tight container, store it in a cool, dry place, and use it within 3–4 months of purchasing.

MEDICINAL AND OTHER USES

Rice is rich in carbohydrate, contains vitamins A and B, some protein and only traces of fat and sugar. It is a more healthy staple food than bread or potatoes. In China, boiled rice gruel, *zhou*, to which many ingredients may be added, is widely used for curing stomach disorders such as diarrhoea and indigestion, and is considered ideal for infants and the elderly, as it is so easily digestible and nutritious. Rice husks are used as animal feed, as is rice straw which also serves as fuel for cooking, and for thatching roofs. Rice flour is used to make rice noodles; other rice by-products include rice wine and rice vinegar.

A farm worker separating the rice husks from the grains

A common sight in all parts of China – an everyday informal meal

CULINARY USES

Rice is served at almost every Chinese meal, but just as you will be hard put to find a recipe for making toast in a Western cookbook, you will not find a recipe for cooking plain rice in a cookbook published in China. Cooking rice is second nature to the Chinese! Boiled and steamed rice are both traditional; boiled rice has a tendency to stick together while steamed rice is firmer in texture and the grains are more separate.

PLAIN RICE

Plainly cooked rice is called white rice. The rice is boiled first, then steamed, either drained of all liquid first then dry-steamed in a steamer, or wet-steamed in the same saucepan until all the liquid has been absorbed. The dry-steaming method produces firm rice with separate grains (and loses starch and nutrients to the liquid) while the wet-steaming method produces a more fluffy rice. The general rule when cooking rice is to use slightly more water than raw grains to produce a firm, fluffy *fan* – the quantity of water decreases proportionally as the quantity of rice increases.

Serves 4
Preparation time 5 minutes
Cooking time 25 minutes

225g (8oz) raw long-grain rice

1 Wash and rinse the rice just once in a saucepan, then add a pinch of salt and enough fresh cold water that when you place your index finger in it with the tip touching the surface of the rice, the water level reaches the first joint of your finger.

2 Cover with a tight-fitting lid and bring to the boil, uncover and stir to loosen the rice sticking to the bottom of the pan. Replace the lid, reduce the heat to very, very low, and leave to cook for 12–15 minutes.

3 The rice will be cooked but not quite ready for serving. Let it stand for 10 minutes off the heat, still covered, and fluff up with a spoon before serving.

Paddy fields in front of the rocky mountains of Guilin

FRESH FISH CONGEE

To make *zhou* (congee) or the universal Chinese breakfast known as *xifan* (thin rice), simmer a small amount of rice in a large quantity of water for at least 30 minutes until it becomes a thick gruel. You can make instant congee by using flaked rice (widely available in supermarkets), thus saving time and fuel. In China, *xifan* is usually served with fermented bean-curd or a relish of pickled vegetables or salted fish. Only on special occasions do we have *zhou* cooked with fresh meat or fish.

Serves 4
Preparation time 10 minutes
Cooking time 35–40 minutes

125g (4oz) long- or short-grain rice, or combination of both
About 1 litre (1¾ pints) chicken stock or water
225g (8oz) firm white fish fillet, skinned
2 tablespoons light soy sauce
1 tablespoon rice wine
2 teaspoons cornflour paste
1 teaspoon finely chopped spring onion
1 tablespoon finely shredded fresh ginger
A few drops sesame oil
Salt and pepper to taste

1 Wash and rinse the rice just once, then place in a saucepan big enough to hold at least 1.5 litres (2½ pints). Add the stock or water and bring to the boil, stir, reduce the heat and simmer gently with the lid mostly covering the pan. Cook for about 30 minutes or until the liquid is reduced by a third and has a smooth, thick consistency.

2 While the *zhou* is cooking, cut the fish fillet into small thin slices or shreds and marinate them with about half of the soy and all the rice wine, cornflour paste, spring onion and ginger.

3 Turn the heat up high, stir in the fish with the remaining soy, blend well and bring back to the boil. Add salt, pepper and sesame oil. Serve hot.

Fresh Fish Congee

糯米 GLUTINOUS RICE

(RUOMI)

While ordinary rice – long- or short-grain – is the daily staple for Chinese people, glutinous rice is regarded as a bit of a luxury in China and is eaten on special occasions. It contains more sugar and fat than ordinary rice, although they are both grown and harvested under the same conditions.

APPEARANCE AND TASTE

The grains of glutinous rice tend to be whiter and rounder than ordinary rice and it tastes much sweeter. It is also a great deal shinier, since it is highly polished.

CULINARY USES

Glutinous rice dishes are usually served as dishes in their own right. The most common way of cooking it is in a form of *zongzi*.

Dragon boat races are held annually to mark Chu Yuan's death in 295 BC

GLUTINOUS RICE WRAPPED IN BAMBOO LEAVES (ZONGZI)

My recipe is for sweet *zongzi*, but they can be made savoury or plain. At the Dragon Boat Festival people eat *zongzi* to commemorate the death of the statesman-poet, Chu Yuan in 295 BC. He drowned himself in protest against government corruption and to draw the fish from eating his corpse, rice and eggs were thrown into the water.

Makes 12
Preparation time about 1 hour, plus 2 hours' soaking time
Cooking time 2 hours

900g (2lb) glutinous rice
1 tablespoon oil
24 dried bamboo leaves
450g (1lb) black or red sweet bean paste
12 strings, each about 1.5m (4½ feet) long
sugar to serve

1 Soak the rice for 2 hours, drain, change water and soak for a further 30 minutes.

2 Drain the rice well, mix in the oil.

3 Soak the bamboo leaves in warm water for 2 hours, rinse in fresh water, then drain and wipe dry.

4 Roll the sweet bean paste into a sausage about 2.5cm (1in) in diameter, cut into 12 sections. Flatten each a little.

5 Place two bamboo leaves side by side, slightly overlapping, and fold the two bottoms over together to form a triangular pouch. Add a portion of the rice and place a section of the bean paste on the rice. Cover with more rice and fold the leaves over the top and round the pouch to produce a plump, triangular-shaped bundle. Tie securely with string, but not too tightly, as the rice will expand during cooking.

6 Simmer the *zongzi* in boiling water for 2 hours.

7 Open the *zongzi* packages at the table and serve hot with more sugar as required. Any leftovers can be reheated unwrapped. *Zongzi* taste even better reheated.

GLUTINOUS RICE CHICKEN

One of my favourite Cantonese specialities – a most aromatic and delicious dish. It is worth taking the extra time to prepare it. Otherwise ask for Lotus Leaf Wrapped Chicken and Rice in a Cantonese restaurant which serves dim sum.

Makes 4 parcels
Preparation time 1 hour
Cooking time 15 minutes

450g (1lb) glutinous rice
1 teaspoon salt
2 tablespoons oil
225g (8oz) chicken, boned and skinned
2 teaspoons light soy
½ teaspoon ginger juice (see Note)
1 tablespoon cornflour paste
125g (4oz) pork fillet
125g (4oz) Char Siu *(cooked)* Pork
or Chinese sausage or ham
125g (4oz) prawns, cooked and peeled
75g (2oz) Chinese dried mushrooms, reconstituted
1 tablespoon rice wine
1 teaspoon sugar
1 tablespoon dark soy
Ground white pepper
4 dried lotus leaves

1 Wash and rinse the rice once, place in a saucepan with about 450ml (16fl oz) water, a pinch of salt and 1 teaspoon oil, bring to the boil and stir. Reduce the heat and cook under a tight-fitting lid for 15–20 minutes. Divide into 8 equal portions.

2 While the rice is cooking, divide the chicken meat into 4 equal portions and marinate with the light soy, ginger juice and about half the cornflour paste for 10–15 minutes. Steam the chicken in a steamer for 5 minutes.

3 Cut the pork fillet, *Cha Siu*, prawns (leave if small), and mushrooms into small pieces.

4 Heat about 1½ tablespoons oil in a pre-heated wok and stir-fry the pork, cha siu, prawns and mushrooms for 1 minute. Add the salt, wine, sugar and a little of the mushroom-soaking water and cook for 2–3 minutes. Add the pepper and thicken the sauce with the remaining cornflour paste. Divide this mixture into 4 equal portions.

5 Soak the lotus leaves in boiling water until soft (about 30 minutes) then rinse in fresh water and shake dry. Spread a leaf on a flat worktop, grease the surface with oil, and place one portion of the cooked rice in the centre. Flatten slightly with your palm. Place one portion of the pork mixture on the rice and a piece of chicken on that. Cover with another portion of rice, again pressing to flatten. Now fold the leaf over its filling to form a neat parcel. Repeat the process until you have made four parcels.

6 Steam in a hot steamer for 15 minutes. Unwrap the hot parcels at the table.

Note: To make ginger juice, mix finely chopped fresh ginger with an equal quantity of water, wrap this pulp in muslin and then twist to extract the juice. Alternatively, crush the ginger in a garlic press. The lotus leaves can be washed and re-used.

米粉 Rice Flour

(MIFEN)

Since rice is the staple food of China, it is not surprising that there should be a multitude of products derived from it. The most popular of these must be rice noodles made from ground rice, commonly known as rice flour. Then there are glutinous and sticky rice flours, normally used for making cakes and other sweet things.

Towers of rice buns for the Festival of the Hungry Ghosts

Sticky rice cakes can be picked up from many road-side stores

Manufacture

Ordinary rice flour is made from low-grade rice, often with a high proportion of millet, which is called *xiaomi* in Chinese, meaning little or minor rice, indicating its inferiority. This reduces the cost considerably. The usual procedure is to wash and soak the grains for anything up to 48 hours, then grind them with water. The resulting paste is poured into fine muslin sacks which are hung up to drain off the liquid. The wet flour is spread out on bamboo mats to dry in the sun before being packaged for market.

Buying and Storing

If stored in a container with a tight-fitting lid, rice flour should keep for several months. The packs in which you buy it should have a 'use by' date stamped on them. You can still use it one or two months after the expiry date, but it will have lost its freshness.

Culinary Uses

Rice flour can be used like other starches: as a thickening agent when mixed with water, or to make a batter for coating food before deep-frying. It can also be used in its dry state to coat food for steaming. A very popular dish in China is *mifen rou* (Steamed Pork with Ground Rice), in which slices of fatty belly pork with the rind on are coated with ground rice and steamed for 3–4 hours until very tender. The steamed pork dish may not appeal to the Western palate because of its fatty nature.

STEAMED BEEF WITH GROUND RICE

This beef dish from Sichuan has proved very popular in my cookery classes, since it is comparatively simple to prepare and cook, and tastes absolutely delicious.

Serves 4
Preparation time 35–40 minutes
Cooking time 15–20 minutes

450g (1lb) beef steak (such as topside rump)
½ teaspoon ground white pepper
2 tablespoons light soy
1 tablespoon chilli bean paste (Toban Jiang)
1 teaspoon ginger juice (p 29)
1 tablespoon rice wine
1 tablespoon vegetable oil
125g (4½oz) ground glutinous rice
225g (8oz) green beans, or any leafy green vegetable
1 teaspoon sesame oil
finely shredded spring onions to garnish

1 Cut the beef steak across the grain to make thin, rectangular slices (about the size of a postage stamp). Marinate with the pepper, soy, chilli bean paste, ginger juice, rice wine and oil for 20–25 minutes.

2 Roast the ground rice in a dry frying pan until fragrant and golden brown, then coat each slice of beef.

3 Line the bottom rack of four small dim sum steamers (or one largish one) with the green vegetable, then arrange the beef slices in neat layers on top.

4 Stack the steamers on top of each other and steam vigorously for 15–20 minutes. Sprinkle with the sesame oil and garnish with the spring onions. Serve hot directly from the steamer, or transfer onto a warmed serving dish. Additional seasonings such as chilli sauce, chilli oil, spicy salt etc may be offered at the table according to individual taste.

米粉

RICE NOODLES

(MIFEN)

The Chinese name for rice noodles is exactly the same as for rice flour: *mifen*. Confusing? Not really – the context tells us which is meant. Rice flour is usually one of many ingredients in a recipe, while rice noodles are the main component of a dish, as in the recipes opposite.

Rice vermicelli

APPEARANCE AND TASTE

There are basically two types of rice noodles: the flat kind about 0.4cm (1/16in) wide, known as rice sticks, and, more common, the very fine strands known as rice vermicelli.

MANUFACTURE

Rice noodles are made from ground rice, not dried rice flour, and the rice used for noodles is usually of a higher grade than that used for flour. The rice grains are washed and soaked before being ground with water into a thin paste, which is drained through a fine sieve into a container. The ground rice settles on the bottom. After some time, the clear liquid is discarded and the thick paste is transferred to a sack to have any residual liquid squeezed out. The semi-dry paste is divided into two; half is made into a dough which is boiled in water for 15 minutes (it need only be half-cooked) before being mixed with the raw half and kneaded into a firm dough. The dough is put through a special press which cuts it into noodles. These are cooked in boiling water for a few seconds only before they are drained, rinsed, cooled in cold water and sold as fresh rice noodles. Dried noodles have been hung up in the sun before being packaged.

BUYING AND STORING

Fresh rice noodles are seldom seen in the West, but dry ones are widely available. The best brand is generally considered to be Kongmoon Rice Vermicelli. Apart from Sha Ho Fun Rice Sticks, most brands of rice sticks are from Thailand and come in several widths – fine, medium, wide and extra wide – of which only the medium ones (about 5mm wide) are suitable for Chinese cooking. Store dried rice noodles in a cool, dry, dark place.

CULINARY USES

While wheat noodles predominate in North China rice noodles are widely used in the South. They will be served in Cantonese teahouses and at road-side takeaway stalls and markets but rarely in restaurants as they are regarded as an everyday home dish.

Fresh rice noodles for sale in a street market

Rice Sticks with Beef in Chilli and Black Bean Sauce

Rice Sticks with Beef in Chilli and Black Bean Sauce

This is one of the most popular rice stick dishes in Cantonese restaurants, where the rice sticks are sometimes called *ho fun*, meaning the noodles are made in a particular district in southern China with river water rather than using well or tap water. (I have it on good authority, however, that almost all Chinese restaurants – at least in Britain – use rice sticks from Thailand!)

Serves 4 as a snack or 2 as a main meal
Preparation time about 15–20 minutes plus marinating time of 2–3 hours or more
Cooking time 10 minutes

1 x 280g (10oz) packet Ho Fun Rice Sticks, or Thai Rice Sticks (5mm)
275–350g (10–12oz) beef steak (such as rump)
1 tablespoon dark soy
2 teaspoons rice wine
½ teaspoon sugar
1 tablespoon cornflour paste
1 small onion
1 small green pepper (capsicum)
About 600ml (1 pint) vegetable oil
1–2 fresh red or green chillies, chopped small
2 tablespoons black bean sauce
2 tablespoons light soy

1 Soak the rice sticks in hot water for 15 minutes, rinse in cold water and drain.

2 Cut the beef thinly across the grain into small postage-stamp size slices. Marinate with the soy, rice wine, sugar and cornflour for at least 2–3 hours.

3 Cut the onion and green pepper (capsicum) into small pieces the size of the beef.

4 Heat the oil in a preheated wok, stir in the beef for about 40–50 seconds, and remove with a strainer as soon as the colour of the meat changes. Drain.

5 Pour off the excess oil, leaving about 2–3 tablespoons in the wok. Add the chillies, onion and green pepper (capsicum) together with the black bean sauce. Stir-fry for about 1 minute, then add the partly-cooked beef. Blend well and stir-fry for another minute. Finally, add the rice sticks with the light soy. Toss and mix for 1–2 minutes, ensuring nothing is stuck to the base of the wok. Serve hot.

Note: This is a basic recipe: the beef and/or vegetables can be varied as you wish.

Fujian Fried Rice Noodles

You will all have eaten, or at least heard of, Singapore Fried Rice Noodles. This world-famous dish was carried to Singapore, and the rest of Southeast Asia, by emigrants from Fujian province.

Serves 4 as a snack, 2 as a main meal
Preparation time 25–30 minutes
Cooking time 10–15 minutes

450g (1lb) rice vermicelli
50g (2oz) dried shrimps, soaked
175g (6oz) lean pork steak
125g (4½oz) celery
125g (4½oz) leeks
3–4 tablespoons oil
2 tablespoons light soy
About 3–4 tablespoons stock or water

1 Soak the vermicelli in boiling water until soft (about 5–8 minutes), rinse in cold water and drain.

2 Drain the shrimps. Thinly shred the pork, celery and leeks.

3 Heat the oil in a preheated wok. Stir-fry the pork with the celery, leeks and shrimps for about 2 minutes, add the stock or water with the vermicelli, blend well and stir until all the liquid has been absorbed.

4 Blend in the soy and serve the dish hot.

面粉

WHEATEN FLOUR

(MIANFEN)

One of the 'five grains' in ancient China, wheat has been cultivated in North China since Neolithic times and today only rice is more widely grown. About one-fifth of China's arable land is devoted to wheat, mainly north of the Huai River.

MANUFACTURE

Like rice, wheat must be hulled before it is edible by man. In ancient times the Chinese would have hulled wheat by pounding it. The rotary mill (made of stone and hand-operated), later revolutionized eating habits, although the techniques required for large-scale flour grinding were unavailable to the Chinese until the second half of the first century BC.

BUYING AND STORING

Up until recently, self-raising flour was not widely available in China since very few households would have bothered to make their own cakes or bread. Nowadays, both plain and self-raising flour can be purchased, either loose or in packets. Store flour in an air-tight container and use within 4–5 months.

CULINARY USES

There used to be a North–South divide in China: wheat products were eaten in the North, rice products in the South. Southerners still believe a proper meal needs rice, and eat more rice in other forms such as noodles, regarding Northern staples such as buns and dumplings made from wheaten flour as mere snacks.

There is a wide range of sweet and savoury wheaten food in China – not just noodles and wontons, but also cakes and buns, almost all steamed rather than baked. Most wheaten food is relatively difficult to make.

GLUTEN

Known as vegetarian or mock meat, gluten is a flour and water dough that has been soaked and kneaded in water to wash out the starch. The end product is spongy and porous like bean-curd or tofu but has a much firmer texture, which makes it ideal for carrying strong flavours.

Canned, ready-cooked gluten in flavours such abalone, mock chicken, vegetarian duck, or just plainly braised gluten is widely available in Oriental stores. Freshly prepared, uncooked gluten can be found in the larger Chinese supermarket.

Braised gluten can be served on its own but is rather bland unless you add extra flavourings such as ginger, spring onions, rice wine, sesame oil etc.

BRAISED GLUTEN

Makes about 300g (10½oz) gluten
Preparation time 30–35 minutes, plus standing time
Cooking time 8–10 minutes

1kg (2lb 4oz) plain flour
2 teaspoons salt
About 500–600ml (18–20fl oz) warm water
Vegetable oil for frying
½ teaspoon salt
1 teaspoon sugar
1 tablespoon light soy
¼ teaspoon MSG (optional)

1 Sift the flour into a large mixing bowl. Add the salt and water gradually to make a firm dough. Knead until smooth, cover with a damp cloth and leave to stand for about 1 hour.

2 Place the dough in a large colander or sieve. Run cold water over it while you press and squeeze the dough with your hands to wash out as much of the starch as possible. After 15–20 minutes of this hard work, you should end up with about 300g (10½oz) gluten. Squeeze out as much water as you can before cutting it into 35–40 small pieces.

3 Heat the oil in a wok or deep-fat fryer until smoking and deep-fry the pieces of gluten in batches for about 3 minutes, or until they turn golden. Remove and drain.

4 Pour off the excess oil, leaving about 1 teaspoon in the wok. Return the fried gluten to the wok. Add the salt, sugar, soy and about 1–2 tablespoons of water. Blend well and bring to the boil. Braise for 2–3 minutes until the liquid has evaporated, and stir in the MSG, if using. Serve hot or cold.

Note: Raw gluten can be stored in the refrigerator for a week or so; it can be cooked by deep-frying, boiling, steaming or baking.

Braised Gluten

饅头

STEAMED BUNS

(MANTOU)

Mantou are the Chinese equivalent of Western bread. They used to be the staple *fan* of North China, where rice was regarded as a luxury food for the better-off.

MANUFACTURE

Made of leavened dough, which is made from wheaten flour and water, *mantou* are steamed rather than baked, and always eaten piping hot.

CULINARY USES

Steamed buns are still widely eaten in China although no longer as a main meal (except for breakfast) but as a snack or part of a meal. Besides plain *mantou*, which usually accompany savoury *cai* dishes, there are two basic types of steamed buns: sweet or savoury *baozi* (filled *mantou*).

STEAMED BUNS

Makes about 24 buns
Preparation time about 1 hour, plus up to 1½ hours' rising time
Cooking time 15–20 minutes

For the dough:
1 tablespoon sugar
2 teaspoons dried yeast
300ml (½ pint) warm water
450g (1lb) self-raising flour
Dry flour for dusting

Sweet filling:
Sweet bean paste (red or black)

Savoury filling:
6 dried Chinese mushrooms
400g (14oz) pork (or lamb or beef)
100g (3½oz) bamboo shoots, drained
1 tablespoon finely chopped spring onions
1 teaspoon finely chopped fresh ginger

Ready-make steamed buns for sale outside a grocer's shop

Steamed Buns (with a sweet filling, indicated by the red dot)

1 teaspoon salt
1 teaspoon sugar
1 tablespoon light soy
1 tablespoon rice wine
½ teaspoon sesame oil

1 Dissolve the sugar and yeast in the warm water for 5–10 minutes until frothy. Sift the flour into a mixing bowl, then gradually stir in the yeast mixture to make a firm dough. Knead for 5 minutes, then cover with a damp cloth and leave in a warm place to rise for 1–1½ hours.

2 To make the savoury filling: soak the mushrooms in warm water for about 45–50 minutes, then squeeze dry and discard any hard stalks. Coarsely chop the mushrooms, meat and bamboo shoots. Mix with the spring onions, ginger, salt, sugar, soy, wine and sesame oil. Blend thoroughly.

3 Knead the dough on a lightly floured surface for about 5 minutes, then roll into a long sausage. Cut into about 24 pieces and flatten each piece with the palm of your hand. With a rolling pin, roll out each piece into a circle about 10cm (4 in) in diameter.

4 Place 1 tablespoon of the filling (sweet or savoury) in the centre of each flattened circle of dough, then gather together the edges to meet at the top around the filling. Twist to enclose the filling. Stand for at least 20 minutes before cooking.

5 Place a piece of wet muslin on the rack of a steamer, arrange the buns 2.5cm (1 in) apart on the muslin, cover and steam vigorously for 15–20 minutes. Serve hot.

Note: In order to distinguish a sweet steamed bun from a savoury one, it is customary to paint a red dot on the top, so it resembles a woman's breast. Someone remarked to me that this is rather rude – my answer was that you just cannot separate food from sex, two of the most essential things in life.

Thin pancakes

薄餅
PANCAKES
(BAOBING)

Pancakes in Chinese cooking can be broadly divided into two categories – the thin and the thick. Traditionally it is the thin that will be used as accompaniments for many Chinese *cai* dishes, while there are several variations, both sweet and savoury, for the thick pancake.

MANUFACTURE

To make thin pancakes at home requires a lot of practice and patience, but a perfect result is possible, as the recipe below I hope demonstrates. Most are made commercially.

APPEARANCE AND TASTE

Thin pancakes, whether frozen or fresh, have an almost translucent look about them and are round.

BUYING AND STORING

Buy ready-made frozen thin pancakes from Oriental stores (many restaurants without a specially trained white chef do). Home-made pancakes can also be frozen.

CULINARY USES

Often called 'duck pancakes', the thin pancakes are widely used for serving Peking duck in Chinese restaurants and as wrappers for a number of other dishes.

Thick pancakes, filled with all manner of delicacies, are eaten as a substantial meal in themselves as well as an accompaniment to the *cai* part of the meal. They are consumed in greater quantities in the North of China than the South.

Making savoury pancakes for passers-by in Beijing

THIN PANCAKES

Here is a recipe for you to try – if you have the time and energy.

Makes 24–30 pancakes
Preparation time about 1 hour plus 30 minutes' standing time
Cooking time 45–50 minutes
450g (1lb) plain flour
About 300ml (½ pint) boiling water
1 teaspoon vegetable oil
Dry flour for dusting

1 Sift the flour into a mixing bowl. Pour in the water very gently, stirring as you pour, then stir in the oil. Knead the mixture into a firm dough. Cover with a damp towel and let stand for about 30 minutes.

2 Lightly dust the surface of a worktop with dry flour. Knead the dough for 6–8 minutes or until smooth, then divide it into 3 equal portions. Roll out each portion into a long sausage, and cut each sausage into 8–10 pieces.

3 Roll each piece into a ball, then, using the palm of your hand, press each piece into a flat pancake. Dust the worktop with more dry flour. Flatten each pancake into a 15cm (6in) circle with a rolling pin, rolling gently on both sides.

4 Place an ungreased frying pan over high heat. When hot, turn the heat to low and place the pancakes, one at a time, in the pan. Remove when little brown spots appear on the underside. Cover with a damp cloth until ready to serve.

Note: If the pancakes are not to be used as soon as they are cooked, they can be warmed up, either in a steamer for 5–6 minutes, or in a microwave oven for 30–40 seconds, depending on the power.

Mu-shu Pork (Pork with Scrambled Eggs)

Mu-shu Pork is one of the most popular dishes in which pancakes are used as wrappers. *Muxi* is the classical Chinese name for the sweet-scented osmanthus, which bears bright yellow flowers in autumn. As explained on p 194, some egg dishes in China are called *muxi* to avoid using the character for egg which has a rather impolite connotation in colloquial Chinese.

Serves 4
Preparation time 25–30 minutes
Cooking time 6–8 minutes

25g (1oz) dried black fungus ('wood ears')
225g (8oz) pork fillet
100g (3½oz) bamboo shoots
175g (6oz) Chinese leaves
3 eggs
1 teaspoon salt
4 tablespoons vegetable oil
2 spring onions, finely shredded
1 tablespoon light soy
2 teaspoons rice wine
A few drops sesame oil
12 thin pancakes to serve

1 Soak the fungus in warm water for 10–15 minutes, rinse and drain. Discard any hard stalks, then thinly shred.

2 Thinly cut the pork, bamboo shoots and Chinese leaves into matchstick-sized shreds. Lightly beat the eggs with a pinch of salt.

3 Heat about 1 tablespoon oil in a preheated wok and scramble the eggs until set, but not too hard. Remove and keep to one side.

4 Heat the remaining oil. Stir-fry the shredded pork for about 1 minute or until the colour changes. Add the fungus, bamboo shoots, Chinese leaves and spring onions. Stir-fry for about 2–3 minutes, then add the remaining salt, soy and wine. Blend well and continue stirring for another 2 minutes. Add the scrambled eggs, stirring to break them into small bits. Add the sesame oil and blend well.

5 To serve: place about 2 tablespoons of hot Mu-shu pork in the centre of a warm pancake, rolling it into a parcel with the bottom end turned up to prevent the contents from falling out. Eat with your fingers.

Note: This dish can also be served with plain rice if so desired.

Spring Onion Pancakes

Spring Onion Pancakes

Popular in northern China, these savoury pancakes can be served on their own as a snack, or as the *fan* part of a meal with other *cai* dishes.

Makes 10–12
Preparation time 30–35 minutes plus 30 minutes' standing time
Cooking time 45–50 minutes

450g (1lb) plain flour
300ml (½ pint) boiling water
About 50ml (2fl oz) cold water
Dry flour for dusting
4–5 spring onions, coarsely chopped
1 tablespoon large-grain sea salt
100g (3½oz) lard or shortening
3–4 tablespoons vegetable oil

1 Sift the flour into a mixing bowl and gently pour in the boiling water. Stir for 5–6 minutes, then add the cold water and knead to a firm dough. Cover with a damp cloth and leave to stand for 25–30 minutes.

2 On a lightly floured surface, roll the dough into a sausage and divide it into 10–12 sections. Roll each section into a flat pancake about 20cm (8in) in diameter. Sprinkle each pancake evenly with the chopped spring onions, salt and lard or shortening. Fold up the pancake from the sides, then roll again to make a 5mm (¼in) thick pancake.

3 Heat the oil in a preheated frying-pan and fry the pancakes, one at a time, over medium heat for 5–6 minutes, turning over once. They should be golden brown and crispy on both sides. Shake and jiggle the pan while cooking so you have a flaky pastry finish.

4 Serve hot. Cut each pancake into small pieces, or tear into pieces and eat with your fingers. The pancakes should have a strong spring onion flavour, with the occasional sharpness of the salt crystals – absolutely delicious.

春卷

SPRING ROLLS

(CHUNJUAN)

Spring rolls are so called because they were originally eaten to celebrate Chinese New Year, which is called Spring Festival as it marks the coming of spring in China.

MANUFACTURE

The wrapping used to be made from a certain starch which ensured a crisper and lighter roll than those made with wheaten flour. Over the years, both filling and skin have changed, so we now have a very wide range of fillings with a wheaten flour skin of varying thickness. The thinner the skin, the crisper the roll, but that is not all: to achieve perfect crispness, the oil temperature and degree of heat are crucial – too hot, the rolls will burn, not hot enough, they become soggy and greasy.

APPEARANCE AND TASTE

These deep-fried crispy rolls served in every Chinese establishment and take-away must be one of the most popular Chinese dishes. The best are crispy and crunchy with a delicious stuffing, the worst can be insipid and soggy.

BUYING AND STORING

Ready-made frozen spring roll skins are widely available. These are usually made of flour and water, but there are certain brands that have had eggs added to the pastry. This may be why spring rolls are sometimes called egg rolls in the USA. These wafer-thin skins come in two sizes: large – about 21.5cm (8½in) square – or small – 17.5cm (7in) square. They usually come in packets of 20 sheets, reasonably priced. Defrost the frozen sheets thoroughly before peeling off each sheet very carefully. Cover under a damp cloth. Unused sheets should be wrapped in cling film and refrigerated – they will keep for several days.

CRISPY SPRING ROLLS

Makes about 20 rolls
Preparation time about 1 hour plus soaking, marinating and cooling time
Cooking time about 10 minutes

6–8 dried Chinese mushrooms
225g (8oz) pork or chicken fillet
1½ tablespoons light soy
1 teaspoon rice wine
1 teaspoon cornflour
125g (4½oz) bamboo shoots, drained
175g (6oz) tender young leeks or spring onions
2–3 tablespoons oil
100g (3½oz) peeled and cooked prawns
½ teaspoon salt
1 teaspoon sugar
20 sheets ready-made spring roll skin
1 tablespoon cornflour paste
Dry flour for dusting
Oil for deep-frying

1 Soak the mushrooms in warm water for about 45–50 minutes, or in cold water for 4–5 hours. Squeeze dry and discard any hard stalks. Cut into matchstick-size shreds.

2 Thinly shred the meat and marinate with about 2 teaspoons soy, the rice wine and cornflour for 25–30 minutes. Thinly shred the bamboo shoots and leeks or spring onions so they are the same size as the mushrooms and meat.

3 Heat the oil in a preheated wok. Stir-fry the leeks or spring onions with the shredded meat for about 1 minute, then add the mushrooms, bamboo shoots and prawns. Stir-fry for

Rhododendrons in flower mark the coming of spring to a forest in northeast China

another minute or so. Add the salt and sugar with the remaining soy, blend well and cook for a further minute. Remove from the heat, drain off any excess liquid and leave to cool.

4 Peel off the skins one at a time and lay diagonally on the worktop. Place about 2 tablespoons of the filling on each one. Shape the filling into a sausage running from your left to right. Lift the corner of the skin nearest you, fold over the filling and roll once away from you. Fold in both ends loosely and roll again – this is an important point, for if you fold the ends too tightly, the roll will not be very crispy when cooked. Brush the last corner with the cornflour paste and roll into a neat package.

5 Lightly dust a tray with dry flour and place the spring rolls in rows with the flap sides down. Repeat the wrapping process until all the filling is used up. Do not cook the spring rolls until a few minutes before serving in order to retain their crispiness. Finished rolls can be kept in the refrigerator for a day or two, or they can be frozen for several months, and then cooked from frozen.

6 To cook: heat the oil in a wok or deep-fryer until smoking a little, then reduce the heat and fry the rolls in batches (3–4 at a time) for 2–3 minutes or until crispy and golden. Remove and drain. They should stay crispy for 15–20 minutes, and in a warm oven will stay crispy for up to 45 minutes before serving.

7 Serve hot with a dip such as soy, rice vinegar, chilli sauce, or plum sauce.

Vegetarian Spring Rolls

Vegetarian Spring Rolls

These small, dainty rolls are ideal as cocktail snacks or at a finger-buffet. A word of warning: you should allow at least four rolls per person, because they are so scrumptious!

Makes 40 rolls
Preparation time about 1½ hours plus cooling time
Cooking time 10–15 minutes

225g (8oz) fresh bean sprouts
2 medium carrots
About 125g (4½oz) sliced bamboo shoots, drained
175g (6oz) fresh white mushrooms
225g (8oz) tender young leeks
3–4 tablespoons oil
1 teaspoon salt
1 teaspoon sugar
1 tablespoon light soy
Pinch of MSG (optional)
40 sheets small spring roll skins, or 20 large ones
2 tablespoons cornflour paste
Dry flour for dusting
Oil for deep-frying

1 Wash and drain the bean sprouts, discarding any husks and small bits. Cut all the vegetables (carrots, bamboo shoots, mushrooms and leeks) into fine shreds, about the same size as the bean sprouts.

2 Heat the oil in a wok and stir-fry all the vegetables for about 2 minutes. Add the salt, sugar and soy, and continue stirring for another minute or so. Add the MSG (if using) and cook for a further 30–40 seconds. Remove from the heat, drain off excess liquid, and leave to cool.

3 The procedure for making the rolls is exactly the same as for the previous recipe, except that the larger sheets should be cut in half diagonally, and when you are filling the roll, place the sheet with the triangle pointing away from you.

4 Cook the rolls as before. You will be able to fry more rolls in each batch as they are smaller, and it will take a little less time to cook them.

餃子
DUMPLINGS
(JIAOZI)

These dumplings were traditionally eaten for breakfast on New Year's Day in North China. Their popularity is such that they are now eaten all year round in every area of China, and indeed all over the world.

MANUFACTURE

Jiaozi making is a sociable affair: on Sundays, families and friends gather to make large quantities of them, amid much banter. When *jiaozi* are served as a full meal, you are supposed to eat at least twenty.

BUYING AND STORING

Frozen pork dumplings made by machine are available in Oriental stores. They are used by most Chinese restaurants for convenience.

***Jiaozi*-making at home in northern China**

Folk dancing in the streets of Beijing during New Year celebrations

POACHED DUMPLINGS

The standard filling of pork and Chinese leaf can be varied: the meat can be lamb or beef, and the vegetable can be spinach or Chinese chives.

Makes 80–90 dumplings
Preparation time about 1½ hours plus 30 minutes' standing time
Cooking time 20–25 minutes

For the dough:
450g (1lb) plain flour
About 425ml (¾ pint) water
Dry flour for dusting

For the filling:
675g (1½lb) Chinese leaf
450g (1lb) minced pork
2 tablespoons finely chopped spring onions
1 teaspoon finely chopped fresh ginger
1 teaspoon salt
1 teaspoon sugar
2 tablespoons light soy
1 tablespoon rice wine
1 tablespoon sesame oil

1 Sift the flour into a bowl, slowly pour in the water and mix to a firm dough. Knead until smooth and soft, then cover with a damp cloth and let stand for 25–30 minutes.

2 Separate the Chinese leaf and blanch in a pan of boiling water for 2–3 minutes or until soft. Drain, finely chop, then mix with the rest of the ingredients to make the filling.

Poached Dumplings

3 Lightly dust a work surface with dry flour. Knead and roll the dough into a long sausage about 2.5cm (1in) in diameter. Cut the sausage into 80–90 small pieces. Flatten each piece with the palm of your hand, then use a rolling pin to roll out each piece into a thin circle about 6cm (2½in) in diameter.

4 Place about 1½ tablespoons of filling in the centre of each circle. Fold into a semi-circle, and pinch the edges firmly so that the dumpling is tightly sealed. Place the dumplings on a tray lightly dusted with dry flour and cover with a damp cloth until ready for cooking. (Any uncooked dumplings should be frozen rather than refrigerated.)

5 Bring 1 litre (1¾ pints) water to a rolling boil, and drop in about 20 dumplings, one by one. Stir gently with chopsticks to prevent them sticking together. Cover and bring back to the boil. Uncover and add about 50ml (2fl oz) cold water, then bring back to the boil once more (uncovered). Repeat this process twice more. Remove and drain the dumplings, and serve hot with a dipping sauce. Any leftovers should be re-heated not by poaching, but by shallow-frying them as for Pot-Stickers – see below.

Grilled Dumplings (Pot-stickers)

Grilled dumplings, also known as Pot-Stickers, are actually shallow-fried on one side, then steamed under cover so you end up with *jiaozi* that are crispy on the base, soft on top and juicy inside. Make the dumplings as in the previous recipe. (Some chefs insist that the dough for Pot-Stickers should be made with boiling water instead of cold water – it does seem to make a difference to the pastry.)

1 Heat about 2 tablespoons vegetable oil in a frying-pan, tilting the pan so that the entire surface is evenly coated with oil.

2 Arrange 8–10 dumplings neatly in rows and fry over a medium heat for 2–3 minutes, or until the base of each dumpling is browned.

3 Pour about 150ml (¼ pint) hot water down the side of the pan. Cover and increase the heat to high. Cook until almost all the water has evaporated.

4 Uncover and continue cooking until all the water has evaporated. Turn off the heat, and use a spatula to loosen the dumplings from the bottom of the pan. Cover the pan with a serving plate and quickly turn the pan over, so that the browned side of the dumplings is uppermost. Serve hot with a dipping sauce (See Note).

Besides poaching and grilling jiaozi, you can also steam them. Place the dumplings on a bed of lettuce leaves on the rack of a bamboo steamer and steam for 10–12 minutes over high heat. Serve hot with a dipping sauce (see Note).

Note: To make a dipping sauce, blend 2 tablespoons light soy sauce with 3 tablespoons rice vinegar, and either add 2 tablespoons finely shredded ginger or 1 tablespoon finely chopped spring onions mixed with 1 tablespoon finely chopped garlic.

Grilled Dumplings (Pot-Stickers)

面條

NOODLES

(MIANTIAO)

First let me dispel the romantic legend that Marco Polo introduced the art of noodle-making to Italy from China. There is evidence that the Italians were making and eating all types of pasta long before Marco Polo even left Venice on his supposed travels to the East (I say 'supposed', because there is a current dispute about whether Marco Polo ever set foot in China – but that is another story). That does not mean there is no link between Chinese noodles and Italian spaghetti: China made contact with the outside world (including the Roman Empire) as early as the second century BC, and it was around the second half of the first century BC that China started to make noodles from wheat flour. There are too many similarities between the various forms of Chinese *mianshi* (noodles and dumplings) and Italian pasta to discount a connection.

A chef in Beijing demonstrates the intricate art of noodle-making

HOW THEY ARE MADE

The Chinese name for noodles is *miantiao* (wheat-flour strips), which is often shortened to *mian*. There are numerous types and shapes of noodles made in China and, until the introduction of modern machinery in the late nineteenth and early twentieth century, almost all noodles were hand-made. I have a vivid memory of watching two chefs (this was around 1938 or '39, in South China) roll out a huge ball of dough by sitting astride the ends of a long wooden pole and seesawing up and down until the dough was an enormous, smooth, thin sheet. They then turned it into noodles by rolling it into a tight bundle and cutting it into fine shreds!

PULLED OR HAND-DRAWN NOODLES

Even today some types of noodles are still made by hand, the best known of which must be *la mian*, meaning pulled or hand-drawn noodles, which were introduced to Beijing from Shandong at the beginning of the fifteenth century during the Ming dynasty. They were much appreciated by the Emperor, who gave them the name Dragon's Whiskers (dragon being the imperial symbol). Making pulled noodles looks like a conjurer's trick: a piece of dough is turned into fine strips of noodles (sometimes as many as a thousand) after only a few minutes' manipulation in the hands of a master chef. It requires great skill and years of practice to achieve this level, one of the reasons why so few chefs are capable of the task. I once asked my good friend Chef But (from Memories of China) exactly how long it took him to acquire his skill, and he told me in all seriousness: sixteen years!

Freshly made noodles suspended on poles to dry

PARED OR PEELED NOODLES

There is another hand-made noodle that I have never seen outside China. Pared or peeled noodles are found mainly in Shanxi province in North China. This singular method of noodle-making requires perhaps even more special skills than pulled noodles, for each 18–20cm (7–8 in) strip is cut by hand in a paring or peeling motion at frenetic speed.

Watching pared noodles being made is the experience of a lifetime. A piece of dough is supported with one hand between the chin and shoulder of the chef – not unlike a musician holding a violin – and by using a curved carving knife, the chef pares off long, thin strips of the dough directly into a large pot of boiling water. If there is a big demand, two chefs may stand side by side and make the noodles simultaneously, for the noodles must not be cooked too long before being drained and served with a sauce or dressing. This is fast food *par excellence*!

APPEARANCE AND TASTE

The following are some of the machine-made noodles that are widely obtainable in the West:

EGG NOODLES

These must be the most common type of noodles in the world. They come in a variety of thicknesses and shapes; they can be flat or round, and are usually coiled into round balls or square packages. They are widely available in dried form, but fresh noodles, which taste much better, are available from Oriental stores. They last a week or ten days in the refrigerator.

Dried egg noodles

LONGEVITY NOODLES

These egg noodles are sold in dried form in long strips and are never coiled as the long strips are supposed to symbolize a long life. As well as being given as presents, they are also served at weddings and birthday celebrations and at festivals. Often the packets are printed with a message that wishes the recipient a long and happy life.

THREAD NOODLES

These are very fine vermicelli made from just wheaten flour and water so are much favoured by vegetarians. They are sold in dried form, always in straight bundles, never coiled up. Hand-made ones have a much more resilient texture than the machine-made ones, since they have to be hand-rolled into thin strips about 2.5cm (1 in) in diameter first, then hung loosely on bamboo sticks and gradually pulled into fine threads. Since the long, thin strips of noodles are dried in the open air by suspending them on bamboo poles, they are also called Suspended Noodles.

YI NOODLES

These are extra-fine egg noodles originally made by the Yi family in Shantou (Swatow) east of Canton. Traditionally served in soup, they are very popular in Cantonese restaurants that specialize in Swatow cooking.

Yi noodles

SHRIMP, SHRIMP ROE NOODLES

These are made from wheaten flour, water, fresh shrimps or shrimp roe, and seasoning, and are always cut into very fine strips like vermicelli, either straight or coiled into small nests. Rather grey in colour, they are pre-cooked, so require soaking in boiling water for 2–3 minutes.

Shrimp roe noodles

Red lanterns, like noodle-eating, all form part of celebrations at New Year, weddings and birthdays

CULINARY USES

In China, noodle dishes are eaten as snacks (*dim sum*) or part of a light luncheon. Traditionally, they are served on birthdays, because the length of noodles represents long life. There are four basic ways of cooking and serving noodles in China:

NOODLES IN SOUP

Noodles immersed in a clear broth with cooked meat and/or vegetables placed on top as a dressing must be the most common presentation in China, always served as a snack, never as a soup course at a main meal. (See also Wontons on p 46–7).
Noodles in soup are sometimes used for medicinal purposes. As a child, when I had a cold my nanny would cook me a large bowl of fine noodles (vermicelli) in steaming hot vegetable soup with masses of ground white pepper. It had a sharp taste and would make my eyes stream with tears, but I always felt much better afterwards. I suppose it had the same effect as an old-fashioned mustard bath.

BRAISED NOODLES, STRAINED NOODLES

A variation on noodles in soup. Braised noodles are served not in a broth, but in a thickened sauce in which they have sometimes been cooked beforehand. In some Cantonese restaurants, they are first boiled in a clear broth, then strained and served with a dressing; the broth is served in a separate bowl as soup.

Longevity noodles

Tossed Noodles

Plainly boiled noodles served with a meat sauce; a selection of shredded fresh vegetables is provided on the table for mixing and tossing with the noodles. In hot summer months, it is often served as a refreshing cold snack – rather like pasta salad in the West.

Dried noodles

Fried Noodles

This must be one of the best-known Chinese dishes in the West. There are two basic types of fried noodles in China: dry-fried and soft-fried, depending on the thickness of the noodles used. Generally speaking, only the fine vermicelli type are used for dry-frying, and the thicker, round or flat noodles for soft-frying. The very popular crispy noodles served in some Chinese restaurants and take-aways are as alien to the Chinese as chop suey.

Vegetarian Noodles in Soup

True Chinese vegetarians will not use egg noodles at all since they will not eat anything connected with living creatures. Instead they will use thread noodles, but you can use either sort.

Serves 4
Preparation time about 15 minutes plus soaking time
Cooking time about 10 minutes

50g (2oz) dried bean curd skin
3–4 dried Chinese mushrooms
40g (1½oz) dried tiger lily buds
175g (6oz) water chestnuts, drained
125g (4½oz) straw mushrooms, drained
125g (4½oz) ginkgo nuts, drained
350g (12oz) fine vermicelli noodles
3 tablespoons vegetable oil
1 teaspoon salt
1 teaspoon sugar
1 tablespoon light soy
570ml (1 pint) vegetable stock (see below)
Pinch of MSG (optional)
2 teaspoons cornflour paste
½ teaspoon sesame oil
Shredded spring onions to garnish

1 Soak the dried bean curd skin in cold water overnight, or in hot water for at least 1 hour, then cut into small pieces. Soak the dried mushrooms in cold water overnight, or in warm water for about 1 hour, then squeeze dry, discard any hard stalks and cut into small pieces. Soak the lily buds in warm water for about 30–40 minutes, top and tail but do not chop. Keep the soaking water to be used as vegetable stock if no other vegetable stock is available.

2 Drain and rinse the canned vegetables. Cut the water chestnuts into thin slices if they are not already sliced. The straw mushrooms and ginkgo nuts can be left whole.

3 Cook the noodles in boiling water for 2–3 minutes, then drain them in a colander and rinse in cold water before placing them in four individual serving bowls (or one large serving bowl).

A bowl of noodles in soup always makes a warming dish

4 Heat the oil in a pre-heated wok and stir-fry the vegetables for 2–3 minutes. Add the salt, sugar and soy, blend well, then add the vegetable stock. Bring to the boil and add the MSG, if using. Thicken the liquid with the cornflour paste. Pour the entire contents of the wok over the top of the noodles, garnish with sesame oil and spring onions. Serve hot.

Cold Tossed Noodles

The dressing for this dish can be varied according to season and personal taste. The basic seasonings are ginger, soy, vinegar, spring onions and sesame oil.

Serves 4
Preparation time 10–15 minutes plus soaking and cooling time
Cooking time 3–4 minutes

2 tablespoons dried shrimps
3 tablespoons rice wine
3 tablespoons light soy
2 tablespoons rice vinegar
1 teaspoon chilli sauce
2 spring onions
450g (1lb) fresh egg noodles or 350g (12oz) dried noodles
1 tablespoon finely chopped fresh ginger
2 tablespoons Chinese Preserved Vegetables (p184)
1 teaspoon sesame oil

1 Soak the dried shrimps in warm water for 10–15 minutes, drain, coarsely chop, then soak in the rice wine for a further 15 minutes.

2 Mix the soy, vinegar and chilli sauce. Finely shred the spring onions.

3 Cook the noodles in a pan of lightly salted water for 2–3 minutes, drain and rinse in cold water. Spread the noodles on a serving dish.

4 Evenly sprinkle the preserved vegetables, shrimps, the soy mixture and ginger. Garnish with spring onions and sesame oil. Mix and toss at the table before serving.

Cold Tossed Noodles

餛飩

WONTON

(HUNTUN)

Wonton, *wanton*, or *wun tun* are romanizations of the Cantonese *wahn tan*, which means 'swallowing clouds'. In the rest of China, *wonton* are called *huntun*, which is derived from *hundun* (chaos), a word describing the beginning of the world according to Chinese folklore.

Their name is the reason why in Beijing and most northern parts of China, wonton are eaten on December 22nd, the winter solstice, known in China as the Arrival of Winter, the day on which ancestors are traditionally remembered. According to legend, the Han Chinese are direct descendants of the Lord of Man, *Hundu* or *Chaos*, and the Chinese worship Hundun as one of their ancestors by devouring *huntun*, his namesake.

Wonton have a long history in China – they were first mentioned during the Three Kingdoms in the third century AD. Up until the Southern Song dynasty (1127–1279) they were eaten only by aristocrats and wealthy households; since then they have become very much food of the people, served in ordinary eating-places, teahouses and road-side stalls rather than high-class restaurants.

Wonton skins

Wontons

MANUFACTURE

As far as I know, nobody makes wonton at home in China – partly because of the bother of making them, and partly because of the availability in China of ready-made wonton skins, which are exactly the same as sheets for egg noodles, i.e. wheaten flour, water and egg.

APPEARANCE AND TASTE

Wonton are small, thin-skinned dumplings with long flapping tails served in soup, and they look like floating clouds which can be easily swallowed or gulped down.

BUYING AND STORING

Factory-made wonton skins (wrappers) are readily available in the West, and frozen ready-made wonton can also be purchased from some Oriental stores. Should you have difficulty in obtaining them, see below for how to make your own.

CULINARY USES

Wonton in clear broth are always served as a snack in China, never as a soup course. Sometimes the broth contains noodles too – an oddity in Chinese cuisine, for two entirely different shapes of food (round wonton and long thin noodles) are rarely served together. The deep-fried version served as an appetizer with sweet and sour sauce is a Western invention, just like chop suey or crispy fried noodles.

A taoist symbol depicting cloud (yin) and fire (yang) – the origins of wonton

WONTON IN SOUP

To be served as a substantial snack, or as part of a light meal with another dish such as fried rice or noodles. Do not serve as a separate soup course at a proper meal.

Makes 24 wonton
Preparation time about 1 hour plus standing time
Cooking time 6–8 minutes

For the wrappers:
1 egg
6 tablespoons cold water
225g (8oz) plain flour
Dry flour for dusting

For the filling:
175g (6oz) pork, not too lean, coarsely chopped
75g (3oz) peeled raw prawns, coarsely chopped
1 teaspoon sugar
1 tablespoon rice wine
1 tablespoon light soy
1 tablespoon finely chopped spring onions
½ teaspoon finely chopped fresh ginger
½ teaspoon sesame oil
Dry flour for dusting

For serving:
600ml (1 pint) good stock (p 71)
1 tablespoon light soy
Salt and pepper to taste
Finely chopped spring onions to garnish

1 Lightly beat the egg and mix with the water until well blended. Stir in the flour and knead together to form a smooth, stiff dough. Cover with a damp cloth and set aside for about 30 minutes.

2 On a lightly floured surface, roll the dough out into a very thin sheet – less than 1.5mm ($^{1}/_{16}$in) thick. Cut out 24 squares, each about 2.5mm x 2.5mm (3in x 3in). Dust each square lightly with flour. If they are not to be used immediately, cover with a damp cloth. (They will keep for several months in the freezer – make sure they are thoroughly defrosted before separating them.)

3 To make the wonton: combine the filling ingredients thoroughly to form a smooth mixture and let stand for 25–30 minutes. Place a heaped teaspoon of the filling in the centre of a wonton skin. Wet the uncovered skin with water and seal the wonton by pressing the edges firmly together. Pull out the outer edges to form a floral shape.

4 To cook: bring the stock to a rolling boil, drop in the wonton one by one and simmer for 6–8 minutes. Add soy, salt and pepper according to taste, garnish with the chopped spring onions and serve hot.

粉絲

BEAN THREADS (VERMICELLI)

(FENSI)

Sometimes known as 'transparent' or 'Cellophane' noodles, these very fine strands of vermicelli are made of mung bean starch – the same green bean which provides the ubiquitous bean sprout. Strictly speaking, bean threads cannot be called noodles since they are not classified as a staple food (*fan*) in China but are used only as an ingredient in *cai* dishes: in vegetarian dishes and, most notably, in the famous Mongolian Hot Pot.

MANUFACTURE

Fensi literally means flour shreds. The manufacturing process involves soaking, husking and grinding the mung beans, straining and cooking the flour, then cooling, kneading and shredding the dough. The *fensi* are hung on bamboo poles to dry in the sun before being packaged.

APPEARANCE AND TASTE

Bundles of Vermicelli ranging from 60g (2oz) to 450g (1lb) in weight are sold tied with string in Cellophane bags. The slightly wrinkly and silvery threads are only about 0.8mm (1/32 in) thick, yet they are firm and very resilient, almost rubber-band like. They have little or no taste until cooked with other ingredients and seasonings, when they acquire a subtle flavour and a wonderfully silky texture.

BUYING AND STORING

Several brands are available but none compares with the Lungkow brand, which is popular worldwide and has been around for almost four hundred years. In a cool, dark, dry place, bean threads will keep almost indefinitely.

CULINARY USES

Bean threads require soaking in warm water before use. In 30–40 seconds they become soft yet resilient, turning almost snow white. They do not expand or go soggy. Drain and rinse them in cold water before cooking.

ANTS CLIMBING TREES

This is a classic dish from Sichuan, so named because the cooked minced meat scattered all over the bean threads resembles ants climbing a tree.

Serves 4–6 as a side dish or 2–3 as a snack
Preparation time 10–15 minutes plus marinating time
Cooking time 8–10 minutes

125g (4½oz) bean threads
225g (8oz) beef steak, or pork fillet if preferred
2 tablespoons light soy
1 tablespoon sugar
1 tablespoon rice wine

Ants Climbing Trees

1 teaspoon cornflour
3–4 tablespoons oil
1 tablespoon chilli bean paste (Toban Jiang)
3–4 tablespoons finely chopped spring onions
1 tablespoon dark soy
About 150ml (¼ pint) stock (p 71)
1–2 small fresh red chillies, shredded

1 Soak the bean threads in warm water for 1 minute. Drain and rinse in cold water, separating any strands that are stuck together. Cut the threads to a shorter, more manageable, length.

2 Finely mince or chop the meat. Marinate with the soy, sugar, rice wine and cornflour for 10–15 minutes, longer if possible.

3 Heat the oil in a preheated wok and stir-fry the meat for about 1 minute or until the colour changes. Add the chilli bean paste, the bean threads and about half the chopped spring onions. Blend well and add the dark soy and stock. Continue stirring until all the liquid has been absorbed. Garnish with the red chillies and remaining spring onions and serve hot.

甘薯

SWEET POTATO

(GANSHU) *Ipomoea batatas*

The common Chinese name for sweet potato is *hongshu* (red potato), on account of the colour of its skin; another name is *shanyu* (hill taro) – the Chinese do not distinguish clearly between taro, yam and potatoes.

HOW IT GROWS

Sweet potato is much cultivated in South China, usually in paddy fields when they lie fallow in winter between rice crops. Its tubers used to be the staple food for the poor, as it is much cheaper to grow than rice and other cereals.

APPEARANCE AND TASTE

The flesh of sweet potato varies from white to pale orange in colour.

MEDICINAL AND OTHER USES

Sweet potato is considered a healthy, strength-giving food, which especially benefits the spleen, stomach and kidneys. Both the plant and tubers are used as animal feed as well as in the kitchen.

CULINARY USES

I have vivid memories of sweet potatoes being used as a *cai* dish, in which they were sliced thinly, fried with spring onions and seasonings, and served with rice. Other ways of eating sweet potatoes include baking them in their jackets, or eating them raw (peeled) like a fruit. In the countryside, sweet potatoes are often sliced then dried in the winter sun; the dried slices can be deep-fried in oil, and eaten like Western crisps.

DEEP-FRIED SWEET POTATO BALLS

This snack was a childhood favourite of mine. It was sold at the road-side, and you ate it piping hot out of its newspaper wrapping – most delicious!

Makes 24 balls
Preparation time about 1 hour
Cooking time 8–10 minutes

450g (1lb) sweet potato
115g (4oz) sugar
175g (6oz) glutinous rice flour
Dry flour for dusting
About 3–4 tablespoons sweet bean paste
Sesame seeds
Oil for deep-frying

1 Boil the potatoes until soft. Peel off the skin, mash the flesh, then mix with the sugar and rice flour to make a stiff dough.

2 Roll the dough into a long sausage and cut into 24 small pieces. Flatten each piece into a small circle. Place about half a teaspoon of sweet bean paste in the middle of each circle, seal by pulling up the edges, then roll into a small ball (about the size of a golf ball).

3 Roll the balls on a bed of sesame seeds until they are completely coated with seeds. Deep-fry in hot oil until golden. Serve hot.

Deep-fried Sweet Potato Balls

POTATO FLOUR

Potato flour (*shengfen*) which is used as a thickening agent and in batter is actually a derivative not of the sweet potato, but of the unsweet variety. This potato (*Solanum tuberosum*) is called *maling shu* or *tudou* (ground legumes) in Chinese. Other names are *penshu* and *yangyu*, indicating its foreign origin. Potatoes are grown in most parts of China, but not as extensively as the sweet variety. I didn't come across them until I was fourteen, when I was given chicken curry, and in my innocence, I thought the potato in that dish was 'curry'!

Apart from being made into flour, potato is used as animal feed for pigs and horses, and in sugar-making and distillation.

芋头
Taro

(YUTOU) *Colocasia esculenta*

This is the same as the taro grown in the South Sea Islands and cultivated for its edible roots. Its Chinese name is *yutou* (taro heads). Several species of *Colocasia* are grown in China, and it has been known since before the Han period (206 BC).

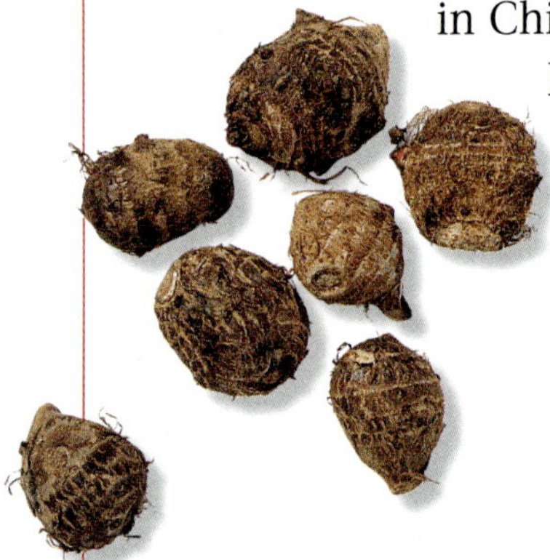

How It Grows

Like other root vegetables (potatoes, yams etc), taro requires warm and damp conditions for growth, so planting usually takes place in summer, harvest in winter. Cultivated all over the world, it is possible to buy taro almost all year round in the West.

Appearance and Taste

Taro comes in several varieties but there are two basic ones: large – about 10cm (4 in) in diameter; and small – 2.5–3.5cm (1–1½ in) in diameter. Both are egg-shaped with brown, hairy skin; the flesh is white with pale purple flecks. Of the two, the smaller variety is more tender and moist with an even texture. Its taste resembles potato in that both are tubers of starchy composition and rather bland, except that the taro has a smoother, almost creamy texture, and is easier to digest.

Medicinal Uses

Taro seeds, leaves and stalks are used medicinally in China. Although the seeds are slightly poisonous, they are recommended for indigestion, flatulence, and for disorders in parturient women. The leaves and stalks are applied to insect bites.

Culinary Uses

Despite its high starch content, taro is never used as a staple food in China, except when baked in its jacket and eaten as a snack. It is usually cooked as a *cai* dish, sometimes on its own (fried then braised with seasonings), sometimes with meat. A popular method, although perhaps not for the Western palate, is to steam slices of taro between layers of sliced belly pork – the taro absorbs the pork fat.

Sweet Taro Purée, Fujian Style

Sweet Taro Puree, Fujian Style

A popular, easy to prepare dessert from Fujian.

Serves 6–8
Preparation time 40–45 minutes
Cooking time about 20 minutes

450g (1lb) taro (the smaller variety, if possible)
115g (4oz) lard
175g (6oz) sugar

1 Wash the taro clean. Steam or boil until soft (about 30 minutes). Remove skin, then mash into a smooth paste.

2 Blend in the lard and sugar, place in a pudding basin, cover with cling film or silver foil, then steam vigorously for 20 minutes. Serve hot.

山藥
YAM

(SHANYAO) *Dioscorea batatas*

The Chinese name for yam, *shanyao* (literally, hill medicine), indicates that it is more often seen as medicine than food. Another common name for it is *tuyu* (native or local taro), for the Chinese do not distinguish clearly between taro, yam and potato, all starchy root vegetables.

Eating yams is thought to contribute to a long life

How It Grows

Yam is more widely grown in northern China than in the South, where taro seems to be more common – maybe because yam requires less water and can withstand a colder climate. Yam is harvested from August onwards, so is primarily available in the cool season.

Appearance and Taste

Like taro and potato, yam has a rough, brownish skin. It is the only vegetable with a four-lobed bottom, and it grows to 12.5–20cm (5–8 in) in length. The flesh is white, crisp, mildly sweet and quite juicy, though sometimes a bit fibrous.

Medicinal Uses

Yam is cooling, with tonic properties which are said to lift the spirits, promote flesh and, when taken frequently, brighten the intellect and prolong life! The capsules or berries have stronger medicinal powers than the rest of the yam: they are an emetic, so are used in cases of poisoning, and they are applied as a poultice to carbuncles, boils, and incipient abscesses.

Culinary Uses

Since yam is regarded more as a medicine than an everyday food, I know of no recipes specifying it. Because of its crispness and light sweetness yam often replaces bamboo shoots, and it is usually stir-fried with pork or prawns and other more colourful vegetables.

Sorting yams on a farm in southern China

玉米
SWEET CORN

(YUMI) *Zea mays*

Cornflour

Sweet corn drying in the sun

Y*umi* (literally jade rice) or *zhenzhu mi* (pearl rice) is a comparatively late addition to the traditional Chinese diet. It is believed to have been introduced from the West some time during the Ming dynasty (1368–1644). The common name for India corn is *liusu*, meaning the sixth grain, indicating it was not one of the original Five Grains.

HOW IT GROWS

Sweet corn is widely cultivated in China, slightly more so in the North, which has a dry climate. In the South, it is mainly a hillside crop; rice is grown in the flatlands, where irrigation can be more easily kept under control.

MEDICINAL AND OTHER USES

Sweet corn is considered nutritious since it contains protein, fat, sugar and vitamins. A decoction of the root and leaves is used to ease urinary difficulties. Regular intake of corn is said to be good for a weak heart and for increasing sexual capacity! The Chinese ferment corn and distil wine and spirit, extract oil and even make flour from it.
It is also widely used as animal feed, particularly in the South.

CULINARY USES

It would be rather difficult to find a recipe featuring sweet corn as the main ingredient – except for the very popular Crab or Chicken and Sweet Corn Soup served in Chinese restaurants abroad (see recipe opposite). Baby corn cobs are now widely used in Chinese cooking, but these are a very recent product, which originated in Southeast Asia.

Corn growing high in the Guangxi province

CORNFLOUR

In Chinese cooking, cornflour is not only used as a thickening agent, but also as a thin batter or marinade for coating food before cooking, when it is mixed with cold water to make a smooth paste. For years, I used to mix roughly one part dry cornflour with one part water, and was quite happy with this until I was told by a master chef that the correct proportion should be 1 part cornflour to 1.2 parts water! He added that, because different flours absorb water differently, one should adjust proportions accordingly. For instance, for water chestnut flour, it should be 1:1.25; and it is 1:1.3 for potato flour. So now you know.

Cornflour is also used as a casing for dim sum, a casing which becomes almost translucent when cooked. The best known of these dim sum is the Cantonese *har kau* (prawn dumplings): fresh prawns with seasoning, wrapped in thin cornflour pastry and steamed in a bamboo basket.

CRAB OR CHICKEN AND SWEET CORN SOUP

This soup originated in the USA, so unless you use canned, creamed sweet corn from America, it will not taste authentic!

Serves 4
Preparation time 10–15 minutes
Cooking time 6–8 minutes

125g (4½oz) crab meat or 175g (6oz) chicken breast meat
½ teaspoon finely minced fresh ginger
2 egg whites
3–4 tablespoons milk
1 tablespoon cornflour paste
600ml (1 pint) good stock (p 71)
1 x 225g (8oz) can creamed sweet corn (American style)
Salt and pepper to taste
Dash of MSG (optional)
Finely chopped spring onions to garnish

1 Flake the crab meat (or coarsely chop the chicken meat), then mix with the ginger.

2 Beat the egg whites until frothy, then add the milk and cornflour paste. Beat again until smooth. Blend in the crab/chicken meat.

3 Bring the stock to a rolling boil, add the creamed sweet corn and bring back to the boil. Stir in the crab or chicken and egg white mixture, adjust the seasoning and stir gently until well blended. Serve hot, garnished with chopped spring onions.

Crab and Sweet Corn Soup

馬蹄粉
WATER CHESTNUT FLOUR

(MATI FEN)

Since water chestnut has a short life span, most of each crop is made into flour, and it is in the powder form that it is extensively used in Chinese cooking.

I have vivid memories of watching farmers in Jiangxi province (where my family took refuge from an advancing Japanese army in the forties) harvesting water chestnuts and making flour.

MANUFACTURE

Water chestnut flour is still made in China, just as I remember it being made more than half a century ago! When a sufficient area had been cleared, the land was levelled and large thatched huts erected. Inside each hut there were several rows of specially constructed wooden seats. A farmer would sit on a seat wearing rubber thimbles on the thumb and finger of each hand, hold a water chestnut by the stalk and crush it against the striated inner side of the large ceramic bowls which were secured on each side of the seat. When the bowls were full, the contents were mixed with water and strained in several stages through muslin in order to extract the starch which is then laid on bamboo mats to dry out in the sun and become flour. The water chestnut harvest was always a great communal affair for the whole village. Women and children worked all day in the fields, picking the chestnuts, while the young men cut the coarse leaves off, loosened the hard earth for the pickers, and carried the water chestnuts to the huts after washing them clean of mud in nearby ponds. After the starch had been extracted, the crushed water chestnuts were used as fodder for domestic animals. Nothing is wasted in China.

CULINARY USES

Water chestnut flour is used not just as a thickening agent or for coating food like cornflour or potato flour, but also for making dim sum and other snacks.

WATER CHESTNUT CAKE

A very popular Cantonese dim sum, this is prepared in homes at Chinese New Year, but restaurants serve it all year round.

Serves 8–10
Preparation time 40–45 minutes
Cooking time 30–35 minutes

225g (8oz) water chestnut flour
300ml (½ pint) milk
450g (1lb) peeled water chestnuts (fresh or tinned)
50g (2oz) lard
225g (8oz) sugar
600ml (1 pint) water

1 Blend the water chestnut flour and milk into a smooth paste.

2 Finely chop the chestnuts into a pulp. Place in a saucepan and mix with the lard, sugar and water. Bring to the boil, add about two-fifths of the chestnut flour and milk paste, blend well and bring back to the boil again. Take off heat to cool for 2 minutes or so.

3 Add the remaining paste gradually, stirring all the time. When it is blended, pour into a medium-sized greased cake tin and steam vigorously for 30 minutes.

4 When it is cool, cut into small squares. Serve cold or heat by frying or steaming.

Water Chestnut Cake

小米
与其它粮食
MILLET AND OTHER GRAINS

(SHAOMI) *Panicum miliaceum*

Ancient texts make much reference to the Five Grains of the Chinese diet – rice, wheat, millet, barley and soya. Nowadays, although the staples which make up the *fan* part of the meal may have changed a little, millet and other grains are still held as important foods. Since they are also eaten by the animals which supply the meat part of the diet, they can even be considered life-giving.

Millet

MILLET

Millet (*Panicum miliaceum*) is an indigenous crop widely cultivated in northern China from the earliest times. Its classical Chinese name *su* used to be the generic term for all kinds of grains. Its common name *xiaomi* means little or lesser rice, for it was regarded as poor man's rice by the more prosperous southerners. The truth is that millet is more nourishing than either rice or wheat – it contains more protein, fat, calcium, iron and vitamins than any other staples – but it is less tasty. Nowadays, millet has become less popular as a staple even in the North, though it is still extensively cultivated in China. As well as being consumed in the form of congee, it is widely used for fermenting and distilling. The stalks provide forage for horses and mules, and the husks are fed to pigs and chicken.

Sorghum

SORGHUM

Sorghum (*Sorghum vulgare*) is a variety of millet that is extensively grown in northern China as food for man and for animals, and for distilling into a spirit. Its classical name is *susu* (Sichuan millet), for the seeds of this plant were brought from Sichuan, but whether it is indigenous there or originally came from further west is not known. The common name *gaoliang* (tall grain) indicates its height. The stalks are used in the construction of fences, huts, mats and so on, in lieu of bamboo reeds from the Yangtze valley.

Sorghum grain is regarded as warming, nutritious, and good for stomach upsets. Its main use is in distilling: it is used to make the famous and very potent alcoholic drink Mou-Tai.

Barley

BARLEY

Barley (*Hordeum vulgare*) is called *damai* (big wheat) in Chinese. Although this cereal has been known in China from very early times, it has not been much cultivated there, despite the fact that it is considered to be very nourishing, preventing fever and giving one strength. It is primarily used for brewing beer.

OATS

Oats (*Avena fatua*) are seldom cultivated in China. The wild variety known as *yanmai* (swallow or birds' wheat) is sometimes collected and used for making bread. The grain is considered to be nutritious, and the shoots of growing grain are supposed to have some medicinal properties: a decoction of the shoots is given to parturient women to induce uterine contractions, in cases of retained placenta.

Oils and Liquid Flavourings

食油

COOKING OILS

(SHIYOU)

Groundnut oil

In the West, one talks about earning one's bread and butter; in China we earn our salt and oil. One of the seven basic daily necessities in China, oil plays a very important role in Chinese cooking. Animal fat has been used since time immemorial, but the extraction of oil from vegetable matter – mainly nuts and seeds – represents a more recent advance. Since animal fats burn at high temperatures, Chinese cooking methods such as stir-frying would not be possible without vegetable oil.

Rapeseed oil

Soya bean oil

VEGETABLE OILS

The most common vegetable oils used in Chinese cooking are rapeseed oil, peanut or groundnut oil and camellia (tea) oil made from the seeds of the wild tea plant (*Camellia*). Other cooking oils are sunflower oil, mustard seed oil, and cotton seed oil. Neither corn oil nor olive oil is produced in China, so I would not recommend them for Chinese cooking.

ANIMAL FATS

The most popular animal fat is pork lard which is a poly-unsaturated fat in China, where pigs are not intensively reared with chemical feeds. Chicken, duck and goose fats (polyunsaturated for the same reason) are also used in Chinese cooking. Beef fat is rarely used, except by Muslims, on account of its rather strong flavour.

CULINARY USES

Before use, every oil must be neutralised so that its flavour does not dominate the food itself. To do this heat the raw oil with a few bits of fresh ginger; when the ginger turns brown, discard it. Another way is to add spring onions and/or garlic to the ginger. Professional kitchens always season an amount of oil in advance, and use it over and over again for different dishes.

OIL-BRAISED CHICKEN

Do not be put off by the title of this dish. It describes a form of deep-frying and the end result is crispy rather than greasy.

Serves 4–6 as a starter, 2 as a main course
Preparation time 15–20 minutes plus marinating time
Cooking time 10 minutes

1 young chicken (poussin) weighing about 500g (1lb 2oz)
3–4 tablespoons light soy
2 tablespoons rice wine
1 tablespoon finely chopped spring onions
1 teaspoon ginger juice
½ teaspoon ground Sichuan peppercorns
1 teaspoon five-spice powder
Oil for deep-frying
Spicy salt and pepper (p 122) and chilli soy for serving

1 Split the chicken down the middle into two halves. Clean well and marinate with the soy, wine, spring onions, ginger juice, Sichuan peppercorns and five-spice for 25–30 minutes or longer.

2 Heat the oil to 160°C/325°F. Remove the chicken halves from the marinade and pat dry before deep-frying for 4–5 minutes. Remove from the oil and place in the marinade again for 10–15 minutes.

3 Reheat the oil to 190°C/375°F and deep-fry the chicken halves for about 5 minutes or until golden brown. (The chicken should be dry.) Remove, drain and chop into small pieces. Arrange on a serving plate.

4 Heat the marinade and pour over the chicken. Serve with spicy salt and chilli soy as dips. The skin of the chicken should be crispy, the flesh tender and aromatic.

Oil-braised chicken

料酒

COOKING WINE

(LIAOJIU)

The cooking wine most widely used in Chinese cooking, is, as you would expect, rice wine. It is generally acknowledged that the best rice wine is made in Shao Xing in southeast China, and that the best known variety is *Hua Tiao Chiew* or *Huadiao Jiu*. The name refers to the pretty patterns carved on the urns in which this brew is matured underground. More details about this and other rice wines are in the chapter on Drinks.

***Shao Hsing Hua Tiao Chiew* Rice Wine**

APPEARANCE AND TASTE

The common name for Chinese rice wine is *huang jiu* (yellow wine), on account of its golden colour – in contrast, Japanese sake, like *Mou-Tai*, is colourless.

BUYING AND STORING

When shopping in Oriental stores for Shao Xing or Shao Hsing wine, read the small print at the bottom of the label: it should state that it is made in Zhejiang, China. Do not be fooled by the fake Shao Hsing wine made in Taiwan and other countries – they pale (literally!) next to the genuine article, in bouquet as well as colour.

CULINARY USES

Should you have difficulty obtaining real Shao Xing Rice Wine, Japanese sake or a dry Spanish sherry is an acceptable substitute. You can also use whisky, brandy and rum. For certain Chinese dishes, *Mou-Tai* or a very strong, clear spirit known as *bai jiu* (white liquor), distilled from sorghum or maize, is sometimes used (p 232).

DRUNKEN CHICKEN

This recipe from Beijing is one of several versions of this very popular dish. Because no liquid other than alcohol is used, the aroma when the dish is brought to the table is quite intoxicating. The chicken should be extremely tender and succulent.

Serves 8–10 as a starter, 4–6 as a main course
Preparation time 30–35 minutes
Cooking time about 1¼ hours

1 young chicken weighing about 1.25kg (2lb 12oz)
1 tablespoon salt
300ml (½ pint) rice wine
50ml (2fl oz) whisky, brandy or rum
4–5 slices peeled fresh ginger root
3–4 spring onions, cut into short sections
Fresh coriander leaves

1 Clean the chicken and blanch in boiling water for 8–10 minutes. Remove and rinse in cold water. Drain.

2 Chop the chicken into small bite-size pieces, and arrange them neatly, skin side down, in a heat-proof bowl.

3 Mix 2 teaspoons salt with the wine, brandy, ginger and spring onions. Pour over the chicken. Cover the bowl with foil and steam for 1 hour.

4 To serve: pour off (and reserve) the liquid from the bowl and discard the ginger and spring onions. Invert the chicken pieces onto a round dish. Boil about half of the juice in which the chicken has been cooked with the remaining salt, then pour it over the chicken. Serve hot.

Drunken Chicken

芝麻油

SESAME SEED OIL

(ZHI MA YOU)

Roasted sesame seed oil

The Chinese character *ma* is properly applied to plants yielding textile fibre known as jute (*Corchorus, Boemeria, Linum*), and also to hemp (*Cannabis sativa*). Hemp seed has been used as food since ancient times, so it is not surprising that *ma* should have been applied to *Sesamum, Linum* and *Cannabis* when General Chang Chien brought seeds of these plants back from India and Central Asia during the Han dynasty.

APPEARANCE AND TASTE

Chinese sesame oil is made from roasted sesame seeds. It is amber in colour and highly aromatic, quite different from the pale yellow sesame oil made in the Middle East and India, which is light and has no aroma.

Raw sesame seeds

BUYING AND STORING

Buy sesame oil in small bottles and use before the expiry date if possible, as it loses its strong aroma. Always store it in a cool, dark place – exposure to strong light and heat may turn it prematurely rancid.

CULINARY USES

Sesame oil will smoke and burn in a matter of seconds over high heat, so is not suitable for stir-frying. We use it to give extra aroma to food: just a few drops sprinkled over a dish and stirred in before it is transferred to a serving platter help to intensify the dish's fragrance. Sesame oil can be used cold as well, such as in salad dressing and in dips. It is much used in Sichuan cooking for the special dry-frying method known as *ganchao*.

DRY-FRIED SHREDDED BEEF

Dry-frying is a unique Sichuan cooking method. The main ingredient is slowly fried over low heat until dry, then very quickly finished off with other ingredients and seasonings over high heat.

Serves 4
Preparation time 20–25 minutes
Cooking time 10–12 minutes

350–400g (12–14 oz) beef steak
3–4 stalks celery (or 2 medium carrots)
3–4 tablespoons sesame oil
2 tablespoons rice wine
1 teaspoon chilli bean paste (toban jiang)
1 tablespoon sweet bean sauce (Hoi Sin sauce)
½ teaspoon chilli powder
½ teaspoon minced garlic
½ teaspoon salt
1 teaspoon sugar
1 tablespoon finely chopped spring onions
½ teaspoon finely chopped fresh ginger
¼ teaspoon ground Sichuan peppercorns
½ teaspoon chilli oil

1 Trim off excess fat from the beef, then cut it into matchstick-size shreds. Cut the celery or carrots into thin shreds.

2 Heat the wok over high heat and add the sesame oil. Before the oil gets too hot, add the beef shreds with about half the wine. Stir-fry until the shreds have separated, reduce the heat and continue stirring until the beef is dry (pour off any excess liquid if necessary).

3 Add the chilli bean paste, sweet bean sauce, chilli powder, garlic, salt and sugar, plus the remaining wine and the celery or carrots. Increase the heat and stir-fry for 2–3 minutes. Add the spring onions, ginger, Sichuan pepper and chilli oil, blend well and serve hot.

Note: I have already reduced the number of hot chillies in the original recipe; you can make further reductions to suit your personal palate.

Dry-Fried Shredded Beef

芝麻醤

SESAME PASTE

Another sesame-based product is sesame paste which is made from ground, roasted sesame seeds. Similar to Middle Eastern tahini, this extremely aromatic paste is primarily used in Sichuan cooking. It is a savoury paste, not to be confused with the sweet sesame paste which is made from black sesame seeds.

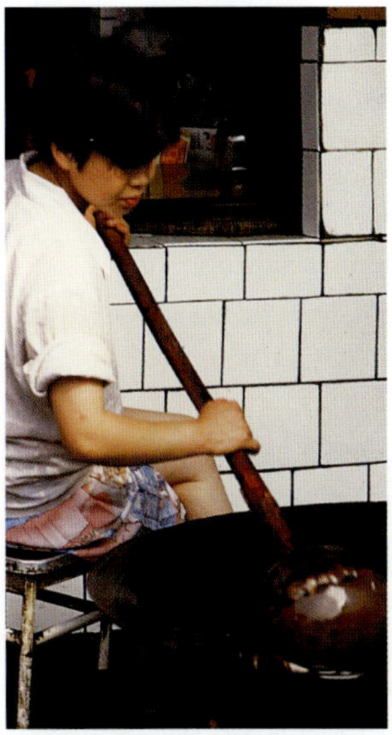

Making sesame paste

APPEARANCE AND TASTE

The paste comes in a glass jar covered with oil; it is hard and resembles cement in colour and consistency and you have to use a really sturdy spoon or blunt knife to scoop it out. Before using, mix with a little sesame oil or hot water to make into a smooth, creamy paste.

BUYING AND STORING

Chinese sesame paste is available from Oriental supermarkets and so long as there is still a good layer of oil over the paste, it should keep for some time. Check the expiry date. Like the sesame oil it should always be stored in a cool, dark place to prevent it going rancid.

CULINARY USES

Bang-Bang Chicken is one of the few recipes in which I use sesame paste. Middle Eastern tahini which looks similar and has the same consistency is an acceptable substitute, but since tahini is not nearly as aromatic as the Chinese product a certain amount of Chinese sesame oil should be added to make it taste stronger.

Bang-Bang Chicken

BANG-BANG CHICKEN

This popular Sichuan dish is known as Bon-Bon Chicken because the meat is tenderized by being banged with a stick (*bon*).

Serves 4–6 as a starter
Preparation and cooking time 30–35 minutes

225g (8oz) chicken meat (boned and skinned)
A few lettuce leaves
2 tablespoons sesame paste
1 teaspoon sesame oil
2 tablespoons light soy
2 teaspoons rice vinegar
1 teaspoon chilli sauce
½ teaspoon sugar

1 Place the chicken meat in a saucepan and cover with cold water. Bring to the boil, reduce the heat and simmer for about 10 minutes. Drain, reserving a little liquid. Beat with a rolling pin until soft, then pull into shreds.

2 Shred the lettuce leaves and place them on a serving dish. Place the chicken meat on top of the lettuce leaves.

3 Mix a little of the liquid in which the chicken has been cooked with the sesame paste. Blend in the soy, vinegar, sesame oil, chilli sauce and sugar. Stir until you have a smooth, creamy paste, pour all over the chicken and serve.

辣油

CHILLI OIL

(LAYOU)

There are two types of this fiery oil, neither of which is used for cooking but as a dressing or a dip.

Red Oil Dipping Sauce

How It Is Made

Heat the vegetable oil to smoking but not boiling point, then allow to cool. Add the chilli flakes (with seeds!) and if making the Cantonese version, add the seasonings of garlic, red onions and salt, and, if liked, dried shrimp and sugar. Cover and remove the pan from the heat. Let the chillies infuse in the oil until it is completely cold – overnight if necessary. To make Sichuan red oil, strain the oil and discard the chillies and seeds. You do not need to use any other seasonings for this oil.

Appearance and Taste

The most common chilli oil is the dark red one served as a dip in Cantonese restaurants. This is made from an infusion of dried red chillies and seasonings in vegetable oil. The Sichuan chilli oil, little seen outside China, is also red and often called *hongyou* (red oil). It has no additional seasonings and the chillies have usually been removed.

Buying and Storing

Chilli oil is sold in small bottles. Several brands are available, and there is even one marketed as XO Chilli Oil, which contains little bits of dried scallops (highly prized by the Chinese) to enhance the flavour. Store chilli oil in a cool, dry, dark place; it will keep for a long time. If you do refrigerate the oil, bring it back to room temperature before serving.

Freshly picked chillies on their way to market

Red Oil Dipping Sauce

This is a basic Sichuan recipe. Other ingredients such as garlic, ginger, spring onions, Sichuan peppercorns and vinegar, either singly or combined, may be added. Use eight parts soy (both light and dark are suitable), three parts red oil and one part sesame oil. Blend well and serve in individual small saucers.

Chillies are left to dry on a roof in Yunnan province

辣椒醬

Chilli Sauce

(LAJIAO JIANG)

Chinese chilli sauce is a very spicy, slightly fruity, hot sauce, which is used both in the kitchen and at table. The main difference between chilli sauce and chilli oil is that only fresh red chillies are used for the sauce, while dried chillies are used for the oil.

Dark or thick chilli sauce

Appearance and Taste

There are two main types of chilli sauce on the market. The most popular one has a loose, light texture which makes it suitable for pouring at table. Apart from hot chillies (usually without the seeds), it may contain rice vinegar, salt, starch and fruit The other (hotter) type of chilli sauce is much thicker and has the seeds left in. It is basically chilli oil with added salt and starch.

Buying and Storing

Light chilli oil is sold in a tall bottle, while thicker chilli sauce comes in a jar. Once opened, both the bottle and jar should be stored in the refrigerator, where they should keep almost indefinitely.

A colourful mound of red chillies to be used in chilli sauce

Culinary Use

Chilli sauce adds an extra zest to any dish, hot or cold, and is ideal not just for Chinese food but also non-Chinese dishes such as stews, curries, salads. It is perfect for marinades. Use the lighter chilli sauce at the table, and the thicker chilli sauce in the kitchen.

Marinade for Barbecue

Mix 1 part chilli sauce with 6–8 parts soy sauce, 2–3 parts rice wine, 1–2 parts sugar, 1 part lemon juice and ½ part sesame oil, and blend well. Marinate spare-ribs, or any other meat or fish, for several hours before grilling. Use the marinade to make a sauce.

Marinade for Barbecue

醬油

SOY

('SOY SAUCE')

(JIANG YOU)

Dark soy

As I said in my Introduction, 'soy sauce' is a mistranslation of this flavouring agent so indispensable to Chinese cooking. *Jiang you* is not a sauce in the strict sense but the liquid extracted from fermented and salted soya beans. The Cantonese call it *chi you* (fermented soya oil or extract).

HISTORY

One of the earliest recorded references to *jiang* is found in the works of Confucius (551–479 BC). The great sage, who was a gourmet of repute, stated categorically in *Lun Yu*, one of his best known works, that one should never eat any meat dishes without *jiang*. By the time of the Han dynasty (206 BC–AD 220), *jiang* was being sold in company with wine, vinegar and other liquids, so it must have been produced on a large scale. Since the Song dynasty (960–1279), *jiang* has been considered one of the seven daily necessities in any Chinese household.

Light soy

MANUFACTURE

The making of *jiang you* (soy extract) is a lengthy and painstaking process. The soya beans are cleaned, soaked until soft, steamed, cooled, mixed with yeast culture and wheat flour, incubated for 3–5 weeks (according to season and local climate), fermented in a brine solution for 6–24 months, baked in the hot summer sun for 100 days, pressed, filtered, pasteurized, and bottled. The quality of the end product depends on the expertise of the soy master, who supervises every stage of the process from start to finish: the selection of the soya beans, the making of the yeast culture, the proportions of the different ingredients, timing and temperature. Not a ten-minute job!

APPEARANCE AND TASTE

Basically, there are two types of soy: light and dark. Light soy or *shengchou* comes from the first pressing (similar to virgin olive oil), so is lighter in colour with a more delicate, purer flavour. Dark soy or *laochou* (literally, old soy) has a longer period of fermentation and is a blend of subsequent pressings, with caramel (burnt sugar) added to give a darker, richer colour.

BUYING AND STORING

Since there are so many different brands of soy available (and within just one brand there can be a range of up-market and down-market products), one has to choose carefully. Avoid brands that are not manufactured in China, Hong Kong or Taiwan, for most of these will have been synthetically made from hydrolysed vegetable protein with corn syrup and other additives, and they do not have the aroma or flavour of naturally fermented products. My personal favourite is the Pearl River Bridge brand from Guangdong, the preferred brand of more than 90 percent of Chinese restaurants in the West.

Like wine and spirits, the quality of a good soy will deteriorate when exposed to oxygen – it will lose its aroma and flavour. Buy a small bottle and use it within 2–3 weeks, less if not stored in a cool, dark place. Or, if you do buy a large one, decant some of the soy into small containers with air-tight lids, and refrigerate. Some types of soy do not contain preservatives, in which case they should be stored in the refrigerator after opening.

CULINARY USES

As a general rule, use light soy for seafood, white meat and most vegetables, also in soups and for stir-frying. Dark soy is for red meat and for braising, roasting and marinating. The ideal mix for dipping soy for the table is two parts light to one part dark – the same proportion used for marinating and stewing. Kikkoman Soy is made for Japanese food, which mainly uses soy at the table. Most Chinese food is pre-seasoned in the kitchen, so although there are certain dishes which require specially prepared dips or sauces, there is no need for additional seasoning.

The Pearl River flows through Guangzhou, capital of Guangdong

Soya Chicken

This is the bright brown chicken seen hanging in the windows of Cantonese restaurants. It is ideal as a starter, or for buffets and picnics.

Serves 8–10 as a starter or 4 as a main course
Preparation time about 15 minutes plus marinating time
Cooking time about 45 minutes plus standing time

1 young chicken weighing about 1.5kg (3lb 5oz)
1 tablespoon ground Sichuan peppercorns
1 tablespoon fresh ginger juice (see p29)
2 tablespoons brown sugar
3–4 tablespoons rice wine
300ml (½ pint) dark soy
150ml (¼ pint) light soy
3–4 tablespoons oil
Lettuce leaves to garnish

1 Clean the chicken well and pat dry with a paper towel. Rub the chicken all over with the pepper and ginger juice, not forgetting the cavity.

2 Marinate the chicken with the sugar, wine and soy in a large bowl for at least 3 hours, turning it over once per hour.

3 Heat the oil in a wok until hot. Brown the chicken all over, then add the marinade, rinsing the bowl with a little water and adding that to the wok too. Bring to the boil, then reduce the heat and simmer, covered, for 30–35 minutes, turning the chicken over several times so that it is cooked evenly on all sides.

4 Turn off the heat and leave the chicken to cool down in the sauce (still covered) for 25–30 minutes. Remove the chicken and chop into bite-size pieces. Arrange them neatly on a bed of lettuce leaves, pour over a little of the sauce and serve at room temperature.

Note: The remainder of the sauce can be stored in the refrigerator for weeks, to be used again and again. (This is the sauce which is sold in bottles as Chicken Marinade.)

Soya Duck

This was one of my childhood favourites. It is from Shanghai and is very rarely seen in the West – only two out of the thousand or so Chinese restaurants in London have it on their menu.

Serves 10–12 as a starter
Preparation time about 30 minutes
Cooking time 45–50 minutes plus cooling time

1 duck weighing at least 2 kg (4lb 8oz)
1 tablespoon salt
2–3 spring onions, cut into short sections
1 tablespoon coarsely chopped fresh ginger
2–3 pieces cinnamon bark
5–6 star anise
2 litres (3½ pints) water
½ teaspoon red colouring (optional)
3 tablespoons rice wine
6 tablespoons dark soy
4 tablespoons light soy
115g (4oz) rock sugar
About 2 teaspoons sesame oil
Coriander leaves to garnish

1 Clean the duck well. Blanch it in a pan of boiling water, remove and pat dry. Cut off the parson's nose, then rub about ½ teaspoon salt inside the cavity.

A picnic is the ideal opportunity to enjoy either of the soya dishes

2 Wrap the spring onions, ginger, cinnamon bark and star anise in a small muslin bag and drop it into a pot of fresh water. Add the red colouring, if using, and bring the water to the boil. Simmer for 15–20 minutes, then remove and discard the bag.

3 Place the duck in the liquid and add the wine, soy, sugar and remaining salt. Bring back to the boil, and simmer gently under cover for 45–50 minutes, turning the duck over several times during cooking. Turn off the heat, and leave the duck in the sauce to cool down, still covered, for at least 2 hours.

4 Take the duck out of the sauce, brush the skin with sesame oil and leave it to cool a little longer. Chop into bite-size pieces and arrange neatly on a serving plate. Reduce the sauce by boiling it over high heat, uncovered, until it thickens. Pour some of the sauce over the duck and serve.

Note: Store leftover sauce in the refrigerator. It will keep for a long time, and can be used again and again, each time replenished with more seasonings (wine, soy, salt and sugar). The older the sauce, the more delicious it will be.

Mushroom Soy

A Cantonese speciality, mushroom soy has a fragrant mushroomy flavour. Again the brand I like best is Pearl River Bridge, which is made with dark soy and straw mushrooms, and has a little sugar added to give it a subtle, sweet taste. Use sparingly in addition to light soy or other seasonings on stir-fried meat and vegetables, in soups and stews. It can be used on its own as a dip at the table. If refrigerated after opening, it should keep for many, many months.

Chilli Soy Sauce

Sold in small bottles, chilli soy is made from light soy flavoured with fresh chilli, usually with sugar and caramel added to balance the peppery hotness. It is more of a dipping sauce for the table, rather than for use in the kitchen. Be warned: it has a long-lasting aftertaste.

Overleaf: Soya Chicken (hanging) and Soya Duck

紹興花彫酒
SHAO HSING
HUA TIAO CHIEW
福
中國

米醋

Rice Vinegar

(MICU)

Vinegar is used extensively in Chinese cooking, and there are two basic types: dark brown – known as red or black – fermented rice vinegar; and clear – known as white – distilled grain vinegar. Grain vinegar is stronger than rice vinegar, so is only used for dips at the table and as a preservative in pickling, rather than for cooking.

Chinkiang rice vinegar

Manufacture

Rice vinegar is made from a mixture of glutinous rice and other grains (which may include rice, wheat, barley and rice husks). The manufacturing process is a cross between that for rice wine and that for soy sauce. It involves soaking, steaming, cooling, primary fermentation with yeast, secondary fermentation with vinegar acid, sunning during the daytime, and exposure to the cool night air (for up to 6–7 months), straining and pasteurization before bottling.

Appearance and Taste

Most rice vinegar has a dark brown, almost black, colour and a beautiful aroma. It has a pleasantly sweetish taste, only mildly sour – not at all sharp like the distilled malt vinegar you get in the West. The average acidity in a Chinese rice vinegar is only about 5–6 percent, and since there is always a residue of sugar from the fermentation process, it is almost drinkable.

Buying and Storing

In China, the common name for rice vinegar is *shaojiu* (lesser wine), and one can buy it 'loose'. Most grocery stores will have big urns of different quality vinegar next to the rice wine and spirit. My nanny used to send me with an empty bottle to our corner shop to have it filled with vinegar. There are many kinds of rice vinegar made in China, but very few are exported. One of the best is the Gold Plum Chinkiang Vinegar, *Zhenjiang xiangcu* (Fragrant Vinegar of Zhenjiang), which because of its reputation (it won the French Laurier d'Or de la Qualité Internationale in 1985) is widely available in the West. Unlike rice wine, rice vinegar can be kept almost forever. Some people say it improves with age, and while I am not so sure about that, I recently came across a ten-year-old bottle of Chinkiang vinegar in a cupboard, and I must admit that it still tasted very good.

Vinegar's medicinal uses have a long association with Buddhism

Medicinal Uses

Rice vinegar is supposed to be good for one's digestion. There is a special vinegar made with herb medicine, first discovered by a seventeenth-century Buddhist monk in Sichuan – he lived to be over a hundred and his longevity was attributed to his daily intake of this medicinal vinegar. It is supposed to reduce high blood pressure, cure coughs and influenza, and prevent other epidemic diseases.

Culinary Uses

As one of the seven basic daily necessities for the Chinese kitchen, vinegar obviously plays a very important role in Chinese cooking, particularly in the northern and western parts of China. Everyone knows about sweet and sour dishes which are more sweet than sour, but there are also hot and sour dishes which use more vinegar than sugar, making them sour rather than sweet. The following recipe is a good example.

Fish in Vinegar Sauce

Hot and Sour Cabbage

Choose a round, pale green cabbage with a firm heart. The white Dutch variety is good – never use loose-leafed dark greens.

Serves 6–8 as a side dish
Preparation time about 15 minutes
Cooking time 5–6 minutes

685g (1½lb) cabbage
A few dried red chillies
3–4 tablespoons oil
12–15 Sichuan peppercorns
1 teaspoon salt
½ teaspoon sesame oil

For the sauce:
2 tablespoons light soy
3 tablespoons rice vinegar
1½ tablespoons sugar

1 Discard the tough outer leaves of the cabbage, then cut it into about 2cm (¾in) square pieces. Chop the chillies finely, discarding the seeds if you don't like your food too hot. Mix the sauce ingredients in a jug or bowl and keep handy.

2 Heat the oil until smoking. Add the chillies and Sichuan peppercorns to flavour the oil, and before they start to burn, quickly add the cabbage and stir-fry for about 2 minutes or until limp. Add the salt and continue stirring for another minute. Pour in the sauce mixture, blend well and continue stirring for 2 more minutes. Add the sesame oil and stir a few more times. Serve hot or cold.

Fish in Vinegar Sauce

This is a sweet and sour dish with a difference: it is subtly vinegary, with a faint touch of sweetness that makes it extremely appetizing.

Serves 4–6 as a starter, 2–3 as a main course
Preparation time about 20–25 minutes plus marinating time
Cooking time 6–8 minutes

450g (1lb) firm white fish fillet (cod, haddock, turbot, halibut or sole etc.)
½ teaspoon salt
2 teaspoons rice wine or brandy
1 egg, beaten
3–4 tablespoons plain flour
Cold water
Oil for deep-frying
Fresh coriander leaves to garnish

For the sauce:
1 tablespoon fresh oil
½ teaspoon finely chopped fresh ginger
1 tablespoon chopped white parts of spring onion
About 125ml (4fl oz) stock or water
2 tablespoons light soy
1 tablespoon rice wine
1 tablespoon sugar
3 tablespoons rice vinegar
1 small fresh red chilli, seeded and thinly shredded (optional)
1 tablespoon cornflour paste
½ teaspoon sesame oil

1 Dry the fish well, then cut it into matchbox-size pieces and marinate with the salt and wine for 10–15 minutes.

2 Mix the egg and flour with a little water to make a smooth batter, and coat the fish pieces with the batter.

3 Heat the oil in a wok or deep-fryer to 170°C/325°F. Add the fish piece by piece, stirring gently to make sure the pieces are separate. Deep-fry the fish for 2–3 minutes or until golden brown. Remove and drain.

4 Wipe clean the wok. Heat the fresh oil until hot, then reduce the heat and add the ginger and spring onion whites to flavour the oil. Before they become brown, add the stock or water and turn up the heat to bring it to the boil. Now add the soy, wine, sugar and about two-thirds of the vinegar. Blend well and simmer for 1 minute before adding the fish pieces. Braise the fish in the sauce for about 2–3 minutes.

5 Add the chilli, if using, and the remaining vinegar. Stir in the cornflour paste to thicken the sauce. Sprinkle the sesame oil all over, blend well and serve while still hot, garnished with the coriander leaves.

甜酸汁

SWEET AND SOUR SAUCE

(TIANSUAN ZHI)

I have news for those who think that sweet and sour dishes are a Cantonese speciality: the first people to use the sugar and vinegar combination in cooking were northerners from the Yellow River Valley well over two thousand years ago, when the southern Cantonese were still regarded as barbarians with no culinary refinement.

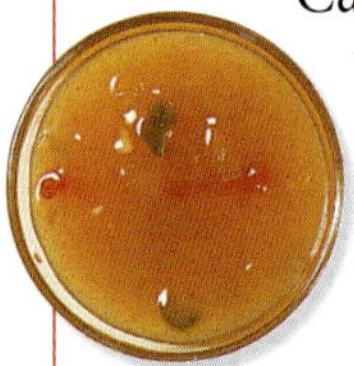

MANUFACTURE

You will never find any commercially prepared sweet and sour sauce in shops in China – it is always freshly prepared for each individual dish. Even in Cantonese restaurants abroad, the sauce is prepared in the kitchen, never bought ready-made. I shall never live down the tale my late wife used to tell our friends, that one of our first meals consisted of a packet of frozen fish fingers served with a bottle of ready-made sweet and sour sauce!

CULINARY USES

Originally, sugar and vinegar (in addition to salt and soy) were used to cook carp from the Yellow River to mask their muddy flavour. This method was later used on mutton and other strongly flavoured foods. Later still, the southeastern Chinese along the Yangtze River delta started to use this mixture for other food – notably prawns and pork spare-ribs. The very popular Sweet and Sour Pork, swamped in tomato ketchup with pineapple, onion and carrots, served in Cantonese restaurants and take-aways throughout the world, has its origin in the West.

Spare-Ribs in Sweet and Sour Sauce

SPARE-RIBS IN SWEET AND SOUR SAUCE

This is the very first Cantonese dish I ever encountered, and I have never forgotten the bright and translucent sauce.

Serves 6–8 as a starter
Preparation time 15–20 minutes plus marinating
Cooking time about 10–15 minutes

450g (1lb) pork spare-ribs
1 teaspoon salt
1 tablespoon light soy
Cornflour paste
Dry cornflour
Oil for deep-frying
3 tablespoons rice vinegar
3 tablespoons sugar
1 tablespoon dark soy
2 tablespoons tomato sauce
1 tablespoon oil
½ teaspoon minced garlic
½ teaspoon finely chopped fresh ginger
1 tablespoon chopped spring onions
1 small fresh red chilli, seeded and finely shredded
½ teaspoon sesame oil

1 Chop the ribs into bite-size pieces. Mix with ½ teaspoon of the salt and light soy and leave to marinate for 10 minutes. Coat each piece of meat with cornflour paste, then roll in dry cornflour.

2 Heat the oil in a wok or deep-fryer to 190°C/375°F, then reduce the heat and let the oil cool down to about 160°C/300°F. Drop the ribs piece by piece into the oil. Deep-fry over high heat for 6–8 minutes, or until crisp and golden, then remove with a perforated spoon. Wait for a few minutes for the oil to become hot again before returning the ribs to be fried again for 1–2 minutes or until golden brown. Remove and drain.

3 Heat the vinegar in a saucepan over low heat, and dissolve the sugar in it. Add the remaining salt with the dark soy and tomato sauce and blend well. This is the sweet and sour sauce.

4 In a clean wok, heat the fresh oil until hot, stir-fry the garlic, ginger, spring onions and chilli for a few seconds, or until fragrant, then add the sweet and sour sauce. Thicken with 1 tablespoon cornflour paste. When the sauce starts bubbling, add the cooked ribs. Mix and toss to make sure that each piece of meat is coated with sauce. Blend in the sesame oil and serve hot or cold.

湯

STOCKS

(TANG)

There is an old Chinese saying: A cook's stock is a singer's voice. Stock in Chinese cooking is paramount – and it can give away a lot about the expertise of the chef!

'Once the stock is ready, then the rest of the meal can be made'

APPEARANCE AND TASTE

There are two basic types of stock used in Chinese cooking. The most common one is known as *qing tang* (clear stock); the other is called *nai* or *nong tang* (milky or thick stock). Chinese stocks are different from the Western version, so commercial stock cubes are no substitute.

MANUFACTURE

Both clear stock and milky stock are made from chicken and pork. We do not have a fish stock. All fish dishes – including soups – are made with meat stock. There is, however, a vegetarian stock known as *bai tang* (white stock), used only in vegetarian kitchens – all vegetable dishes served in non-vegetarian Chinese restaurants are cooked with meat stock, explaining in part why they taste so delicious!

CULINARY USES

It is impossible to do any cooking without stock in a professional kitchen. Stock is the very first item a Chinese cook prepares when starting work in the kitchen each morning. It is used not only as the basis for soups, but also in general cooking instead of water whenever liquid is required.

CLEAR STOCK

To upgrade this basic stock to *gao tang* (high or superior stock), add a duck. For those who don't eat pork, substitute lamb or veal (but not beef) in the ingredients. And if you would prefer a chicken stock, use just extra chicken and no red meat at all.

Makes about 4 litres (7 pints) stock
Preparation time 10–15 minutes
Cooking time about 4 hours

1 chicken weighing about 1 kg (2lb 4oz)
1 kg (2lb 4oz) pork spare-ribs
4–6 spring onions, white parts only
50g (2oz) fresh ginger, crushed
3–4 tablespoons rice wine

1 Trim and discard excess fat from the chicken and spare-ribs. Place the meat in a large pot. Add about 6 litres (10½ pints) cold water. Bring to a rapid boil over high heat and skim off the scum.

2 Add the spring onions, ginger, and rice wine. Reduce the heat and simmer gently, covered, for 3½–4 hours.

3 Remove and discard all the solid ingredients, then strain the stock. It is now ready for use.

Note: If you do not possess a pot large enough to hold 7 or more litres of water, by all means reduce the ingredients proportionately. If refrigerated when cool, the stock will keep for up to 4–5 days. Alternatively, it can be frozen in small containers and defrosted as required.

MILKY OR THICK STOCK

Use the same ingredients as for the clear stock, though some chefs use fresh pigs' trotters as well as spare-ribs for extra flavour. Follow the instructions for Clear Stock through Step 1, then boil over a medium heat, uncovered, for 2 hours. Keep at no more than a rolling boil so the stock does not boil away. During the second hour, the stock will turn milky. After 2 hours it will be thick, and have reduced by two-thirds. It will set like jelly when refrigerated.

VEGETARIAN STOCK

This delicate vegetarian stock can be enriched with dried Shiitake mushrooms, which result in a much darker colour and fragrant aroma.

Makes 2 litres (3½ pints) stock
Preparation time 5–10 minutes
Cooking time 30 minutes

225g (8oz) fresh soya bean sprouts
2 litres (3½ pints) cold water
3 spring onions, white parts only (optional)

1 Dry-fry the sprouts in a preheated wok or pan over medium heat for a few minutes to eliminate the sharp 'beany' smell.

2 Pour in the water and bring to the boil. Add the spring onion whites, if using, and simmer gently, covered, for 30 minutes. Strain, discarding the sprouts and spring onions. Refrigerate any leftover stock. It will keep for several days.

SEASONINGS

精盬

SALT

(JINGYAN)

Salt has become an essential part of our diet all over the world; it must be one of the earliest forms of seasoning, heralding the arrival of the art of cookery.

MANUFACTURE

Some people believe that our primitive ancestors discovered salt purely by chance: hunters left their kill on the seashore to dry, and it was sometimes covered by the tide. When the tide had gone down, salt crystals were left behind, and when the food was cooked, it tasted better than usual. Thus was salt discovered! An interesting story, but it does not explain how people who lived inland, miles from the sea, discovered salt in underground mines. Perhaps they were actually digging for coal or iron, and found salt by chance that way.

CULINARY USES

Common salt is used not just as a seasoning in Chinese cooking but also to preserve vegetables, fish and meats. There is a famous Cantonese dish known as Salt-Baked Chicken, which is not that difficult to cook at home – try it, and see how it is done.

SALT-BAKED CHICKEN

Because the chicken is wrapped in fine muslin or cheesecloth, it never tastes too salty – the meat is succulent, and the skin is firm but not crisp. I have no idea who invented this method of cooking or when, but it might have its origin in the very popular dish known as Beggar's Chicken, in which a whole chicken is encased in clay and baked in hot ashes. It is a dish which has been on the menu of good Cantonese restaurants for well over a hundred years.

Serves 6–8 as a starter or 3–4 as a main course
Preparation time about 25–30 minutes plus drying time
Cooking time about 1½ hours

1 young chicken, weighing about 1.25kg (2lb 12oz)
2 tablespoons light soy
2.25kg (5lb) coarse salt

For the marinade:
1 teaspoon finely chopped fresh ginger
1 tablespoon finely chopped spring onions
2 pieces star anise, crushed
½ teaspoon salt
50ml (2fl oz) Mei Kuei Lu Chiew or brandy, rum, vodka etc*

For serving:
1 tablespoon oil
1 teaspoon minced fresh ginger root
1 tablespoon finely shredded spring onions
½ teaspoon salt
About 50ml (2fl oz) milky (thick) stock (p 71)

1 Clean the chicken well, then blanch in boiling water for a few minutes. Remove and drain. Brush the whole chicken with soy, then hang it up to dry for at least 2 hours.

Salt-Baked Chicken

2 Mix together all the marinade ingredients and pour into the cavity of the chicken. Wrap the chicken firmly with a single layer of cheesecloth, making sure the overlap is on top of the breast, so it is easier to unwrap for serving.

3 Heat the coarse salt in a wok or large casserole until very hot (the ideal dish for salt-baking is the Chinese casserole known as a sand or clay pot), then turn off the heat and remove about half of the salt. Make a good-sized hole in the middle of the salt in the pot, and place the wrapped chicken in it, breast side up. Cover it with the salt removed earlier, so the chicken is completely buried in the salt. Cover the pot tightly.

4 Turn the heat to medium high for 15 minutes, then reduce to very low, and cook the chicken gently for 50–55 minutes. Take it off the heat, but do not uncover for at least 15–20 minutes.

5 Make the dipping sauce by heating the oil in a small saucepan over low heat. Add the ginger, spring onions, salt and stock, blend well and place in two small saucers on the table.

6 Remove the chicken from the salt (the salt can be re-used). Unwrap it and chop it into small bite-size pieces. Arrange them neatly on a serving dish. Serve hot or cold.

Mei Kuei Lu Chiew is a delicate and fragrant spirit made from sorghum with specially grown rose petals (*mei gui* being the Chinese name for rose) (p233).

味精

MSG (Monosodium Glutamate)

(WEIJING)

The use of MSG (monosodium glutamate) is one of the most controversial aspects of Chinese cooking. Extensive research conducted worldwide demonstrates that, if used correctly, MSG is safe for human consumption, since it contains less sodium than the refined salt we use every day.

Manufacture

The Chinese have been using MSG as a flavour enhancer in its liquid form of soy (sauce) for centuries, but it was the Japanese who first discovered it could be extracted from seaweed to create what they call *Aji-No-Moto* (the element of taste). From 1923 the Chinese then began to make their own MSG from wheat protein, which was called *Ve-Tsin* or *weijing* (the essence of taste), also known as Gourmet Powder. Its popularity was phenomenal: within years it became an indispensable item to both the catering trade and middle-class households, for as the makers claim on the package: 'A sprinkling of *Ve-Tsin* will bring out the full natural flavour of your dishes and render them surprisingly delicious.' Glutamic acid is one of the most abundant amino acids and is one of the most commonly used of the 23 or so we find in proteins. The salts it forms with sodium (MSG), potassium, calcium and so on are collectively referred to as glutamates and occur naturally in meat, fish, milk (particularly breast milk), cheese, vegetables, tomatoes and mushrooms.

Culinary Uses

Some Chinese restaurants may claim that they do not use any MSG in their dishes, but they do use soy (sauce), oyster sauce, and the other bean pastes, all of which contain MSG – that is why they taste so delicious! When using MSG at home, you must observe a few basic points: you only need a tiny amount – no more than a pinch, or about half a teaspoon at most – at any one time, and should not use it in every single dish you are serving at the meal; it should never be added to food until the end of cooking, because when heated above 160°C/325°F for an extended period – more than 2–3 minutes, say – it changes chemically and becomes poisonous; and it should not be sprinkled on at table, for to have the correct effect, it has to be dissolved completely in the food seconds before the end of cooking (see the recipe below).

Emerald and White Jade Soup

This humble soup of spinach and bean-curd (tofu) has been given a rather poetic name – a good example of the Chinese penchant for hyperbole. It is also a good example of the Chinese way of making a most delicious soup out of simple ingredients – thanks to MSG!

Emerald and White Jade Soup

Serves 4
Preparation time 5–10 minutes
Cooking time 5 minutes

1 cake bean-curd
Salt
225g (8oz) fresh spinach leaves
1 tablespoon oil
About 600ml (1 pint) water
½ teaspoon MSG
Sesame oil to garnish

1 Cut the bean-curd into 16 small cubes. Blanch in a pan of lightly salted water for 2–3 minutes, remove and drain.

2 Cut the spinach into small pieces – baby spinach leaves can be left whole.

3 Heat the oil and stir-fry the spinach for 1 minute. Add ¼ teaspoon of salt and continue stirring for 10–15 seconds. Add the water and bring to the boil. Add the bean-curd cubes and cook for 2 more minutes, then sprinkle over the MSG with about 1 teaspoon salt. Blend well and serve hot with a few drops of sesame oil.

Note: If you happen to have ready-made chicken or other meat stock to hand, it will improve the flavour of the soup immensely. But even if you use plain water and MSG as recipe above, you will be surprised by how good the dish is.

白糖

SUGAR

(BAITANG)

Partly refined sugar

Although sugar was not included in the original 'seven basic daily necessities' it has became an indispensable item in the Chinese kitchen today. By sugar we of course mean sucrose, a simple carbohydrate produced by green plants. The most common type of sugar, and some would say the best, is made from sugar cane (*Saccharum officinarum*), a perennial tropical reed that accumulates sucrose in its tissue fluids to an unusually high degree: about 15 percent.

MANUFACTURE

The earliest record of sugar cane in China dates from the second century BC, but it wasn't until the middle of the ninth century, during the Tang dynasty, that the method of boiling the juice of crushed cane to make sugar was introduced into Sichuan and other parts of China from Turkestan or Central Asia. The Chinese character for sugar, *tang*, is made up of the name of the dynasty combined with the food or rice radical. Li Shih-chen's description of how sugar was manufactured, published in 1578, hardly differs from what I witnessed in Jiangxi province in the forties. The cane is cut down and stripped of its leaves. It is then crushed between rollers to extract its juice, which is heated and filtered to produce a clarified and thickened juice. This is then boiled until a mix or *massecuite* of crystals and mother syrup is produced. The sugar crystals (raw cane sugar) are separated from the residual syrup (molasses).

Sugar cane grows all over China

Blocks of brown sugar for sale in a Yunnan village

APPEARANCE AND TASTE

The raw sugar has to go through one final process: refinement. The sticky, brown, impure substance is cleaned and transformed into pure, white sugar, which can be stored forever. Although the Chinese name for sugar is *baitang*, meaning white sugar, it is usually only partly refined, so it is really brown sugar. What you call light brown sugar is called *huangtang* (yellow sugar) in China and dark brown sugar is *hongtang* (red sugar). Very little Chinese sugar is exported except the crystals known as rock sugar.

CULINARY USES

The Chinese use sugar not just in sweet foods as in the West, but in almost all savoury dishes. This is partly to redress the yin-yang balance with salt, and partly to enhance the natural sweetness of the food being cooked, since sugar occurs naturally in all foods, particularly in vegetables. A soft light brown sugar such as Demerara is ideal for nearly all Chinese cooking.

THOUSAND-LAYER CAKE

Here is another example of Chinese hyperbole. Of course there are nothing like a thousand layers in this cake, but then there are not that number in French *millefeuilles* either. There are, in fact, no fewer than 81 layers in this Chinese version – pretty impressive, don't you think?

Makes about 40–60 small pieces
Preparation time about 30 minutes plus standing time
Cooking time 50–60 minutes

700g (1lb 8oz) plain flour
200g (7oz) sugar
2 teaspoons dried yeast
About 350ml (12fl oz) warm water
115g (4oz) lard or shortening
3–4 tablespoons crushed walnuts
Dry flour for dusting

1 Sift the flour into a mixing bowl and add the sugar. Mix well. Dissolve the yeast in warm water and slowly pour it into the bowl. Knead for 5 minutes, then cover the dough with a damp cloth and let stand for 3 hours or until it doubles in volume.

2 Dust a work surface with flour and divide the dough into three equal portions. Roll out each portion into a thin rectangle about 30cm (1ft) x 20cm (8in). Spread some lard and sprinkle some chopped walnuts on the surface of one portion, then place another portion on top to make a sandwich. Spread some lard and walnuts on top of the sandwich, and place the third portion on top to form a double-decker sandwich.

3 Roll this sandwich flat until it measures about 35cm (2½ft) x 30cm (1ft). Spread some lard and walnuts over the middle third of the surface of the dough. Fold one third over to cover the middle section, and spread lard and walnuts on top of that. Fold the other third over.

4 Turn the dough around so that the folded edge faces you. Repeat the rolling, spreading and folding twice more so that you end up with the dough measuring roughly 30cm (1ft) x 20cm (8in) again, but this time with 81 layers. Let it stand for about 30 minutes.

5 Place the dough on a wet cloth on the rack inside a hot steamer, and steam, covered, over boiling water for 50–60 minutes.

6 Remove the cake from the steamer and let it cool down a little. Cut into 40–60 squares or diamonds before serving.

Toffee Apples

This has to be the Number One dessert in Chinese restaurants. Toffee banana is very popular too, but it lacks the crunchiness of apple. This dish may appear quite simple to prepare and cook, but it requires practice to achieve perfection.

Serves 4–6
Preparation time 25–30 minutes
Cooking time 3–4 minutes

3–4 medium green cooking apples
About 4 tablespoons plain flour
2 tablespoons cold water
1 egg, beaten
Oil for deep-frying
2 tablespoons sesame oil
175g (6oz) sugar
1 tablespoon sesame seeds (optional)

1 Peel, core and cut each apple into 8–10 wedges. Roll them in dry flour.

2 Make a smooth batter by mixing the flour with the water and egg. Dip the apple wedges in the batter to coat them evenly.

3 Heat the oil in a wok or deep-fryer until very hot and smoking (about 190°C/375°F) and drop in the pieces of apple one by one. Stir to make sure that they do not stick together. Fry for about 3 minutes until golden, scoop out with a strainer and drain.

4 Clean the wok and heat the sesame oil over medium heat. Add the sugar and stir constantly, slowly at first, then quickly, until the mixture turns golden and caramelized. Turn the heat down to very, very low, and add the apples to the toffee. Stir and add the sesame seeds, if using. Make sure each piece of apple is evenly coated with toffee. Dip each piece in icy cold water for a few seconds to harden the coating, so that the toffee does not stick to your teeth, and serve immediately.

The first 3 stages are straightforward; the crucial stage is the toffee-making. The secret lies in timing and heat control. The caramelization happens very suddenly – it is vital that you don't look away or stop stirring even for a second!

Note: If using bananas, choose firm, under-ripe ones. Peel and cut into 2.5cm (1in) pieces. Sprinkle with dry flour and proceed as for apples.

Toffee Apples

梅子酱

PLUM SAUCE

(MEIZI JIANG)

Plums, like apricots, cherries, and peaches, are a member of the genus *Prunus*. The Chinese variety (*P. mume*) is said to be indigenous to north China, but is now found in many other parts of the country, both wild and cultivated. Most people know that cherry blossom is the national emblem of Japan, but perhaps not many people are aware that plum blossom is the Chinese national emblem.

MANUFACTURE

Half-ripe plums are pickled with a salt and sugar solution, then dried. They are called *hua mei* (preserved prunes). Ripe plums are put in a press and the juice extracted, to be added to water as a cooling summer drink. It can also be blended with water, sugar, salt, vinegar and starch to make a thickish plum sauce.

APPEARANCE AND TASTE

Plum sauce has a smooth consistency with a colour which can range from pale beige to light brown, because different brands use different thickening agents. One of the more popular thickening agents is sweet potato flour. Some brands also add seasonings such as chilli, garlic and ginger to the basic plum sauce, so it tastes fruity and tangy.

BUYING AND STORING

Plum sauce is usually sold in small glass bottles or jars; it is widely available in Oriental stores and supermarkets. There are at least half a dozen different brands on the market, ranging from the really awful to the wonderfully good. Read the label: it should state where the product is made and list the ingredients. Try them out (they are comparatively inexpensive), and decide which brand you like best. All bottles should have a use-by date on them. Once opened, store in the refrigerator, where it will keep for a very long time.

Light plum sauce

Dark plum sauce

CULINARY USES

I have to admit that I have never came across 'plum sauce' as you know it anywhere in China. Like black bean sauce (p 90), plum sauce seems to have originated in Hong Kong. I am not saying that plum sauce is not genuinely Chinese, and indeed, I really like some brands of the sauce. It is quite versatile: you can use it as a dip – for deep-fried food such as spring rolls, spare-ribs and crispy duck – or use it for stir-fried dishes.

DUCK WITH PINEAPPLE

There are two different versions of this popular Cantonese dish: one is steamed, using a whole raw duck, the other is stir-fried, using cooked duck, which is much easier to reproduce at home. Ideally, you should use the meat of a roast duck, because the dark skin gives this dish extra colour.

Duck with Pineapple

Serves 4
Preparation time about 10 minutes
Cooking time 6–8 minutes

175–225g (6–8oz) cooked duck breast meat, boned but not skinned
3 tablespoons oil
1 small onion, thinly sliced
1 small carrot, thinly shredded
1 tablespoon Chinese pickled ginger
1 spring onion, cut into short sections
About 115g (4oz) pineapple rings, drained and cut into small slices
½ teaspoon salt
2 tablespoons plum sauce
2–3 tablespoons syrup from the pineapple
2 teaspoons cornflour paste

1 Cut the duck meat into thin shreds or slices.

2 Heat the oil in a preheated wok, stir-fry the onion slices until opaque, add the carrot, stir-fry for about 2 minutes.

3 Add the duck with the ginger, spring onion, pineapple, salt and plum sauce. Blend well and stir-fry for 1–2 minutes. Add the syrup from the pineapple, bring to the boil and thicken the sauce with the cornflour paste. Serve hot.

蠔油

OYSTER SAUCE

(HAOYOU)

A Cantonese speciality, oyster sauce is an oyster-based flavouring sauce. The Chinese word *you*, which also appears in the term for soy, means 'extraction' rather than 'sauce'. 'Oyster Flavoured Sauce' is the same as 'Real Oyster Sauce'.

MANUFACTURE

Oysters from the Pearl River delta are mentioned as early as the Tang period (618–907), but oyster sauce as we know it is reputed to have been created by Mr Lee Kum Sheung in a coastal village in the Pearl River Delta in 1888 (a very lucky number among the Chinese). Mr Lee went on to establish the leading sauce firm Lee Kum Kee, which has been operating in Hong Kong since 1932 (the year of my birth – another lucky year!). Different brands use different ingredients in varying proportions, but the basic combination is oyster extract, salt or soy (sauce), thickening starch, sugar and caramel. Since it is naturally so flavoursome it does not now require the addition of MSG.

APPEARANCE AND TASTE

Oyster sauce is a smooth brown sauce, available in large and small-sized bottles; taste and texture vary according to brand. Like oysters, it is highly delicious.

BUYING AND STORING

The more expensive brands are greatly superior to the cheaper brands and have a far richer flavour. Once the bottle is opened, always keep it in the refrigerator, whether it contains preservatives or not. It keeps for a long time.

Quails Eggs and Mushrooms with Oyster Sauce

CULINARY USES

Oyster sauce adds extra flavour to almost any food, be it meat, poultry, fish or vegetables. But treat it with great respect – it should not be used indiscriminately. It is a cooking sauce, it should be added to food only at the last minute of cooking.

QUAILS' EGGS AND MUSHROOMS WITH OYSTER SAUCE

This is a very delicate and colourful dish. It may appear rather complicated, but it is in fact not difficult.

Serves 4–6
Preparation time 30–40 minutes, plus soaking time
Cooking time 30–35 minutes

20 small dried Chinese mushrooms
1 tablespoon light soy
1 tablespoon finely chopped spring onion
½ teaspoon finely chopped fresh ginger
About 3–4 tablespoons stock
24 quails' eggs
2 tablespoons oil
24 asparagus tips
24 baby corn cobs
½ teaspoon salt
1 teaspoon sugar
2 tablespoons oyster sauce
2 teaspoons cornflour paste

1 Soak the mushrooms in warm water for 25–30 minutes (or in cold water for 1 hour), squeeze dry and discard any hard stalks. Place the mushrooms in a bowl with the soy, spring onion, ginger and stock, and steam vigorously for 15 minutes.

2 Hard boil the quails' eggs for 5 minutes, then cool in cold water and peel.

3 Heat the oil and stir-fry the asparagus and baby corn with the salt and sugar for 2–3 minutes. Arrange them alternately around the edge of a large serving plate. Remove the mushrooms from the liquid and place them in the centre of the vegetables; place the quails' eggs in the centre of the mushrooms, so you have a three-tier pyramid of vegetables, mushrooms and quails' eggs.

4 Warm the sauce in which the mushrooms have been steamed with the oyster sauce. Add a little more stock or water if necessary, then thicken with the cornflour paste. Pour evenly over the quails' eggs. Serve hot.

蜂蜜

HONEY

(FENGMI)

Honey, a natural product, must be the oldest sweetening substance – it has been known in China since ancient times. There is recorded evidence of honey having been used as a seasoning from the second century BC, but it must have been used in Chinese kitchens hundreds, if not a thousand, years before that.

MANUFACTURE

Although honey can be made artificially from dextrose, flavourings and colouring substances, natural honey is of course made by bees from the nectar they gather from flowers. The human input comes in removing the honey from the combs. Traditionally the wax combs are cut by hand to remove the honey. When commercially processed, the honey is spun from the combs using centrifugal force. The honey is then pumped into a strainer, filtered and packed.

APPEARANCE AND TASTE

Honey is the true essence of flowers, and different flowers produce distinctly different-tasting honey. I do not remember ever seeing honey sold in the comb in China, only in liquid form, which ranges from very thin to almost solid – and from pale white to golden, amber and dark brown.

MEDICINAL USES

The first time I had honey was as a medicine – a great improvement on the traditional, foul-tasting, herbal medicine and it certainly cured my dry cough. Later I was to discover that honey is used in China to treat constipation, stomach ache, insomnia and even heart disease.

Honey-coated pork hanging in the window – a common sight in China

CULINARY USES

The use of honey in Chinese cooking seems to have been superseded by malt sugar (maltose) – quite why is difficult to explain. Maybe malt sugar is always of a consistent quality, while honey, as a natural product, is not. When cooking with honey bear in mind that not only do its sugars tend to caramelize very quickly when heated, but the exact timing varies from honey to honey, usually depending on the glucose content.

BARBECUE (CHAR SIU) PORK

Also known as Honey-Roasted Pork, these are the strips of shining red meat seen hanging in the windows of Cantonese shops and restaurants.

Serves 8–10 as a starter. It is never served on its own as a main course, but can be used as an ingredient in a number of dishes.
Preparation time 20–25 minutes plus marinating time
Cooking time 25–30 minutes

675g (1lb 8oz) pork fillet
About 150ml (¼ pint) boiling water
2–3 tablespoons honey, dissolved in a little hot water
Shredded lettuce to serve

For the marinade:
1 tablespoon sugar
1 tablespoon crushed yellow bean sauce
1 tablespoon Hoi Sin sauce
1 tablespoon oyster sauce
1 tablespoon dark soy
1 tablespoon red fermented bean curd (see p 102)
2 tablespoons Chinese spirit, or brandy, rum etc
1 teaspoon sesame oil

1 Cut the pork into strips about 3cm (1¼in) wide and 18–20cm (7–8in) long. Place in a shallow dish and add the marinade. Blend well so the pork strips are coated all over. Cover and leave to marinate for at least 2 hours, turning occasionally.

2 Preheat the oven to 220°C/425°F/gas mark 7. Arrange the pork strips on a rack over a baking tin (reserving the marinade), with the boiling water in the bottom of the tin. Cook for 12–15 minutes.

3 Reduce the oven to 180°C/350°F/gas mark 4. Baste the pork with the marinade and turn the strips over. Cook for a further 8–10 minutes.

4 Remove pork from the oven, brush with the honey syrup, and lightly brown under a medium grill for 3–4 minutes, turning once or twice.

5 To serve, allow pork to cool before cutting it across the grain into thin slices. Arrange the slices neatly on a bed of lettuce leaves. Make a sauce by boiling the marinade for a few minutes with what has collected in the baking tin. Strain and pour over the pork.

Candied Fritter

I do not have a sweet tooth, but I have adored this most delectable snack since I was a small child. Its Manchurian name is rendered in Chinese as: *sa* (Buddha) *qi* (riding) *ma* (horse).

Makes about 40–50 pieces
Preparation time about 45 minutes
Cooking time 20–25 minutes

350g (12oz) plain flour
2 teaspoons baking powder
3 eggs, beaten
Dry flour for dusting
Oil for deep-frying
225g (8oz) sugar
175g (6oz) honey
About 200ml (7fl oz) water

1 Sift the flour and baking powder onto a work surface. Form a hollow in the centre, pour in the eggs and blend well. Knead the dough thoroughly until it is smooth.

2 Roll out the dough with a rolling pin until it is like a big pancake about 3mm (⅛in) thick, then cut it into long, thin strips 5cm (2in) wide. Dust with dry flour to prevent them sticking together.

3 Heat the oil in a wok or deep-fryer to about 160°C/325°F and deep-fry the strips in batches for 45–50 seconds or until light golden. Remove and drain. Place in a bowl.

4 Place the sugar, honey and water in a saucepan. Bring to the boil, then simmer, stirring gently, until the mixture is like syrup. Pour it over the fried strips and mix thoroughly until each strip is coated with syrup.

5 Turn out the strips into a pre-greased cake tin and press down to form one big cake. When cool, cut into squares. Serve cold.

Fruit Jam

This is a sweet, thick fruit preserve usually made with ripe fruit and sugar, but since sugar-making was not introduced to China until the middle of the ninth century, we have to assume that jams were made with cooked fruit and honey in the olden days. Apart from being used as a sweet filling for cakes and buns, fruit jams feature very little in everyday Chinese life. The only two fruit jams I can think of are Plum Sauce and Lemon Sauce, neither of which are sweet jams as we know them in the West, but are used instead for cooking savoury dishes.

Candied Fritters

飴糖

Malt Sugar

(YITANG)

Malt sugar, or maltose, is made from fermenting germinated grains of barley, hence another Chinese name for it is *maiya tang* (sprouting barley sugar).

Appearance and Taste

Malt sugar is quite thick, golden brown in colour and has a unique, strong flavour. If you have any difficulty in obtaining malt sugar, try molasses or honey as a substitute.

Culinary Uses

Malt sugar's use in Chinese cooking is rather limited, though it does feature in one of the most famous dishes in the world: Peking Roast Duck. This dish is often confused with the very popular Aromatic and Crispy Duck, partly because they are both served wrapped in pancakes with sauce and vegetables. This is only done by Cantonese restaurants abroad, however. In China, Aromatic and Crispy Duck is not roasted, but steamed and deep-fried, and is always chopped into small bite-size pieces and served with a dry spicy salt dip. Peking Roast Duck is crispy, but it is not really aromatic, its fragrance coming from the natural flavour of the duck, plus perhaps the coating of malt sugar applied to the skin before cooking.

Only specially reared ducks can be used for an authentic Peking Roast Duck

Beijing's sophisticated Fanshan Restaurant, which specializes in imperial-style cuisine

Peking Roast Duck

Strictly speaking, it is almost impossible to reproduce this dish at home in the West for two reasons. Firstly, the genuine article is a specially reared species of duck which is brought by several stages of force-feeding and special care to exactly the right degree of plumpness and tenderness before it is ready for the oven. Secondly, the duck should be cooked in a specially constructed kiln-like oven, with wood from the Chinese date tree as fuel. But don't despair: people who have travelled all the way to Beijing and sampled the duck there have hardly been able to tell the difference between authentic Peking Roast Duck and that served in the West! You will be surprised by the simplicity of the whole process, and the end result should be entirely satisfactory if you follow all the steps correctly.

Serves 10–12 as a starter or 6–8 as a main course
Preparation time 35–40 minutes plus drying time
Cooking time 1¾ hours

1 oven-ready duckling weighing about 2.25g (5lb)
2 tablespoons malt sugar (or molasses or honey) dissolved in 2 tablespoons water

For serving:
20–24 Duck Pancakes (p 36)
125ml (4fl oz) Duck Sauce (p 93)
6–8 spring onions, thinly shredded
½ cucumber, thinly shredded

1 Clean the duck well, removing the wing tips and any feather stubs, as well as the lumps of fat from inside the vent.

2 Blanch the duck in boiling water for 2–3 minutes. Remove and drain. Dry thoroughly and while the skin is still warm, brush the duck all over with the malt sugar (or honey) and water solution. Hang it up to dry in a cool and airy place for at least 6–8 hours or overnight – the drier the skin, the crispier the duck when roasted.

3 To cook: heat the oven to 200°C/400°F/gas mark 6. Place the duck, breast side up, on a rack in a roasting tin, and cook on the middle rack of the oven for 1½–1¾ hours, without basting or turning.

4 Half an hour before the duck is cooked, prepare the sauce (p 93) and place it in two individual small bowls. Place the shredded spring onions and cucumber on two small plates. Warm up the pancakes either by steaming for 10–12 minutes, or in the microwave for 25–30 seconds on high.

5 To serve: peel off the crispy skin in small slices with a sharp carving knife, then carve the meat into thin strips. Arrange the skin and meat on separate serving plates.

6 To eat: spread about 1 teaspoon of the duck sauce in the middle of a warm pancake, add a few strips of spring onions and cucumber, then top with 2–3 slices each of duck skin and meat (some people prefer to eat the skin and meat separately). Roll up the pancake and turn up the bottom edge to prevent the contents from falling out. Eat with your fingers. The point to remember here is NOT to have too much sauce or meat at one go (greedy people beware!): too much sauce will overpower the delicate duck, and too much meat will cause the parcel to break up.

Note: Traditionally, the duck carcass is made into a delicious soup to be served at the end of the meal. To do this, use the following recipe:

Break up the carcass and place it in a pan with a few bits of fresh ginger. Add water to cover and bring to the boil. Simmer gently, covered, for about 30 minutes, then add about 450g (1lb) Chinese leaves cut into small pieces. Cook for 10–15 minutes before serving hot, seasoned with salt and pepper. Garnish with either fresh coriander leaves or chopped spring onions.

Peking Roast Duck

Brown slab sugar

冰糖

ROCK SUGAR

(BINGTANG)

Chinese rock sugar is similar to coffee sugar, except that the lumps are much larger – the Chinese name *bingtang* literally means 'ice' sugar, suggesting that it is like icebergs.

Yellow rock sugar with white crystal sugar

MANUFACTURE

The irregular rock-shaped pieces are produced by the slow crystallization of a saturated sugar liquor.

APPEARANCE AND TASTE

There are two types, the most common of which is Yellow rock sugar. It is widely available and is made from light brown sugar; it has a unique, mild sweetness not unlike maltose. The other type is the darker slab sugar, made with dark brown sugar and sold in thin, rectangular blocks; it has a caramel taste.

CULINARY USES

Rock sugar imparts a special sheen to long-cooked dishes, such as stews (known as red cooking) and soy-braised food. It has to be broken into smaller pieces before being added to the pot. The best way to do this is to wrap several large rocks in a tea towel and bash them with a hammer – if you use a wooden rolling pin, you will only damage the rolling pin's smooth surface! Break up a large amount at a time so you don't have to do it each time a recipe calls for rock sugar. The rocks, large or small, will keep forever, provided they are stored in a cool, dry place.

PORK SHOULDER WITH ROCK SUGAR

This is a typical red-cooked dish from southeast China – a must for any celebration, big or small. I suppose it is the nearest equivalent to a traditional Sunday roast, although I think this more flavoursome. Pork shoulder is usually sold with the bone in and the rind on.

Serves 10–12 when served with other dishes as part of a meal; will feed at least 6 as the main course when served with vegetables and rice

Preparation time 10–15 minutes
Cooking time 2½ hours

1 pork shoulder weighing about 1.5–2kg (3–4lb 8oz)
50ml (2fl oz) rice wine
50g (2oz) crushed rock sugar
5 tablespoons dark soy
3 tablespoons light soy
2–3 spring onions, cut into short sections
1 tablespoon peeled fresh ginger slices

1 Clean the joint well, making sure the skin is hair-free. Use a sharp pointed knife to make a few deep cuts through to the bone, to shorten the cooking time.

2 Place the joint in a large pot with the skin side down. Add enough cold water to cover and bring to the boil over high heat. Skim off the scum, add all the other ingredients and simmer gently, covered, for half an hour or so.

3 Turn the joint over so the skin side is upward. Continue cooking under cover for 2 more hours, by which time the juice should have reduced by about three-quarters. Increase the heat to high, and cook for 5 minutes, uncovered, to reduce and thicken the gravy further.

4 Traditionally, the pork is served whole in a large bowl with the gravy poured over it. When it is cooked to perfection, the skin and meat should be tender enough to be easily pulled off the bone with chopsticks or a spoon. Any leftovers can be cut into thin slices and served cold.

The candyman and fortune teller making candy figures out of caramelized sugar

虾酱

SHRIMP PASTE

(XIAJIANG)

The fermented essence of pulverized shrimp, shrimp paste is definitely an acquired taste – few Chinese restaurants in Britain would serve a dish containing shrimp paste to their non-Chinese customers!

APPEARANCE AND TASTE

Shrimp paste on its own is very salty and pungent and I must admit it is not a taste I am very keen on. I believe that there are many others who share my view, for it is very rarely featured on the menus of Chinese restaurants.

BUYING AND STORING

Chinese shrimp paste, not to be confused with the bland Western variety, is only available in Chinese supermarkets. Once opened it will keep best in the refrigerator.

CULINARY USES

Of the few dishes that do contain shrimp paste, only one or two actually mention it by name in the title of the dish, such as Crispy Pork with Shrimp Paste Casserole, and Fried Squid with Shrimp Sauce. Should you wish to give this delicacy a try at home before sampling it in a restaurant, here is a simple recipe that actually tastes very good and looks quite stunning.

Shrimp paste

Stir-fried Squid Flowers with Shrimp Paste

STIR-FRIED SQUID FLOWERS WITH SHRIMP PASTE

Ideally the squid for this recipe should be not less than 15cm (6in) long. Prepare the squid as described on p 174.

Serves 4
Preparation time 25–30 minutes
Cooking time 5–6 minutes

350–400g (12–14oz) cleaned squid
1 small onion
3 tablespoons vegetable oil
1 tablespoon thinly shredded fresh ginger
1–2 spring onions, cut into short sections
2 teaspoons rice wine
1 tablespoon shrimp paste
2 tablespoons stock or water
A few drops sesame oil

1 Prepare and blanch the squid as for the recipe on page 174. Cut the onion into small thin slices.

2 Heat the oil in a preheated wok. Stir-fry the onion slices until opaque, then add the squid-flowers with the ginger and spring onions. Stir-fry for about 1 minute, then add the wine and shrimp paste with the stock or water. Bring to the boil, stirring constantly.

3 Blend in the sesame oil and serve hot. As you can see, quite stunning.

虾干 虾米

DRIED SHRIMPS

(XIAGAN, XIAMI)

Sun-dried shrimps play an important role in Chinese cooking. Because of their strong aroma and flavour, they are used as a seasoning rather than as an ingredient in their own right.

APPEARANCE AND TASTE

In China there are two basic categories of dried shrimps: shelled and headless ones, or unshelled ones with their heads still attached. The latter are tiny – too small to be peeled – and are rarely seen outside Southeast Asia. A variety of different-sized dried shrimps is available in the West. They can be divided into three types: large, medium and small, though even the so-called large ones are no bigger than 1cm (½in) long, and the small ones are really tiny, about the size of a grain of rice. Another Chinese term for dried shrimps is Sea Rice, for no freshwater prawns or shrimps are dried.

Shrimps being sorted on the quay to be laid out to dry

BUYING AND STORING

In China, dried shrimps are usually sold loose, while in the West they are sold packed in air-tight plastic bags. Once opened, they will keep for many months if stored in an air-tight container.

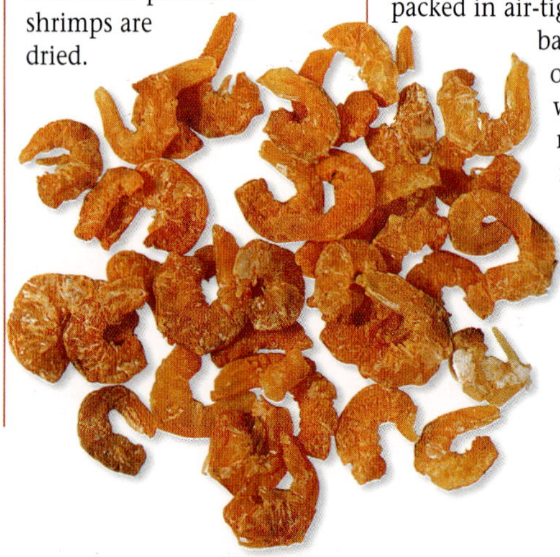

Shelled dried shrimps

CULINARY USES

Before they can be used, dried shrimps must be washed and cleaned in cold water, and any bits and pieces discarded before they are soaked in warm water, or better still, rice wine, for at least an hour. Reserve the liquid for use later on. Dried shrimps have a strong flavour which may not appeal to everybody. Nevertheless, they do give an exotic taste to many dishes, such as salads, stews and soups, and they are one of the Eight-Treasure ingredients for stuffing etc.

EIGHT-TREASURE DUCK

The eight treasures refer to the eight items used for the stuffing.

Serves 6–8
Preparation time 40 minutes
Cooking time 1¼ hours

1 duck, weighing not less than 2kg (4½lb), cleaned
2–3 tablespoons dark soy

For the stuffing:
115g (4oz) glutinous rice
175g (6fl oz) boiling water
2 tablespoons dried shrimps, soaked
4–5 medium Chinese dried mushrooms, soaked
Duck giblets (gizzard, heart and liver)
115g (4oz) bamboo shoots
55g (2oz) Chinese bacon, ham or pork sausage
2 tablespoons oil
1 tablespoon finely chopped spring onions
½ teaspoon salt
1 tablespoon light soy
1 tablespoon rice wine

1 Clean the duck well, inside and out. Pat dry and brush the skin with the dark soy.

2 Soak the rice in boiling water for 25–30 minutes. Cut the soaked shrimps, mushrooms, gizzard, heart, liver, bamboo shoots, bacon or ham etc into small cubes.

3 Heat the oil in a preheated wok. Stir-fry the shrimps, mushrooms, giblets, bamboo shoots, and bacon with the spring onions and salt for about 2 minutes. Add the rice, the water, light soy and wine, blend well and bring to the boil. Reduce the heat and cook for 8–10 minutes, or until all the liquid has been absorbed.

4 Preheat the oven to 200°C/400°F/gas mark 6. Pack the stuffing into the duck cavity and close the tail opening.

5 Place the duck on a wire rack in a roasting tin and cook in the oven for 30 minutes. Reduce the heat to 180°C/350°F/gas mark 4 and cook for a further 45 minutes.

6 To serve: scrape out the stuffing and place on the centre of a platter. Chop the duck into bite-sized pieces and arrange neatly around the stuffing.

Fresh celery

Celery Salad with Dried Shrimps

The Chinese seldom eat raw vegetables, since manure is used extensively as fertilizer. Most salads in Chinese cuisine are lightly cooked, then served cold with a dressing. Vegetables grown in the West, by modern methods, can be served raw quite safely.

Serves 4–6
Preparation and cooking time
10 minutes plus soaking time

2 tablespoons dried shrimps
2 tablespoons rice wine
1 head celery
1 teaspoon salt

For the dressing:
1 tablespoon light soy
1 tablespoon sugar
1 tablespoon rice vinegar
1 teaspoon sesame oil
1 tablespoon finely chopped fresh ginger

1 Wash and clean the dried shrimps, then soak in rice wine for 1–2 hours.

2 Discard the tough outer sticks of celery and cut the rest into thin strips about 4cm (1½in) long. Blanch in a pan of salted boiling water for 1–2 minutes, then rinse in fresh cold water. Drain and place on a serving dish.

3 Make the dressing by combining the soaked shrimps with the wine in which they have soaked, the soy, sugar, vinegar, sesame oil and ginger. Blend well and pour over the celery. Toss and mix just before serving.

Celery Salad with Dried Shrimps

豆豉

SALTED BLACK BEANS

(DOUCHI)

These fermented, salted, soft, black soybeans are a wonderful seasoning agent for Chinese cooking. They are very popular all over China, especially in rural households in the South. Salted black beans are the oldest recorded 'soy food' in Chinese history – they are, in fact, the noble ancestor of soy sauce, and, indeed, the water in which the beans have been soaked is often used as a soy substitute by less well-off people, since it is more economical to do so.

MANUFACTURE

Detailed instructions for the preparation of fermented soy beans were given over two thousand years ago. The process involves boiling black soybeans until soft, then soaking them in water over night; steaming them for 2–3 hours the next morning, and inoculating them with the *Aspergillus oryzae* mould to ferment for 15–21 days; covering them with a brine solution and alcohol to mature for at least six months, then spreading them out to dry in the sun; steaming them again until they are soft and spreading them out to dry in the sun once more. After this steaming and sunning process has occurred three times, the product is finally ready for use.

Loose salted black beans

APPEARANCE AND TASTE

Salted black beans do not have an attractive appearance: dull, dark grey in colour, they have an odour which may not appeal to the uninitiated, but once they have been heated during the cooking process, they turn a shiny black and have a wonderful aroma, as well as a savoury flavour.

BUYING AND STORING

Ordinary salted black beans are sold loose, sometimes in sealed polythene bags; the named brands are either in vacuum-packed plastic bags or in cardboard cartons. Once opened, store in an air-tight container. They will keep for 5–6 years if stored in a cool, dark, dry place.

A Cantonese cook at work – stir-fried dishes often require high heat and split-second timing

Seasoned salted black beans

CULINARY USES

Salted black beans are most versatile in the kitchen. They can be used whole in stews, or crushed for steamed and stir-fried dishes. Strongly flavoured seasonings such as ginger, garlic, chilli and wine are often blended with black beans to give an extra dimension. Classic recipes using black beans include steamed fish, braised lobster, steamed pork spare-ribs, stir-fried beef and chicken dishes.

LOBSTER WITH CHILLI BLACK BEAN SAUCE

This is one of the most popular dishes in Cantonese restaurants, where one can sometimes choose a live lobster from the fish tank. A Chinese chef would never dream of using ready-cooked lobsters as they will have been boiled for far too long, thus losing much of their delicate flavour and texture. At any rate, the Chinese method of chopping off the head of a lobster with one blow, thus killing it instantly, is by far the most humane way of killing it – it is estimated

that it takes anything up to six minutes to kill a lobster by the boiling in a pot method.

Serves 4–6
Preparation time 20–25 minutes plus marinating time
Cooking time 10–15 minutes

1 large or two medium lobsters
1 tablespoon chopped white parts of spring onions
5–6 small slices of peeled fresh ginger
3 tablespoons rice wine
2 tablespoons light soy
Oil for deep-frying
Fresh coriander leaves to garnish

For the sauce:
2 tablespoons salted black beans
1–2 fresh red chillies
2 cloves garlic
2–3 spring onions
2 tablespoons rice vinegar
1 tablespoon sugar
4 tablespoons good stock (p 71)
2 eggs, beaten
2 tablespoons cornflour paste
1 teaspoon sesame oil

1 Chop off the head of the lobster, be it dead or alive, then cut in half lengthways. Discard the legs, intestines, and the feathery lungs. Remove the claws and crack them with the back of the cleaver, and cut each half of the body into 3–4 pieces.

2 Marinate the lobster pieces with the white parts of the spring onion, the ginger, wine and soy for 15–20 minutes.

3 For the sauce: soak the black beans in warm water for 5 minutes, then drain and mash. Finely shred the chillies and spring onions, and finely chop the garlic. Mix the vinegar and sugar with the stock in a bowl.

4 Heat the oil in a wok until hot. Deep-fry the lobster pieces for about 3 minutes (if you are using uncooked lobster, its colour will turn from grey to bright orange), remove and drain.

5 Pour off the excess oil, leaving about 1 tablespoon in the wok. Add the chillies, spring onions, garlic and mashed black beans and stir-fry over low heat for about 30 seconds or until fragrant. Add the vinegar, sugar and stock mixture. Blend well, turn up the heat and bring to the boil, stirring constantly. Now return the lobster pieces to the wok, toss for 1–1½ minutes, then add the beaten eggs. Cook for 30 seconds, stirring. Thicken the sauce with the cornflour paste and sprinkle on the sesame oil. Serve hot, garnished with the fresh coriander leaves.

Note: This dish should be served on its own and eaten with fingers, so provide finger bowls and plenty of paper napkins for the table.

STEAMED SCALLOPS WITH BLACK BEAN SAUCE

Fresh scallops in their shells are quite expensive and not all that widely available – but a good fishmonger will always obtain them for you if you order in advance.

Serves 6–8 as a starter
Preparation time 40–45 minutes
Cooking time 8–10 minutes

12 fresh scallops in their shells

Steamed Scallops with Black Bean Sauce

For the sauce:
1½ tablespoons salted black beans
2 tablespoons oil
1 teaspoon finely chopped garlic
1 tablespoon finely chopped fresh ginger
1 tablespoon finely chopped spring onions
1 tablespoon finely chopped fresh red chillies
½ teaspoon ground Sichuan peppercorns
2 tablespoons soy (light or dark)
1 tablespoon rice wine
2 tablespoons good stock (p 71)
½ teaspoon sesame oil

1 Scrub the scallops under cold running water, then open them and discard the flat, empty half of each shell. Prise off the flesh but leave it in the shell.

2 Soak the black beans in warm water for 5 minutes, drain and mash. Prepare the rest of the ingredients for the sauce.

3 Place the scallops in their shells on two separate heat-proof dishes. Place the dishes on the racks of two layers of hot bamboo steamers, and steam for 8–9 minutes.

4 While the scallops are being steamed, make the sauce by heating the oil in a small saucepan over a low heat. Add the garlic, ginger, spring onions, chillies, Sichuan peppers and black beans, and stir-fry for about 30 seconds or until fragrant. Add the soy, wine and stock, and continue stirring for 15–20 seconds or until the sauce starts to bubble. Sprinkle on the sesame oil and simmer gently for about 1 minute.

5 To serve: put about 2 teaspoons of the sauce over each scallop and serve them in the shells. The flesh can easily be removed from the shell with chopsticks or a fork, and the remaining sauce drunk from the shells. Absolutely delicious!

豉汁醬

BLACK BEAN SAUCE

(CHIZI JIANG)

I have a strong suspicion that commercial black bean sauce (liquidized, salted black beans seasoned with soy sauce, salt, sugar and spice) is a Hong Kong invention concocted mainly for the convenience of Westerners. I cannot remember ever seeing it in China, nor can I find any mention of its existence in any Chinese publication, past or present.

APPEARANCE AND TASTE

Commercial black bean sauce is less aromatic than the fresh paste one makes oneself, but still has the same lovely glossy black colour. Some varieties also include added orange peel, ginger, chillies or garlic.

BUYING AND STORING

There are a number of different brands available, all tasting slightly different – try them out for yourself. You may end up going back to using dried salted beans, but it is always useful to have a jar of your favourite brand as a standby, just in case you run out of any of the ingredients necessary to make your own sauce.

A fast-food stand doing brisk business at lunch time

CULINARY USES

I must admit to using ready-made black bean sauce myself, but only in demonstrations and cookery classes – for convenience, I hasten to add! One of the most popular variations is black bean and garlic sauce. This actually contains far more salted beans than black bean sauce so tastes much 'beanier' as a result.

STEAMED SPARE-RIBS WITH BLACK BEAN SAUCE

This is one of my favourite Cantonese dim sum dishes, but if you cook it in sufficient quantity and serve it with rice plus one or two other dishes, it can be an ideal main course.

Serves 4–6
Preparation time 10–15 minutes plus marinating time
Cooking time 25–30 minutes

675g (1½ lb) pork spare-ribs
1–2 fresh red chillies, finely shredded
2 spring onions, cut into short sections

For the marinade:
1 teaspoon finely chopped garlic
½ teaspoon finely chopped fresh ginger
½–1 teaspoon finely chopped fresh red or green chillies
2 tablespoons black bean sauce
1 tablespoon light soy
1 tablespoon rice wine
2 teaspoons cornflour

1 Trim off any excess fat from the ribs, then chop them into small bite-size pieces. Cover with the marinade for at least 1 hour – the longer the better.

2 Spread the spare-ribs out on a heat-proof platter and steam them in a hot steamer over a high heat for 25–30 minutes.

3 Remove the platter from the steamer and place it on top of a larger dish or plate. Garnish with the chopped chillies and spring onions. Serve hot.

Mixed Seafood with Vegetables

The Chinese term *sanxian* (three delicacies) originally referred to the combination of sea cucumber, prawns and chicken. In most Chinese restaurants in the West, it is customary to use squid, prawns and scallops for this dish.

Serves 4–6
Preparation time 25–30 minutes
Cooking time 10 minutes

175–225g (6–8oz) cleaned squid
150g (5½oz) uncooked prawns, peeled
½ egg white
4–6 fresh scallops
½ teaspoon salt
1 tablespoon cornflour paste
About 300ml (½ pint) oil
½ teaspoon finely chopped fresh ginger
1–2 spring onions, cut into short sections
2 tablespoons black bean and garlic sauce
2 stalks of celery, thinly sliced diagonally
1 medium carrot, thinly sliced diagonally
1 small red pepper (capsicum), cut into small pieces
½ teaspoon sugar
1 tablespoon rice wine
Stock or water
½ teaspoon sesame oil

1 Prepare and blanch the squid as described on p 174. Cut each prawn in half lengthways. Cut each scallop into 3–4 slices.

2 Mix the prawns and scallops with a pinch of the salt, the egg white and about half the cornflour paste.

3 Heat the oil in a preheated wok until medium hot. Blanch the seafood for about 30–40 seconds, remove and drain.

4 Pour off the excess oil, leaving about 2 tablespoons in the wok. Stir-fry the ginger and spring onions with the black bean and garlic sauce over low heat for about 30 seconds, or until fragrant. Turn the heat up high again and add the vegetables to be stir-fried for about 2 minutes. Return the seafood to the wok with the remaining salt, the sugar and wine. Blend well and add a little stock or water, stirring constantly. When the juice starts to bubble, thicken it with the remaining cornflour paste. Sprinkle on the sesame oil and serve hot.

黃醬

YELLOW BEAN SAUCE

(HUANG JIANG)

Sometimes labelled brown bean sauce or ground bean sauce (*mochi jiang*), this is the soybean paste made from crushed or ground, salted and fermented yellow soybeans, which are sweeter and less salty than black beans. To this basic bean sauce, spices and other seasonings are added, giving many varieties. Seasonings and spices are added to it in different proportions in different regions of China: Hoi Sin sauce is one example (p 94), and Guilin Chilli sauce is another (p 95).

MANUFACTURE

The process of fermenting yellow soybeans differs slightly from the process for black beans. It involves soaking the soybeans for 16 hours; steaming them until soft; fermenting them for about 5 days, stirring and turning them every other day; blending the beans with salt, sweet glutinous rice wine and dark brown sugar; filling a pottery jar with them – not too tightly, nor too loosely; letting the jar stand for two days with the opening tightly sealed; and leaving the jar upside-down in a cool, dry place for the beans to ferment for a further 3 months. The beans are then ready to be used on their own, or to be ground and blended with additional seasonings.

APPEARANCE AND TASTE

Yellow bean sauce is a beautiful brown colour with a wonderful aroma. The basic sauce usually has just salt, sugar, flour and water or soy sauce added to it and there are no set rules governing the amount of seasoning or spice added – it is a question of regional taste.

BUYING AND STORING

Yellow bean sauce comes in different-sized cans and jars, and there is no standard name for it: besides simple yellow bean sauce, there is crushed yellow beans, brown bean sauce and ground bean sauce. They are all basically the same, each with a very slightly different taste. Jars of yellow bean sauce are readily available; once opened, store them in the refrigerator and use by the date stamped on them. Cans are usually stocked only by Oriental stores (and cost less). Once opened, transfer the sauce to a plastic or glass container with an air-tight top. If refrigerated, it will keep for many, many months.

CULINARY USES

There is a wide range of Chinese dishes in which yellow bean sauce is used, and of course it is the basis for a number of well-known sauces, such as duck sauce for the famous Peking Duck, and the very popular Cantonese Hoi Sin sauce.

Evening sun falls on a corner of the Imperial Palace

Sweet-as-Honey Lamb

SWEET-AS-HONEY LAMB

There is an interesting story to this dish. It is supposed to have originated in the Imperial Palace kitchen in the autumn of 1772, when Emperor Qian Long shot three deer while hunting. The Palace kitchen devised this recipe for the venison and the Emperor declared it as sweet as honey.

Serves 4
Preparation time 15–20 minutes plus marinating time
Cooking time 5–6 minutes

300–350g (10–12oz) boned leg of lamb
2 tablespoons yellow bean sauce
Oil for deep-frying
½ cucumber, thinly sliced
½ teaspoon sesame oil

For the sauce:
1 teaspoon finely chopped fresh ginger
1 tablespoon light soy
1 tablespoon rice wine
2 tablespoons sugar
1 tablespoon rice vinegar
About 2–3 tablespoons stock or water
1 tablespoon cornflour paste

1 Cut the lamb into thin slices about the size of a postage stamp. Marinate with the yellow bean sauce for 10–15 minutes – longer if possible.

2 Mix the ingredients for the sauce in a small bowl.

3 Heat the oil in a wok until medium hot. Deep-fry the lamb slices for about 1 minute, stirring continuously to separate the slices. Scoop out as soon as the colour of the meat changes and drain.

4 Pour off the excess oil, leaving about 1 tablespoon in the wok. Return the lamb to the wok and stir-fry for about 1 minute, then add the sauce mixture. Blend well and stir for about 1 minute. Add the cucumber slices with the sesame oil, stir and toss a few times more. Serve hot.

BRAISED SPARE-RIBS IN BROWN SAUCE

This dish is one of my personal favourites for serving to family and friends. It has a wonderful aroma and is extremely succulent. If the meat comes away from the bone too easily, you have over-cooked it.

Serves 4–6
Preparation time 20–25 minutes, plus marinating time
Cooking time 15–20 minutes

675g (1½lb) pork spare-ribs
¼ teaspoon ground Sichuan peppercorns
2 tablespoons sugar
1 tablespoon light soy
1 tablespoon dark soy
2 tablespoons rice wine
1 tablespoon cornflour
3–4 tablespoons oil
2 cloves garlic, chopped
2–3 spring onions, cut into short sections, with white and green parts separate
2 small fresh red chillies, cut into small pieces
2–3 tablespoons yellow bean sauce
About 150ml (¼ pint) stock or water
1 small green pepper (capsicum), cubed

1 Trim off any excess fat from the ribs, then chop each rib into 3–4 bite-size pieces. Marinate with the pepper, sugar, light and dark soy, wine and cornflour for about 30–35 minutes – the longer, the better.

2 Heat the oil in a preheated wok or pan and lightly brown the spare-ribs for 2–3 minutes. Remove with a perforated spoon.

3 In the same oil, stir-fry the garlic, the white parts of the spring onions, the chillies and the yellow bean sauce for about 30 seconds, or until fragrant. Return the ribs to the wok, stirring constantly, until each piece of rib is coated with sauce. Add the stock or water and blend well. Boil, then reduce the heat and simmer under cover for 10–12 minutes, stirring occasionally.

4 Add the green pepper (capsicum) and the green parts of the spring onions. Increase the heat and cook uncovered for 1–2 minutes more, stirring continuously. Serve hot.

DUCK SAUCE

Traditionally, Peking Duck is served with a sweet fermented wheatflour sauce called *Tian Mian Jiang*. For some unknown reason, this is not available in the West, so most restaurants use Hoi Sin sauce as a substitute, which is not quite right. Some non-Cantonese restaurants use a version of Duck Sauce based on either Hoi Sin sauce or yellow bean sauce. Commercially made Peking Duck Sauce is not widely available. This is my recommended recipe.

2 tablespoons vegetable oil
125g (4oz) yellow bean sauce
2–3 tablespoons sugar
1 teaspoon sesame oil

Heat the oil in a small saucepan. When hot, add the bean sauce and stir over low heat for 2–3 minutes. Add the sugar and about 2–3 tablespoons water, and continue stirring for 2–3 minutes more. Finally, add the sesame oil and stir for 30 seconds or so more.

海鲜酱

HOI SIN SAUCE

(HAIXIAN JIANG)

Also known as Barbecue Sauce, this very popular Cantonese speciality has become almost as familiar as soy in most households. The Chinese name (*haixian* in Mandarin, *hoisin* in Cantonese) literally means sea-delicious, which is just as enigmatic as the Sichuan cookery term *yuxiang* (fish-flavour) for a certain style of seasoning.

MANUFACTURE

Hoi Sin sauce is made from yellow beans seasoned with sugar, vinegar, salt, chilli, garlic, sesame oil and red colouring, with flour and water as a thickener. Different brands contain different amounts of seasoning and spices, and vary in flavour.

CULINARY USES

Hoi Sin sauce's popularity is perhaps due to its versatility: as well as a seasoning, it makes a great marinade and it can be used as a dip at the table. (The practice of serving Hoi Sin sauce with Crispy and Aromatic Duck or Peking Duck is incorrect. Use instead a specially prepared Duck Sauce – see p 93.)

BARBECUED PORK SPARE-RIBS

This is a simplified way of cooking the half saddle of pork spare-rib seen hanging in some Cantonese restaurants.

Serves 6–8
Preparation time about 20 minutes plus marinating time
Cooking time 30–45 minutes

1kg (2lb 4oz) pork spare-ribs
2 teaspoons five-spice powder or 1 tablespoon curry powder
225g (8oz) Hoi Sin sauce
4–5 tablespoons rice wine

1 Trim off excess fat from the ribs, and cut each rib into 7cm (3in) long pieces. Marinate with the five-spice powder or curry powder, Hoi Sin sauce and wine for 3–4 hours at room temperature, or refrigerate overnight, turning now and again.

2 Cooking method 1: Barbecue the ribs over a hot grill for about 15 minutes, turning frequently, and basting with the marinade.

3 Cooking method 2: Place the ribs in a baking tin with a little water or stock and roast in a preheated hot oven (230°C/450°F/gas mark 8) for 15–20 minutes. Turn the ribs over, reduce the heat to 200°C/400°F/Gas mark 6, and cook for 25–30 minutes more. Serve hot or cold.

BRAISED CHICKEN WINGS

This is a very popular dish in Cantonese restaurants. The sweetness of the Hoi Sin sauce goes well with the soy and honey.

Serves 4–6
Preparation time 10 minutes plus marinating time
Cooking time 13–15 minutes

12 chicken wings, without the pinions
2 teaspoons sugar
1 tablespoon each of dark soy, light soy and rice wine
About 300ml (½ pint) oil
½ teaspoon finely chopped fresh ginger
1 tablespoon finely chopped spring onions
2 tablespoons Hoi Sin sauce
About 150ml (5fl oz) stock
1 tablespoon honey

1 Marinate the chicken wings with the sugar, dark and light soy, and wine for at least 1 hour, longer if possible, turning occasionally.

2 Heat the oil until hot. Reserving the marinade, deep-fry the chicken wings for about 2–3 minutes, or until golden brown. Drain.

3 Pour off the excess oil, leaving about 1 teaspoon in the wok. Add the ginger, spring onions and Hoi Sin Sauce. Stir-fry for 30–40 seconds, add the chicken wings with the marinade and blend well. Add the stock and bring to the boil. Reduce the heat and braise for 8–10 minutes, covered, stirring once or twice.

4 Uncover, turn the heat up and reduce the sauce until it is thick and sticky. Add the honey and blend well. Serve hot or cold.

Barbecued Pork Spare-Ribs

桂林辣椒醬

Guilin Chilli Sauce

(Guilin Lajiao Jiang)

Guilin in Guangxi is famous for its scenery, its rivers and tall, pointed mountains. Its cuisine has never been of note compared to that of its distinguished neighbours, Hunan and Guangdong. It has, however, produced a chilli sauce with a worldwide reputation, thanks to some entrepreneurs who produced it for the international market.

Manufacture

Apart from fermented and salted beans, the main ingredient is of course fresh red chillies. Other ingredients are garlic, vinegar, sugar and starch, making it quite different from all other chilli sauces. As with many of these manufactured sauces, different brands can have different colours.

Buying and Storing

Some of the Hong Kong brands which are available in the West use black beans, while the Guilin product uses yellow beans, which have quite a different flavour. My favourite Guilin brand, Mount Elephant, comes in a rustic brown earthenware pot and is occasionally obtainable in the West. Look out for it.

Chicken Cubes with Chilli Bean Sauce

The original recipe for this dish calls for chicken breast, but a chef friend tells me that he always uses thigh meat in his restaurant, as he found it has a much stronger flavour than the rather bland breast.

Serves 4
Preparation time 20–25 minutes plus marinating time
Cooking time 8–10 minutes

400–450g (14oz–1lb) chicken thigh meat, skinned and boned
½ teaspoon ground Sichuan peppercorns
1 tablespoon sugar
1 tablespoon rice wine
1 tablespoon light soy
2 teaspoons cornflour
About 300ml (½ pint) oil
2–3 spring onions cut into short sections, with white and green parts separated
2 tablespoons Guilin chilli sauce
1 small green peppe (capsicum)r, cut into small pieces

Chicken Cubes with Chilli Bean Sauce

1 Trim off excess fat from the chicken, then cut into 1.5cm (¾in) cubes. Marinate with pepper, sugar, wine, soy and cornflour for 25–30 minutes.

2 Heat the oil in a preheated wok to medium hot. Lightly brown the chicken cubes for 2–3 minutes. Remove, drain.

3 Pour off the excess oil, leaving 2 teaspoons in the wok. Stir-fry the white parts of the spring onions with the chilli sauce over low heat for about 30 seconds, until fragrant. Return the chicken to the wok. Turn up the heat and stir-fry for another minute, adding a little stock or water if it starts getting too dry. Continue stirring until the juice starts to bubble, then add the green pepper (capsicum) with the green parts of the spring onions. Blend and cook for 1 more minute. Serve hot.

Dusk at Yangshou, south of Guilin, famous for its karst limestone mountains

柱侯醬

CHU HOU BEAN PASTE

(CHUHOU JIANG)

Ling Chu-hou was a chef who worked in Foshan near Canton around the beginning of the last century. He is credited with creating this special sauce, which became so famous that not only was this delicious sauce named after him, but also several dishes. For many of the regional ones, however, consumption is restricted to the province of origin.

MANUFACTURE

Chu Hou bean paste is made with yellow soybeans, wheat flour, sugar, fat and sesame. Lard was used originally, but the Pearl River Bridge brand of the paste, which is mainly for export to the West, uses peanut oil instead of lard. Other brands from Hong Kong all use vegetable oil for the same reason.

Poultry is a major source of protein for many country-dwellers

CULINARY USES

Chu Hou bean paste is used in poultry and seafood dishes.

CHU HOU CHICKEN

Pigeon, duck and goose can all be prepared and cooked by this method, but remember to adjust the seasonings and the cooking time.

Serves 4–6
Preparation time 10–15 minutes
Cooking time about 1 hour

1 young chicken, weighing about 1.25kg (2lb 12oz)
25g (1oz) lard or 1 tablespoon vegetable oil
4–6 tablespoons Chu Hou bean paste
About 50ml (2fl oz) Chinese spirit, or brandy, whisky, rum etc

Chu Hou Chicken

About 1 litre (1¾ pints) stock or water
1 teaspoon MSG or 2 teaspoons salt
1 tablespoon cornflour paste
½ teaspoon sesame oil
Shredded spring onions to serve

1 Clean the chicken well and pat dry both inside and out.

2 Heat the lard or oil in a pot or wok over low heat. Stir-fry the Chu Hou paste with the spirit for a few seconds, then add the stock or water. Bring to the boil over high heat, immerse the chicken in the liquid and simmer gently, covered, over a low heat for 30–35 minutes.

3 Lift the chicken out of the liquid and drain the liquid back into the pot or wok. Bring the liquid back to the boil and immerse the chicken in it again. Empty and immerse the chicken five more times, which will take about 20 minutes to complete, by which time the chicken should be cooked.

4 Remove all the bones of the chicken before cutting it into small pieces for serving. Put the bones back into the liquid and boil for a few minutes to reduce the sauce. Remove the bones and add the MSG or salt. Thicken the sauce with the cornflour paste, blend in the sesame oil and pour it over the chicken. Serve with the shredded spring onions.

豆沙

SWEET BEAN PASTE

(DOUSHA)

Although there are two different coloured sweet bean pastes (red and black), they are both made from red beans. I discovered this unexpected fact only very recently, while researching this book.

MANUFACTURE

Basic red bean paste is made by gently boiling red beans in water until soft, grinding them into a pulp, cleaning and straining them to get rid of the skin then filtering and pressing them. This will give you unsweetened paste. For sweet red bean paste, crushed rock sugar is mixed in, and for sweet black bean paste, additional sugar is used with lard or oil – it has to be heated, mixed and stirred until the colour turns black. More often than not, essence of various fragrant flowers such as roses or s sweet-scented osmanthus (cassia) is blended in with the black paste.

APPEARANCE AND TASTE

Sweet bean paste is a thick, smooth purée. The red variety is really red-brown in colour, and does not taste very sweet; the black bean paste is a shiny black because it contains fat. It is more fragrant and tastes sweeter than the dull-looking red bean paste.

BUYING AND STORING

Sweet red bean paste is readily available in tins from Oriental stores; I have never came across black paste in the West. Once the tin is opened, transfer the contents to a plastic or glass container with an air-tight lid and store in the refrigerator where it will keep forever.

Red Bean Paste Pancakes

CULINARY USES

Sweet bean paste is widely used as a filling for steamed buns (*baozi*), cakes and other desserts. In China, sweet black bean paste is far more popular than the red variety, and as a child, I always preferred the sweeter taste of the former.

RED BEAN PASTE PANCAKES

This is a popular dessert served in most non-Cantonese restaurants. It is very easy to prepare and cook at home, provided you use commercially made pancakes, which are readily available in most supermarkets. Otherwise you can follow the recipe for Thin Pancakes given on p 36.

Serves 4–6
Preparation time 10–15 minutes if using ready-made pancakes
Cooking time 4–5 minutes

8 Thin Pancakes (p 36)
About 8 tablespoons sweet red bean paste
1–2 tablespoon vegetable oil
Granulated or caster sugar to serve

1 Spread a pancake on a flat surface, then smear about 1 tablespoon red bean paste evenly over most of the pancake's surface.

2 Roll the pancake over the filling three or four times to form a flattened roll.

3 Carry out steps 1 and 2 on the other seven pancakes.

4 Heat the oil in a frying pan, then reduce the heat to low and shallow-fry the pancake rolls until golden brown on both sides.

5 To serve, cut each roll into 3–4 pieces, sprinkle with sugar and serve hot.

豆瓣醬

CHILLI BEAN PASTE

(TOBAN JIANG)

What distinguishes this seasoning from other thick sauces is the fact that it is made with broad beans rather than soya beans. Pixian County lies in the heart of the Chengdu Plains (Chengdu is the capital of Sichuan province), where the land is extremely fertile and broad beans of very high quality are grown. It is here that *toban jiang* originated over a hundred years ago.

MANUFACTURE

Toban jiang is made in many other regions of China, but none can match the aroma and flavour of the product from Pixian. In Pixian, *toban jiang* is made in large earthenware tubs, from broad beans, fresh red chillies, plain flour, salt and water. The process involves two periods of fermentation, the first lasting roughly a week, the second lasting 3–5 months,with 40–50 days spent drying in the sun in between. Hot Broad Bean Paste from Anqing in southeast China is sweeter and less hot because it contains sweet rice wine and fewer chillies.

Planting peppers in Sichuan

APPEARANCE AND TASTE

Toban jiang is a beautiful, rich, reddish-brown, speckled with lots of chilli seeds. It varies from almost sweet to mildly hot to quite hot. It is never mouth-numbing because unlike ordinary chilli sauce, which is more of a dipping sauce for the table, *toban jiang* is used only in the kitchen.

BUYING AND STORING

Unfortunately, Pixian *toban jiang* is rarely seen in the West. What is widely available is chilli bean paste made in Hong Kong, Taiwan, and Singapore. Some brands are quite good, but they cannot compare with the genuine article. Different brands have different degrees of hotness – you will have to try them out to find one that suits your taste. If you store the jar in the refrigerator after opening, it should remain good for many months, provided you always use a clean spoon.

CULINARY USES

As I said earlier, chilli bean paste is not to be confused with the very popular chilli sauce: the two are not interchangeable. *Toban jiang* is an essential seasoning in Sichuan cuisine, notably in dishes such as Toban Fish, Braised Bean Curd, and Twice-Cooked Pork. Some Sichuan chefs would even go so far as to say that without Pixian *toban jiang*, it is not possible to produce authentic Sichuan food.

TOBAN FISH

This is a variation on the classic Sichuan fish dish called Dry-Fried Fish, often translated as Braised Fish in Spicy Hot Bean Sauce, or Chilli and Garlic Sauce. If you are not used to cooking a whole fish, by all means use fish steak or fillet, but a fish cooked whole with its head and tail intact always looks most impressive on the table and I believe tastes better. Make sure you have a big enough wok.

Serves 4–6
Preparation time 10 minutes
Cooking time 10 minutes approximately

Toban Fish

1 carp, bream, perch, mullet, or sea bass, about 700g (1lb 9oz), gutted and cleaned
½ teaspoon salt
3–4 tablespoons oil
2 tablespoons chilli bean paste (toban jiang)
1 teaspoon finely chopped fresh ginger
½ teaspoon finely chopped garlic
1 teaspoon finely chopped white of spring onion
1 tablespoon soy
1 tablespoon rice wine
About 150ml (¼ pint) stock or water
2 teaspoons sugar
1 tablespoon cornflour paste
1 tablespoon rice vinegar
1 tablespoon finely chopped green of spring onion
½ teaspoon sesame oil

1 Clean and dry the fish well. Score both sides of the fish as far as the bone, making diagonal cuts at intervals of about 2.5cm (1in). Rub the fish with the salt, inside and out.

2 Heat the oil in a preheated wok and fry the fish for about 3–4 minutes, turning over once, or until golden brown on both sides.

3 Push the fish to one side of the wok, add the bean paste, ginger, garlic and the white of the spring onion white and stir-fry for 15–20 seconds until fragrant. Add the soy, wine, stock and sugar, then move the fish back to the middle of the wok and bring to the boil. Reduce the heat a little and braise, covered, for about 5 minutes.

4 Gently lift the fish out and place on a serving platter. Thicken the sauce with the cornflour paste and blend in the vinegar, spring onion green and sesame oil. Pour the sauce over the fish and serve hot.

Home-Style Braised Bean Curd

Not to be confused with the world-famous *Ma Po Doufu*, which uses salted black beans (p 197). Here the bean-curd is cooked with pork rather than beef.

Serves 4
Preparation time 10 minutes
Cooking time 8–10 minutes

2 cakes bean curd
3–4 tablespoons oil
½ teaspoon salt
115g (4oz) pork, thinly sliced
1 tablespoon chilli bean paste
1 leek, cut into short sections
2 spring onions, cut into short sections
1 tablespoon light soy
3–4 tablespoons stock
1 tablespoon rice wine
2 teaspoons cornflour paste
A few drops sesame oil

1 Split each cake of bean curd crossways into 3–4 slices, then cut each slice diagonally into two triangles. Blanch the bean curd in a pan of boiling water. Remove and drain.

2 Heat the oil in a preheated wok and fry the bean curd slices with the salt for 2–3 minutes, turning once. Remove and set aside.

3 Stir-fry the pork slices until the colour changes from pink to pale white. Add the bean paste, leek and spring onions, blend well, then add the stock and soy with the bean curd. Bring to the boil and braise gently for 3–4 minutes.

4 Add the rice wine and thicken the sauce with the cornflour paste. Sprinkle over the sesame oil and serve at once.

西红柿酱

TOMATO SAUCE

(XIHONGSHI JIANG)

Tomatoes ripening on the vine

The tomato (*Lycopersicum esculentum*) is not indigenous to China, but is of foreign origin, as its common name, *panqie* (foreign aubergine), indicates. Just when it was introduced is uncertain; the earliest mention of it dates from the end of the seventeenth century.

APPEARANCE AND TASTE

I first encountered tomato in its hard, green form, sliced and stir-fried with scrambled eggs, and to this day, I still prefer my tomatoes to be hard and green, cooked rather than raw – although I do love the very tasty tomato salads of Mediterranean countries.

CULINARY USES

Tomato sauce used in Chinese cooking should be either tomato paste (purée), or a lightly seasoned tomato-based sauce, not the ubiquitous tomato ketchup, much used in sweet and sour dishes by some Chinese restaurants. Tomato ketchup and tomato sauce (paste) are not interchangeable in Chinese cooking.

STIR-FRIED PRAWNS IN TOMATO SAUCE

This is a most delicious dish, simple and easy to prepare. It can be served as a starter or as part of the main course when combined with other dishes.

Serves 4–6 as a starter
Preparation time 15–20 minutes
Cooking time 8–10 minutes

300g (10oz) peeled prawns, uncooked
1 teaspoon salt
½ egg white, beaten
2 tablespoons cornflour paste
2–3 firm tomatoes
1 clove garlic, finely chopped
2 spring onions
About 300ml (½ pint) oil
2 tablespoons tomato paste (purée)
2 teaspoons sugar
1 tablespoon light soy
2 teaspoons rice wine
About 125ml (4fl oz) good stock
½ teaspoon sesame oil
Fresh coriander leaves to garnish

1 Blend the prawns with a pinch of the salt, the egg white, and about half the cornflour paste.

2 Skin the tomatoes and cut each one into small wedges. Cut the spring onions into short sections, separating the white and green parts.

3 Heat the oil in a preheated wok or pan. Stir-fry the prawns for about 1–1½ minutes, remove with a strainer and drain.

4 Pour off the excess oil, leaving about 1 tablespoon in the wok or pan. Stir-fry the garlic, the tomatoes and white parts of the spring onions for about 30 seconds, then add the remaining salt together with the tomato paste, sugar, soy, rice wine and stock. Blend well and bring to the boil.

5 Add the prawns with the green parts of the spring onions. Blend well and thicken the sauce with the remaining cornflour paste. Sprinkle on the sesame oil and serve hot, garnished with coriander leaves.

Stir-fried Prawns in Tomato Sauce

柠檬酱

Lemon Sauce

(NINGMENG JIANG)

It is common knowledge that the sweet orange (*Citrus sinensis*) originated in China, but nobody seems certain about the origins of the lemon (*Citrus limon*), which is not widely used in China. It is a mystery to me how the very popular Cantonese dish called Lemon Chicken came into being – you will never find it on the menu of any restaurant in mainland China.

Manufacture

I do not have the exact formula for commercially produced lemon sauce (no one makes their own), but it is a simple matter of mixing water with lemon juice, lemon rind, sugar, salt, and thickening it with starch.

Appearance and Taste

Most bottled lemon sauce is quite attractive. Some, if not most, brands add artificial colouring to make the sauce bright yellow. The flavour is deliciously piquant.

Lemon sauce

Buying and Storing

Bottled lemon sauce from Hong Kong is widely available in Oriental stores. Once opened, store in the refrigerator, where it should keep for a very long time. Each bottle should have a 'use by' date stamped on it.

Culinary Uses

Lemon sauce features in just one Chinese dish: the ubiquitous Lemon Chicken that appears on the menu of every Cantonese restaurant and take-away in the West. I have no idea what else you can do with it – you could try it with fish dishes and see what happens.

Lemon Chicken

Perhaps what makes this dish so appealing to the Western palate is the fact that it is a refreshing change from strong-tasting sweet and sour sauce.

Serves 4
Preparation time 15–20 minutes plus marinating time
Cooking time 8–10 minutes

450g (1lb) chicken breast fillet
Salt and pepper
1 tablespoon rice wine
1 egg, beaten
2 tablespoons plain flour
Oil for deep-frying
Lettuce leaves
1 tablespoon oil
About 200ml (⅓ pint) ready-made lemon sauce
Slices of fresh lemon to garnish

1 Trim off any excess fat from the chicken. Marinate with the salt, pepper and rice wine for 25–30 minutes.

2 Make a batter with the beaten egg and flour, adding a little water if necessary.

3 Heat the oil in a wok or deep-fryer to 180°C/350°F. Coat the chicken with the batter and deep-fry for 4–5 minutes or until golden brown. Remove and drain.

4 Cut the chicken into bite-size slices and arrange on a serving dish on a bed of lettuce leaves.

5 Heat about 1 tablespoon oil in a wok or saucepan over low heat. Mix in the lemon sauce, blend well and pour evenly over the chicken pieces. Garnish with the lemon slices and serve hot.

Lemon Chicken

Red fermented bean curd

豆腐乳

FERMENTED BEAN CURD

(DOUFU NAI)

Doufu nai, literally 'bean-curd milk', is a Chinese speciality little appreciated by Westerners. It is definitely an acquired taste, and has often been compared to strong cheese: you either love it (as does almost everyone in China) or hate it (as does almost everyone elsewhere). But everybody loves it when it is disguised as a seasoning. Another Chinese name for fermented bean-curd is *jiang doufu*, *jiang* being the Chinese term for soy and all the other 'sauces' which have been through some form of fermentation.

LEGEND

One day a street bean-curd seller came across two old gentlemen playing a game of chess outside a teahouse. Stopping to watch, he put down his baskets of bean curd by the roadside. It was a long and exciting match, and when it was all over, the young lad discovered to his horror that his bean curd had gone mouldy. He was so distressed that he burst out crying, so the two chess players rushed over and whispered some instructions to his ears, then disappeared into thin air. The young lad realized that he had had an encounter with two Immortals, and hurried back home to carry out the instructions by marinating the bean curd with salt and spices. The next day, the mouldy bean curd had turned into aromatic and delicious *doufu nai*!

Passing the time outside a teahouse, Sichuan

Since the fifteenth century Fengdu fermented bean curd has held an excellent reputation and today there are two leading brands: one is called The Immortals, and the other, The Two Immortals! The teahouse in which the chess game took place still exists, and has been renamed as 'The House of The Two Immortals'.

MANUFACTURE

There are three stages to making *doufu nai*: the first stage is to make the bean curd by soaking, grinding, filtering, heating, cooling, setting, pressing and cutting soybeans. The second stage involves laying out the bean curd on beds of rice straw for fermentation, renewing the rice straw regularly. The actual period of fermentation usually lasts about five days in the spring, and seven to eight days in winter. The final stage is to dry the mouldy bean curd in the sun before marinating with salt, sorghum spirit and spices. It is stored in brine in sealed earthenware urns to be matured for at least six months before going on sale.

APPEARANCE AND TASTE

There are two basic types of fermented bean curd: red and white. The red one has ground red rice instead of spice added to it, and the colour is on the surface only; the spice used for the white type is often ground hot red chillies. Both types are very salty, the one with chilli tasting quite hot and spicy.

BUYING AND STORING

In China, fermented bean curd can be bought loose, and it is often home-made. In the West, it is widely available in tins or jars; once opened, the contents should be transferred to a plastic or glass container with an air-tight lid, and refrigerated. Glass or earthenware jars should also be refrigerated after opening. Both home-made and bought varieties will keep for many years.

Culinary Uses

The most common way of serving fermented bean curd in China is for breakfast with rice congee. The milder tasting red fermented bean curd is used as a seasoning agent in marinating and cooking.

Pork Chops with Red Fermented Bean Curd

The best cut for this dish is known as 'English spare-rib chop', which, unlike Chinese or American spare-ribs, is all meat with hardly any bone attached. Failing that, use pork steak.

Serves 4–6
Preparation time 20–25 minutes
Cooking time 10–15 minutes

450g (1lb) pork spare-rib chops or steaks
Salt and pepper
1 tablespoon rice wine
2 teaspoons cornflour paste
1 small onion
1 small green pepper (capsicum)
Oil for deep-frying
1 teaspoon minced garlic
1 tablespoon light soy
2 teaspoons sugar
1 tablespoon red fermented bean curd, mashed
½ teaspoon sesame oil

1 Cut the pork into thin strips about the size of French fries. Marinate with the salt, pepper, wine and cornflour for about 10 minutes.

2 Thinly shred the onion and green pepper (capsicum).

White fermented bean curd

3 Heat the oil in a wok or deep-fryer and fry the pork strips for 2–3 minutes, stirring to separate them. Remove and drain.

4 Pour off the excess oil, leaving 1 tablespoon in the wok. Stir-fry the onion and garlic for about 1 minute, then add the green pepper (capsicum), pork, soy, sugar and fermented bean curd. Blend well and stir-fry for 2–3 minutes. Sprinkle on the sesame oil and toss a few times more. Serve hot.

Sichuan-Style Fried Green Beans

Green or French beans (*Haricots verts*) are known in Sichuan as 'four-season' beans since they are grown all year round in this part of the world.

Serves 4–6
Preparation time 10–15 minutes plus soaking time
Cooking time 6–8 minutes

1 tablespoon dried shrimps
450g (1lb) green (French) beans
Oil for deep-frying
1 teaspoon finely chopped fresh ginger
2 tablespoons fermented bean curd (with chilli), mashed
½ teaspoon salt
1 teaspoon sugar
2 tablespoons stock or water
1 tablespoon finely chopped spring onions
1 tablespoon rice vinegar
½ teaspoon sesame oil

1 Soak the dried shrimps in warm water for about 30–40 minutes. Rinse and drain, then finely chop.

2 Top and tail the beans, cutting them in half. Heat the oil and deep-fry the beans for 1–2 minutes. Scoop out and drain.

3 Pour off the excess oil, leaving about 1 tablespoon in the wok. Stir-fry the chopped ginger, dried shrimps and fermented bean curd for about 30 seconds. Now add the beans with the salt, sugar and stock or water. Stir-fry for 1–2 minutes more, then add the spring onions and vinegar. Blend well. Add the sesame oil and serve hot or cold.

Sichuan-Style Fried Green Beans

卤水料

MASTER SAUCE MIX

(LUSHUI LIAO)

The specially prepared sauce or gravy known as *lushui zhi* is sometimes loosely translated as 'master sauce or gravy', because it can be used again and again. The making of master sauce is quite simple to start with, but it takes several years before it can be said to be truly mature. The sauce is enriched by being used to cook different ingredients over a long period of time; it is supposed to bear the mark of each individual chef.

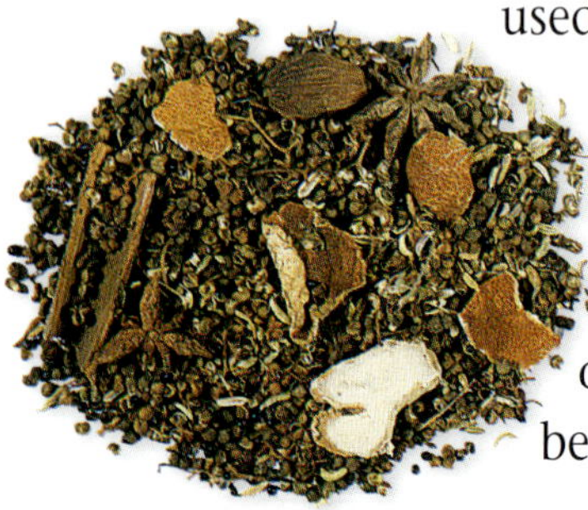

MANUFACTURE

The ingredients for a master sauce can be simple or complex: the average home cook would just use salt, soy, rice wine, rock sugar, spring onions, ginger and the ubiquitous star anise, while a professional chef would use more than ten different spices in addition to the basic seasonings, and the 'secret recipe' would be passed down from chef to apprentice. The truth is that there aren't really any secret recipes for making master sauce, for a good sauce depends not so much on the basic ingredients used to start with, but on the poultry, meat and other foods that have been cooked in it.

BUYING AND STORING

It is possible to obtain ready-mixed spices for master sauce on the open market. The brand that is widely available from Oriental stores in the West is Wah Loong's Mixed Spices, which is a blend of star anise, cinnamon, cardamom, clove, fennel seeds, ginger, Farchiew (Sichuan peppercorns) and liquorice. This mixture is very similar to standard five-spice powder, except that the various spices are not ground up but left either whole or in small pieces. Commercially produced master sauce in bottles is also available, usually labelled as Lo Sui Marinade (*lo* being Cantonese for *lu*). It may not be as good (or mature!) as home-made, but I have tried it and the result is quite acceptable.

CULINARY USES

The Chinese cookery term *lu* is very difficult to define. Basically it involves cooking a whole chicken or duck, large pieces of meat, offal and giblets etc in the master sauce. The process of cooking *lu* food is very simple. The raw ingredient is first cleaned, then blanched or par-boiled before being slow-cooked in the master sauce. After a relatively short time, the heat is turned off, and the food is left to cool in the sauce for several hours in order to continue cooking in the diminishing heat of the liquid.

MASTER SAUCE

Makes about 3 litres (5¼ pints) master sauce
Preparation time 10–15 minutes
Cooking time 25–30 minutes

2.5 litres (4½ pints) water
15g (½oz) star anise
15g (½oz) liquorice root
15g (½oz) cinnamon bark
15g (½oz) orange peel
7.5g (¼oz) fennel seeds
7.5g (¼oz) dried ginger
7.5g (¼oz) Sichuan peppercorns
7.5g (¼oz) cloves
500ml (18fl oz) soy
250ml (9fl oz) rice wine
350g (12oz) rock sugar
1½ tablespoons salt
3–4 spring onions, each tied into a knot
3–4 large pieces fresh ginger

Poplars line the Silk Road, the former trade route for Asian spices

1 Bring the water to a boil in a large pot. Put all the dried spices into a muslin or gauze sack, tie it up and immerse it in the boiling water.

2 Add the soy, wine, sugar, salt, spring onions and ginger to the pot. Reduce the heat and bring back to the boil slowly, then simmer gently for about 20–25 minutes until it is fragrant and dark brown in colour.

3 Strain and discard all the bits and pieces. This is the 'raw' master sauce, and it becomes 'mature' only after a number of different ingredients have been cooked in it. These must include chicken, duck, meat and offal.

Note: Store in the refrigerator when cool, but remember to re-use it or just boil it at least once a week, to keep it in good order. It will keep in the freezer almost indefinitely, but will not mature unless you cook with it frequently.

Herding ducks to water in Guangdong

Braised Chicken/Duck Giblets

In Western cooking terms, giblets means the head, neck, heart, pinions, feet, gizzard, kidneys and liver of poultry. These are normally used for making stock. In China, we use the head, neck, pinions and feet for stock-making, but the heart, kidneys, gizzard and liver are regarded as delicacies, and are usually used in special dishes. This is one.

Serves 4 as a starter
Preparation time 10–15 minutes
Cooking time 25–30 minutes plus cooling time

4–6 eggs (optional)
4–6 chicken/duck wings
The liver, hearts, and gizzard of two or more chickens/ducks
About 2 litres (3¼ pints) Master Sauce
Sesame seed oil and fresh coriander leaves to garnish

1 Hard boil the eggs, if using, for about 8–10 minutes, then soak in cold water for a few minutes before peeling.

2 Clean the wings, the liver, hearts and gizzard well. Blanch in a pot of boiling water for a few minutes, then remove, rinse in cold water and drain.

3 Place all the ingredients, including the Master Sauce, in a pot or pan. Bring to the boil slowly over low heat, simmer gently for 20–25 minutes, then turn off the heat and leave the ingredients to cool in the sauce, covered, for at least 3–4 hours.

4 To serve, remove the food from the sauce. Cut each egg in half or into quarters, and the rest, except the wings, into small thin slices. The wings should be left whole or chopped in half. Serve cold, garnished with sesame oil and coriander leaves.

Note: It may be necessary to replenish the Master Sauce with more seasonings such as soy, wine and sugar from time to time. Should the aroma become weak, more spices, spring onions and ginger may also be required.

Herbs and Spices

青葱

SPRING ONIONS (SCALLIONS)

(QING CONG) *Allium fistulosum*

The Chinese term for the spring onion or scallion is 'green onion' (*qing cong*), usually shortened to *cong* (onion). The common onion of the West (*Allium cepu*) is referred to as *yang cong* (foreign onion).

MEDICINAL USES

Spring onion tea is given to people suffering from catarrh, fever, headache, cholera, diarrhoea, dysentery, urinary infections and rheumatic disorders. It is also used as a sedative for children. Abscesses and fractures are smeared with the bruised bulb, or anointed with the juice. Every part of the plant is supposed to have some special therapeutic property.

Small spring onions

Large spring onions

HOW IT GROWS

Spring onion is native to Siberia and Mongolia, and is now cultivated all over China and almost everywhere in the world. Several species are grown, ranging from the kind with little round bulbs at the root to the one with almost non-existent, flat 'bulbs'. It is a mystery how spring onion came by its English name, since it is grown all year round – perhaps people associate the colour green with spring. Spring onions are also labelled 'salad onions' in some stores.

APPEARANCE AND TASTE

Spring onions have long green tubular leaves with pale green stalks and white bulbs; they are usually sold with roots still attached. The taste can vary from very mild to quite pungent with a touch of sweetness – the Chinese would describe it as fragrant.

Spring onion stalks

Spring onions growing

BUYING AND STORING

Spring onions are usually sold in bunches. Store them in a plastic box rather than a plastic bag so they can breathe; that way they will keep longer without going soggy. In a refrigerator they should keep for up to a week.

CULINARY USES

In China, spring onions are used as a vegetable as well as a flavouring, and in some parts of China, the filling for spring rolls consists entirely of spring onions. When used as a flavouring, the green leaves and white parts are usually cooked separately, with the white parts added to the dish at an earlier stage of cooking, while the green parts, often finely chopped, are added at the last minute or so. In some dishes they are used as a garnish and scattered raw, so they do not lose their delicate flavour.

CRAB WITH SPRING ONIONS AND GINGER

In my opinion any recipe that uses crab can equally well be made with lobster, so feel free to use either shellfish in both this and the Lobster with Chilli Black Bean Sauce (p 88).

Serves 4
Preparation time 15–20 minutes, plus marinating time
Cooking time 8–10 minutes

1 large or 2 medium crabs
2 tablespoons rice wine
1 egg, beaten
1 tablespoon cornflour paste
3–4 tablespoons oil
1 tablespoon thinly sliced fresh ginger
1 tablespoon white parts of spring onions, cut into short sections
2 tablespoons light soy
2 teaspoons sugar
1 tablespoon rice vinegar
About 100ml (4fl oz) stock or water
2 tablespoons green parts of spring onions, cut into short sections
½ teaspoon sesame oil

1 Cut the crab in half from underneath. Open the shell and discard the feathery gills and the sac. Break off the claws and legs, crack open with the back of the cleaver and cut the body into pieces.

2 Marinate the claws, legs and body pieces with the wine, egg and cornflour paste for 15–20 minutes.

3 Heat the oil in a preheated wok and stir-fry the pieces of crab with the ginger and spring onion whites for 2–3 minutes. Add the soy, sugar, vinegar and stock or water, blend well and bring to the boil. Braise for 4–5 minutes, stirring constantly.

4 Add the spring onion greens with the sesame oil. Stir a few times more and serve hot.

Note: Like the lobster dish on p 88, this dish should be served on its own and eaten with fingers, so provide finger bowls and paper napkins for the table.

Crab with Spring Onions and Ginger

RAPID-FRIED LAMB WITH SPRING ONIONS

This recipe originated in Shandong. The rapid cooking method known as *bao* means 'explosion', and is even quicker then standard stir-frying.

Serves 4
Preparation time 10–15 minutes plus marinating time
Cooking time 5 minutes

350g (12oz) leg of lamb fillet
About 600ml (1 pint) oil
6–8 spring onions, cut into short sections
3–4 small bits of fresh ginger
1 tablespoon yellow bean sauce
1 tablespoon Worcestershire Sauce

For the marinade:
½ teaspoon sugar
Pinch of ground white pepper
1 tablespoon dark soy
1 tablespoon rice wine
2 teaspoons cornflour paste
1 teaspoon sesame oil

1 Cut the lamb across the grain into slices the size of large postage stamps, then marinate for several hours.

2 Heat the oil in a preheated wok until smoking. Stir-fry the lamb in the oil for about 30–40 seconds until the meat changes colour. Then remove the slices and drain.

3 Pour off the excess oil, leaving about 1 tablespoon in the wok. Stir-fry the spring onions and ginger with the yellow beans for about 30 seconds, then return the lamb to the wok, blend well and add the Worcestershire Sauce. Stir-fry for about another minute and serve hot.

Note: The timing and temperature are vitally important in this dish: the heat must be very high at all times and the cooking should be extremely rapid!

姜 (薑)

GINGER

(JIANG) *Zingiber officinale*

An indispensable ingredient in Chinese cookery, ginger is not native to China. Its name *jiang*, is derived from the Chinese word for boundary or border, indicates that ginger originally came from outside the Middle Kingdom. Some sources trace ginger back to the tropical jungles of Asia, from where it was introduced to China more than two thousand years ago.

How It Grows

Ginger is cultivated in the central and southern provinces of China, practically all the year round. Ginger root is the rhizome of a plant grown on sandy soil, which bears small yellow and purple flowers. The roots are dug up while still young and tender, as they become fibrous if left too long.

Ginger plants showing roots

Appearance and Taste

The fresh ginger roots are golden-beige in colour with a smooth, dry skin. Pieces are usually about 2cm (¾in) in diameter but can vary in size from small bits to whole knobby 'hands' of 7.5–10cm (3–4in) long and wide. The flesh is pale yellow, and has a sweet, pungent flavour.

Buying and Storing

Fresh ginger roots are readily available all year round nowadays – in supermarkets as well as Oriental stores. Choose ginger roots that are firm and smooth, and avoid those with dry and wrinkled skin. Store in a cool, dry, dark place – not in the refrigerator, unless in an air-tight container. Ginger roots should keep for up to two weeks, if bought in prime condition.

Medicinal Uses

Fresh ginger is used to suppress objectionable odours, stimulate digestion, quell nausea and check coughs. It is a carminative and an astringent and is also thought to counteract the effects of mushroom poisoning. Dried ginger has similar properties, and may be used to treat urinary problems, haemorrhages, constipation and dysentry.

Culinary Uses

Ginger is often paired with spring onions to create a balance in seasoning – the 'hot' yang ginger is offset by the 'cool' yin spring onions. When used alone ginger is highly valued for its aromatic flavour which will complement (and mask if necessary) the strong flavours and odours of meat and seafood. Ginger is also used to 'season' raw oil as described on page 58, and features widely in pickles and preserves. To prepare: scrape or peel as much of the rhizome as you need, cut across the grain in long diagonals, then slice, shred or finely chop. Furthermore

Selecting the firmest roots of ginger

some recipes such as Glutinous Rice Chicken call for ginger juice. See p 29 for how to make this.

SHREDDED BEEF WITH ONION AND GINGER

This dish originated in Sichuan, and like so many other dishes from that province, it has now become an international favourite. Pork or lamb can be substituted for beef.

Serves 4
Preparation time 15 minutes
Cooking time approximately 4 minutes

300g (10oz) beef steak
1 medium onion
About 25g (1oz) fresh ginger root, peeled
3 tablespoons oil
1 tablespoon chilli bean paste
1 tablespoon light soy
1 teaspoon sugar
1 tablespoon rice wine
1 teaspoon rice vinegar
½ teaspoon sesame oil

1 Cut the beef into thin shreds; thinly shred the onion and ginger root.

2 Heat the oil in a preheated wok or pan until smoking, stir-fry the onion and ginger for about 1 minute, add the beef, and continue stirring for another minute or until the colour of the meat changes.

3 Add the chilli bean paste, blend well, then add the soy, sugar, rice wine and vinegar. Cook for 30–40 seconds more. Sprinkle on the sesame oil, toss to incorporate and serve hot.

GINGER-FLAVOURED LYCHEE SORBET

This is the most refreshing sorbet imaginable. Ginger can also be added to other types of sorbet, such as lemon, coconut, kiwi fruit, or mango.

Serves 4–6
Preparation time 10–15 minutes
Freezing time approximately 2¾ hours

60g (2oz) rock sugar and 100ml water (if using fresh lychees instead of canned ones)
450g (1lb) fresh lychees in their shells or a 450g can of lychees in syrup or natural juice
1 tablespoon grated fresh ginger root

1 Make a syrup, if using fresh lychees, by dissolving the rock sugar in boiling water, then leaving to cool.

2 Peel the fresh lychees and remove the stones. Place the lychees and ginger in a food processor or blender with the syrup, or juice from the can, and process to a smooth purée.

3 Pour the purée into a freezer-proof container, and place in the freezer for about 2 hours or until almost set.

4 Break up the iced mixture and beat until smooth. Return mixture to the freezer for 30–45 minutes to set solid before serving.

Ginger-flavoured Lychee Sorbet

蒜

GARLIC

(SUAN) *Allium sativum*

Garlic has been known to the Chinese from very early on – it is mentioned in the Calendar of the Xia, written in about 2000 BC. It is now called *xiao suan* (little garlic) to distinguish it from the rocambole (*Allium scorodoprasum*), a cross between a spring onion and leek called *da suan* (big garlic) or *hu suan* (foreign garlic).

Garlic clove

HOW IT GROWS

Garlic is a bulbous perennial of the onion family with flat, green leaves and small white flowers. The bulb has anything from 6 to 20 individual cloves. About a month after the seed stalks emerge, the tops start to turn yellowish-brown and the bulbs are pulled out of the earth. The bulbs are sold without the leaves.

APPEARANCE AND TASTE

Garlic is known for the crescent shape of its cloves and white or purplish-pink papery husks. The flavour is distinctive: strong and pungent, with a touch of sweetness. Its aroma is much stronger than that of onions. The non-bulbous rocambole is more highly-flavoured than the Western leek. Because its green leaves and white stems taste garlicky, it is referred to as 'garlic sprouts' by the Chinese.

BUYING AND STORING

Garlic is available all year round. Store it in a dry, airy place at room temperature, in a plastic bag to prevent shrivelling – not in the refrigerator. Damp conditions will cause garlic to sprout. I have not found rocambole in the West.

Garlic bulb

MEDICINAL USES

The medicinal virtues of garlic are many. It is good for the spleen, stomach and kidneys, acting as a sedative and removing poisons, and will prevent goitre. It is supposed to neutralize the noxious effect of unwholesome water and putrid meat and fish. It is customary to eat whole cloves of garlic on Dragon Boat Festival day to fend off evil spirits and demons.

CULINARY USES

In Chinese cookery, garlic ranks third most important after spring onion and ginger. A crushed clove of garlic (sometimes with a few bits of ginger) is often added to hot oil to flavour it, then removed and discarded before the meat, seafood or vegetables are added. Garlic is also used in marinades and sauces. Garlic cloves should be peeled before using. If you crush a clove with the flat side of the blade of a Chinese cleaver the papery husk will slip off easily.

'CRYSTAL-BOILED' PORK WITH GARLIC SAUCE

'Crystal boiling' is a unique Chinese cooking method used for white meats such as chicken and pork that are very fresh and tender. The raw ingredient, usually in large pieces (a whole chicken or a joint of pork), is cooked in boiling water for a relatively short time, then the heat is turned off, and it is left to continue cooking in the warm pot.

Serves 10–12 as a starter or 6–8 as a main course
Preparation time 10 minutes
Cooking time 50 minutes plus cooling time

1kg (2lb 4oz) leg of pork, boned but not skinned

For the sauce:
2 tablespoons finely chopped garlic
1 tablespoon finely chopped spring onions
1 teaspoon sugar
4 tablespoons light soy
1 tablespoon distilled spirit
2 teaspoons sesame oil
1 teaspoon red chilli oil

Pungent garlic for sale

1 Place the pork, tied together in one piece, in enough boiling water to cover it. Bring back to the boil, skim off the scum and simmer, covered, for about 50 minutes.

2 Leave the pork in the liquid to cool, covered, for at least 2–3 hours before removing it to cool further, skin side up, for another hour or so.

3 To serve: cut off the skin, leaving a very thin layer of fat on top, as on a ham joint. Cut the meat across the grain into small, thin slices and arrange neatly on a plate. Mix the sauce ingredients, and pour the sauce evenly over the pork.

In Shanghai, the meat is served cold and the sauce does not contain any chilli, while in Sichuan, the meat is served warm and, of course, the sauce has chilli oil in it. Any leftovers can be used in a number of dishes, such as the famous Twice-Cooked Pork with Bamboo Shoots (p 147).

STEAMED AUBERGINE WITH GARLIC

This is good for the health, as both aubergine and garlic are powerful restoratives and preventatives for all sorts of conditions.

Serves 4
Preparation time 10 minutes
Cooking time about 1 hour plus cooling time

450g (1lb) aubergine (eggplant)
4 garlic cloves, crushed
½ teaspoon salt
1 tablespoon light soy
1 tablespoon rice vinegar
2 teaspoons sesame oil

1 Peel the aubergines, cut in half lengthways, thinly slice.

2 Place the slices on a plate or in a bowl. Steam for at least an hour until soft. Remove to cool.

3 Mix the crushed garlic with the rest of the ingredients to make a dressing. Serve the aubergines mashed with the dressing.

Steamed Aubergine with Garlic

香菜 芫荽

CORIANDER (CHINESE PARSLEY)

(XIANGCAI/YUANSUI) *Coriandrum sativum*

Whoever called coriander 'Chinese parsley' must have an odd sense of humour, because the Chinese name for parsley is 'Foreign coriander'! Coriander is not in fact native to China, as one of its Chinese names, *xiyuan*, indicates (*xi* meaning Western): it was introduced from Central Asia over two thousand years ago by the Han general, Zhang-qian.

HOW IT GROWS

A member of the carrot family, coriander is both an annual and perennial plant that grows up to 20cm (8in) tall, and has several stalks. It bears white flowers that mature into seeds; these offer a spice that is rarely used in Chinese cooking.

APPEARANCE AND TASTE

Fresh coriander has a cluster of serrated, dark green leaves with pale green stems. The seeds, which are categorized as a spice, have a sweet, pungent taste and aroma, while the herbal leaves are bitter and refreshing.

BUYING AND STORING

Fresh coriander (known as *cilantro* in Latin America and certain other markets) is usually sold in a cluster of long stalked leaves with a small taproot at the base. It is available from Oriental stores and greengrocers. It is also sold in supermarkets, packed in small plastic containers without the root, but much more expensively.

Store the bundled fresh coriander with root in water, and the rootless one in the refrigerator. Both should keep for 3–4 days after purchase.

MEDICINAL USES

The leaves, stems and seeds are all used medicinally. The leaves are actually considered to be slightly harmful if eaten in excess. Carminative and relaxing properties are attributed to the plant, and it is recommended in cases of ptomaine poisoning.

CULINARY USES

Whole fresh coriander leaves, never chopped up, are used extensively as a garnish in Chinese cooking, and the leaves with stems attached are also sometimes used as a vegetable. The seeds are an ingredient in curry powder, and are used in the marinade for satay.

Coriander seeds are left when the blossom dies on the tree

Fish Slices and Coriander Soup

Fish Slices and Coriander Soup

I learnt to make this most delicious soup from my good friend Mr Ke, the famous Peking chef who has sold his very popular restaurant in London and now lives and works back in China. We still see each other now and again, but I do miss his cooking very much indeed.

Serves 4
Preparation time 10 minutes
Cooking time 3–4 minutes

225–300g (8–10oz) white fish fillet, such as lemon sole or plaice
½ egg white, lightly beaten
2 teaspoons rice wine
2 teaspoons cornflour paste
700ml (1¼ pints) stock or water (p71)
1 tablespoon light soy
About 115g (4oz) fresh coriander leaves, without too much stalk
Salt and pepper to taste

1 Cut the fish into small slices, each about the size of a matchbox. Mix with the egg white, wine and cornflour paste.

2 Bring the stock or water to a rolling boil, and poach the fish slices for about 1½–2 minutes.

3 Add the soy and coriander leaves and bring back to the boil. Adjust the seasoning and serve hot.

Note: If using water instead of stock, a pinch of MSG should be added to the soup.

Stir-Fried Chicken with Coriander

This is a most delicate and colourful dish. The recipe was passed on to me by the late Kenneth Lo, the eminent Chinese gourmet and a long-standing family friend. I regret that I never found out its origin, but I suspect that it must have came from Ken's home province of Fujian in Southeast China.

Serves 4
Preparation time 20 minutes
Cooking time 3–4 minutes

225–300g (8–10oz) chicken breast fillet
1 teaspoon salt
½ egg white, lightly beaten
1 tablespoon cornflour paste
About 300ml (½ pint) oil
1 tablespoon thinly shredded fresh ginger
2–3 spring onions, finely shredded
1 bunch fresh coriander leaves, washed, roots removed
½ teaspoon sugar
½ tablespoon rice wine
Pinch of MSG (optional)
½ teaspoon sesame oil
A few sprigs fresh coriander leaves to garnish

1 Cut the chicken into thin shreds. Mix with a pinch of salt, egg white and cornflour paste, in that order.

2 Heat the oil in a preheated wok or pan until warm. Stir-fry the chicken shreds for 30–40 seconds until the colour changes, stirring to separate the shreds. Remove and drain.

3 Pour off the excess oil, leaving about 2 teaspoons in the wok. Stir-fry the ginger and spring onions for a few seconds, then return the chicken shreds to the wok with the remaining salt, the coriander leaves, sugar, wine and MSG, if using. Continue stirring for about 1 more minute, adding a little stock or water only if necessary. Sprinkle on the sesame oil and serve hot, garnished with the sprigs of coriander.

陳皮

ORANGE PEEL

(CHENPI) *Citrus aurantium v. nobilis*

Dried tangerine or Mandarin orange peel is primarily a medicinal herb, but it is also used as a spice in cooking. China produces several species of orange and tangerine with many varieties.

MANUFACTURE

Only ripe fruit is used. The peel is dried naturally in the sun, and seasoned with salt and sugar. A warm and dry winter climate is needed, so the majority of dried orange peel comes from southern China, mostly Guangdong (Canton) and Fujian.

APPEARANCE AND TASTE

Dried orange peel does not have a very attractive appearance: dull and shrivelled, the dark red strips have a pale white underbelly and bear no resemblance to the bright orange peel of the fresh fruit. But the dried peel has a lovely aroma with a fragrant, tangy flavour.

BUYING AND STORING

Dried orange peel is usually sold in Oriental stores in plastic bags. Once opened, the bags should be resealed and stored in an air-tight container. The peel should keep for many months, if not years, provided it is in a cool, dry, dark place.

MEDICINAL USES

Dried orange peel is regarded by Chinese doctors as a panacea for all sorts of ills. Among the qualities attributed to it are stimulant, anti-inflammatory and antispasmodic. It is also recommended for treating fish and lobster poisoning, pin worms, and even breast cancer.

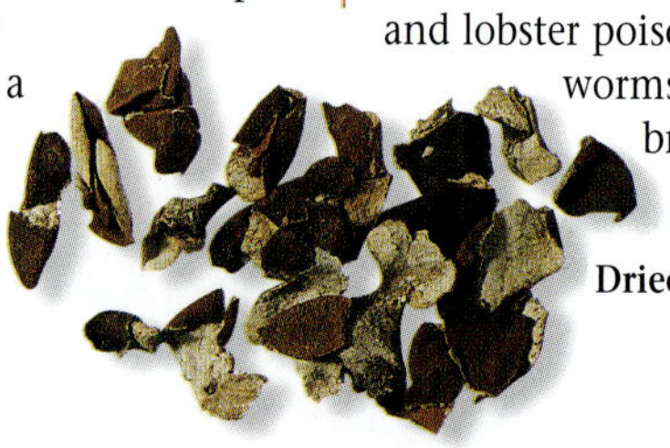

Dried orange peel

Hot and Sour Mutton Stew

CULINARY USES

Dried orange peel is used primarily as a seasoning, like star anise and cinnamon bark, when braising meat. It is usually discarded after cooking, except in some Sichuan and Hunan dishes, in which the peel is shredded or chopped (after soaking) and stir-fried with the sauce.

HOT AND SOUR MUTTON STEW

This delicious dish is almost a soup but it is served as part of a main course.

Serves 4–6
Preparation time 30 minutes
Cooking time about 1 hour 15 minutes

- *700g (1lb 9oz) lean mutton or lamb*
- *3–4 small pieces dried orange or tangerine peel*
- *2–3 pieces star anise*
- *1 teaspoon whole Sichuan peppercorns*
- *5–6 dried whole red chillies*
- *1–2 spring onions, cut into short sections*
- *½ tablespoon fresh ginger slices*
- *1 tablespoon oil*
- *2 tablespoons chilli bean paste*
- *About 600ml (1 pint) meat or chicken stock*
- *2–3 tablespoons rice wine*
- *450g (1lb) Chinese turnip or carrot, cut into small diamond-shape pieces*
- *2 tablespoons rice vinegar*
- *Coriander leaves to garnish*

1 Cut the meat into 2.5cm (1in) cubes. Blanch in boiling water for 2–3 minutes, remove and drain.

2 Place the peel, star anise, Sichuan peppercorns, chillies, spring onions and ginger in a muslin bag.

3 Heat the oil in a wok or pot. Stir-fry the chilli bean paste over moderate heat until fragrant, then add the stock and bring to the boil over high heat. Add the meat, rice wine and bag of spices. Reduce the heat and simmer gently for 45–50 minutes.

4 Add the turnip or carrot pieces, braise for 10–15 minutes, then remove and discard the bag of spices. Add the vinegar and blend well. Serve hot, garnished with the coriander leaves.

八角

STAR ANISE

(BAJIAO) *Illicium anisatum v. verum*

One of the most important spices used in everyday Chinese cooking, star anise is not indigenous to China. It probably came from the East Indies or Japan, brought by sea to Canton many centuries ago. Although similar to fennel seed and aniseed in aroma and taste, it comes from a quite different plant.

HOW IT GROWS

Star anise is the fruit of an umbelliferous tree of the magnolia family which reaches a height of 8–15m (25–45ft). It grows mainly in Guangxi in southern China; other provinces such as Guangdong, Fujian, Taiwan, Guizhou and Yunnan have successfully cultivated it.

APPEARANCE AND TASTE

This beautiful octagonal spice is mahogany in colour, and the eight boat-shaped petals form a perfect star – hence its name. Each petal is compressed laterally, and opens at the top, disclosing a solitary, shining seed in the smooth cavity. Its aroma and sweet taste is more pronounced than aniseed.

BUYING AND STORING

Star anise is always sold whole in dried form, in plastic bags. Some petals will be broken, but do make sure the majority have eight petals intact: some unscrupulous merchants have tried to pass off a five-petal 'bastard star anise' which is poisonous. Reseal the packet once opened, and store in an air-tight container. It should keep well for many months.

MEDICINAL USES

The seeds of star anise are recommended as a diuretic, and for constipation, lumbago, hernia, and bladder complaints. It is carminative, soothing to the stomach, and an essential flavouring in cough mixtures.

Spicy Tea Eggs

CULINARY USES

For everyday cooking in China, star anise is usually used whole or broken into smaller pieces, never crushed. It is used in stews and marinades, and is not eaten but discarded after cooking. The exception is when it is ground into fine powder to make the famous 'five-spice powder' (see p 124).

SPICY TEA EGGS

In order to achieve the beautiful marble pattern, you must not use newly laid eggs. By all means buy fresh eggs, but keep them for several days before using, so that the shell comes off the egg easily, leaving a smooth, marbled pattern.

Allow 2 eggs per person as a snack, or 1 egg per person as part of a meal
Preparation time about 20 minutes
Cooking time 45–50 minutes plus cooling time

12 eggs
1 teaspoon salt
2 tablespoons light soy
1 tablespoon dark soy
3–4 whole star anise
3–4 tablespoons good quality black China tea leaves

1 Hard boil the eggs for 8–10 minutes. Remove and soak in cold water to cool a little before tapping each shell gently with a spoon, or rolling the eggs on a hard surface, until they are finely cracked all over.

2 Place the eggs all together in a saucepan and cover with water. Add the salt, light and dark soy, star anise and tea leaves. Bring to the boil, then simmer gently, covered, for 45–50 minutes. Leave the eggs to cool in the liquid for several hours: the longer the infusion, the stronger the flavour.

3 To serve: remove the eggs from the liquid (which should be discarded as it cannot be re-used) and carefully peel off the shell to reveal the beautiful marble pattern. Serve the eggs whole, or cut in halves with the yolk side down.

桂皮 肉桂

CASSIA (CHINESE CINNAMON)

(GUIPI/ROUGUI) *Cinnamomum cassia*

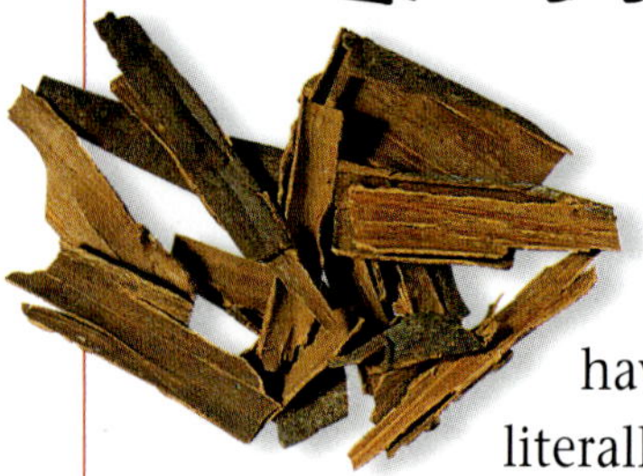

The Chinese name *gui*, by which cassia or Chinese cinnamon is generically known actually embraces four quite different plants! We have cassia bark, *guipi* in Chinese, then we have cassia or *rougui* which literally means fleshy cinnamon; we also have *guihua*, cassia flower of the *Osmanthus fragrans*, and finally there is *guiye*, the leaf of the laurel tree (*Laurus nobilis*). In the West the more readily available cinnamon is often used as a substitute for cassia, but it is important to understand that these are not interchangeable spices.

HOW IT GROWS

Both the common cinnamon and cassia trees are members of the laurel family – the latter is native to southern China, the former originated in Sri Lanka. The Chinese variety grows to a height of 3–5m (10–16ft) with glossy green leaves that bear tiny white, yellow or red flowers. The bark, which we use as a spice, is stripped off and dried. The Sri Lankan tree in comparison can grow as high as 10m (35ft).

APPEARANCE AND TASTE

Chinese cinnamon bark is dark brown and rough on the outside, and pale brown and smooth on the inside. The unscraped bark of the tree is the product we call *rougui* (cassia); the scraped bark of the tree is the genuine *guipi* (Chinese cinnamon). Both have a distinctive, bittersweet flavour, but cassia tastes more woody and less pungent.

BUYING AND STORING

Cassia bark and cinnamon are sold in small pieces in plastic bags. The Chinese variety can be obtained only from Oriental stores. Keep either in an air-tight container, and store in a cool, dark, dry place. It should be good for several months, if not years.

MEDICINAL USES

Stomachic, stimulant, carminative, astringent and sedative qualities are attributed to Chinese cinnamon bark. It is especially recommended for colic, excessive sweating and post-partum difficulties. The bark may also be applied to poisonous snake bites.

A cassia (Chinese cinnamon) tree

Aromatic and Crispy Duck

CULINARY USES

Chinese cinnamon bark is an important spice for Chinese cooking, second only to star anise, with which it is often paired. It is an essential ingredient in the five-spice blend, as well as in Master Sauce (p 104).

AROMATIC AND CRISPY DUCK

This is one of the most popular dishes in Chinese restaurants in the West. The cooking method for the famous Peking Roast Duck (see p 82) is different.

Serves 10–12 as a starter or 6–8 as a main course
Preparation and initial cooking time 8 hours plus cooling time
Final cooking time 6–8 minutes

1 duck weighing about 2.25kg (5lb), cleaned
Oil for deep-frying

For the marinade:
6 tablespoons light soy
3 tablespoons rice wine
1 tablespoon whole Sichuan peppercorns
3–4 star anise
2–3 sticks Chinese cinnamon bark
1 teaspoon whole cloves
3–4 spring onions, cut into short sections
1 tablespoon small pieces fresh ginger

For serving:
20–24 thin pancakes (p 36)
125ml (4fl oz) plum sauce
6–8 spring onions, thinly shredded
½ cucumber, thinly shredded

1 Remove the wing tips and the lumps of fat from inside the vent. Split the duck in half lengthways down the backbone and clean the inside well.

2 Combine the ingredients for the marinade in a deep dish or bowl. Place the two halves of the duck in the marinade and leave to marinate for at least 4 hours, turning the duck from time to time.

3 Steam the duck with the marinade in a hot steamer over high heat for 4 hours. Top up with fresh boiling water when necessary.

4 Remove the duck from the liquid and leave to cool for at least 6–8 hours. This is most important, for unless the duck skin is cold and dry, it will not be crispy.

5 To serve: deep-fry the duck halves, skin side down in hot oil, for 6–8 minutes or until crisp and golden, turning once in the last minute or so. Remove and drain. Shred the meat and skin with a spoon and fork, and wrap it in the pancakes with plum sauce, spring onions and cucumber, just as when eating Peking Roast Duck (p 36). Alternatively, use crispy lettuce leaves (Webb or Iceberg) instead of pancakes.

咖喱粉 CURRY POWDER

(GALIFEN)

A number of Chinese restaurants and take-aways offer a selection of curry dishes and these are very popular with their Western customers, who claim that they taste quite different from those served in Indian establishments. This is not surprising since we use a different method of cooking as well as our own special blend of spices.

MANUFACTURE

Chinese curry powder is a stronger and spicier version of the five-spice powder. This is the formula: 300g (10½oz) turmeric, 60g (2oz) white pepper, 60g (2oz) cinnamon/cassia bark, 40g (1½oz) coriander seeds, 40g (1½oz) fennel seeds, 25g (1oz) star anise, 15g (½oz) ginger, 15g (½oz) Sichuan peppercorns. Pulverize the spices into a fine powder, then blend and heat with a vegetable cooking oil.

APPEARANCE AND TASTE

Because of the large amount of turmeric and other light-coloured ingredients, Chinese curry powder is yellow rather than brown and the taste is much milder than Indian or Thai curry powders. The heat in a cooked curry dish usually comes from the addition of Chinese chilli sauce.

BUYING AND STORING

It is hard in the West to find commercially produced Chinese curry powder, so almost all restaurants use a mild blend from India – standard Mild Madras Curry Powder is very popular. All brands contain some chilli powder, so they are not as mild as the standard Chinese mix. The majority of these brands are sold in jars, rather than plastic bags. Powder sold in bags should be stored in an air-tight container, and kept away from heat and from strong light.

CULINARY USES

In China, curry powder is usually used for making 'curry-flavoured oil', which is not unlike the 'curry paste' of the West. As well as using curry powder in curries, a Chinese cook often adds a pinch to marinades for roasted and barbecued dishes instead of, or in addition to, five-spice powder.

CURRIED CHICKEN

A Chinese curry dish usually contains potatoes, though these are omitted in most Chinese restaurants in the West. Any other meat or seafood can be substituted in this recipe.

Serves 4
Preparation time 15 minutes plus marinating time
Cooking time 25–30 minutes for chicken (10–15 minutes for prawns; 40–45 minutes for red meat)

450g (1lb) chicken meat (boned and skinned)
Pinch of ground white pepper
1 teaspoon sugar
1 tablespoon light soy
1 tablespoon rice wine
1 tablespoon cornflour
3 tablespoons oil
1 clove garlic, chopped
1 medium onion, chopped
2–3 tablespoons mild curry powder
About 300ml (½ pint) stock or water
1 teaspoon salt
1 tablespoon dark soy
1–2 teaspoons chilli sauce (optional)

1 Cut the chicken meat into small cubes, and marinate with the pepper, sugar, soy, wine and cornflour for 25–30 minutes.

2 Heat the oil in a wok or pan. Stir-fry the garlic and onion over a low heat until opaque, then add the curry powder. Mix well and cook until fragrant. Add a little stock or water and stir to a smooth paste.

3 Add the chicken cubes with the salt, dark soy and the rest of the stock. Blend well and bring to the boil over high heat, stirring constantly. Reduce the heat and braise, covered, for 20–25 minutes, stirring now and again. Add the chilli sauce, if using, and serve hot with plain boiled rice and vegetables.

Curried Chicken

芥

MUSTARD

(GAI) *Brassica juncea; Sinapis alba*

Mustard is a member of the cabbage family. It has been grown in China since ancient times, but it was mainly used as a leafy vegetable (p 134) until the Tang dynasty (618–907), when the use of mustard seed as a spice was introduced from the West, probably by Arab traders.

HOW IT GROWS

The mustards grown in China are mostly varieties of the indigenous *Brassica juncea*; the only imported variety is *Sinapis alba*, which is known as 'white or foreign mustard' in Chinese. Mustard is a green-leafed vegetable with clusters of bright yellow flowers.

APPEARANCE AND TASTE

There are basically three types of mustard seeds: white, yellow and brown. Black mustard is very rare, certainly never seen in China. They all taste much the same: sharp, nutty, slightly bitter and aromatic.

BUYING AND STORING

As far as I know, whole mustard seeds are never used in Chinese cooking; they are usually only available in ground form. Commercially prepared mustard sauce is not really suitable for the Chinese table. It is better – and much cheaper – to make your own mix using the powder (see below). Store the powder in a cool, dark, dry place, where it should keep for quite a long time.

Mustard fields in Hunnan

Shredded Chicken in Mustard Sauce

MEDICINAL USES

The leaves, stalk and seeds of the mustard plant all have medicinal properties. They are recommended as corrective, digestive, and expectorant remedies. They are also used to relieve toothache and ulcers, and to calm nerves.

CULINARY USES

As mentioned earlier, it is mainly the leaves and stalks of the mustard plant which are used as a vegetable in Chinese cooking. The seeds are used to make oil, and the rest ground into fine powder to be mixed into mustard sauce, either as a dip for the table, or blended with other ingredients into a sauce for cold seafood, meat and poultry dishes.

SHREDDED CHICKEN IN MUSTARD SAUCE

For best results, use the bright yellow-coloured mustard powder known as English mustard, mix it with cold water to form a thin paste, then let it mellow for about 30 minutes before using.

Serves 4
Preparation time 10–15 minutes plus cooling time
Cooking time 2–3 minutes

250–300g (9–10oz) chicken breast meat, boned and skinned
Pinch of salt
2 egg whites, lightly beaten
1 tablespoon cornflour paste
About 150ml (¼ pint) oil
1 lettuce heart, shredded

For the sauce:
2 tablespoons mustard powder mixed with an equal amount of cold water (see above)
1 tablespoon light soy
1 tablespoon rice vinegar
2 teaspoons sesame oil

1 Thinly shred the chicken and mix with the salt, egg whites and cornflour paste.

2 Heat the oil in a preheated wok or pan. Stir in the chicken over medium heat, separating the shreds so they do not stick together. As soon as the colour changes from pink to pale white (about 2 minutes), scoop out with a perforated spoon and drain. Let the chicken cool, then place on a bed of shredded lettuce leaves on a serving dish.

3 Mix all the sauce ingredients in a little bowl. Blend well and pour evenly all over the chicken just before serving.

花椒

SICHUAN PEPPERCORNS

(HUAJIAO) *Zanthoxylum piperitum v. bungei*

Sichuan peppercorns do not belong to the same family as Western black and white peppercorns, as the botanical name shows. Their most common Chinese name, *huajiao* (*farchiew* in Cantonese), literally means 'flower pepper'; other names are *chuan jiao* or *shu jiao*, which both mean 'Sichuan pepper'; and *ye* (*shan*) *jiao* or 'wild (mountain) pepper'. In English, it is often called 'Chinese pepper', 'brown pepper' or 'red pepper'.

HOW IT GROWS

Sichuan peppercorns are the berries of a spiny shrub which grows from 1.2 to 1.5m (4–5ft) high. It takes about three years before the tree starts to bear fruit (berries), and it usually has a life span of forty to fifty years. The Sichuan species used to grow wild, but it is now widely cultivated in western China.

APPEARANCE AND TASTE

Sichuan peppercorns have a purplish-red husk and a shiny, aromatic, black seed, which has a peculiar, pungent flavour and a benumbing, acrid aftertaste, quite different from the common Western peppercorn.

BUYING AND STORING

Sichuan peppercorns are available in all Oriental stores, much more cheaply than in a specialist gourmet shop or supermarket. If bought in a plastic bag from an Oriental store, keep in an air-tight container and store in a cool, dark, dry place. They should keep for many months if not years, but like most spices, the aroma will diminish with age, so try not to buy too many at a time.

MEDICINAL AND OTHER USES

The leaves and berries are recommended for treating certain gastro-urinary disorders. Externally, they are used to stimulate the skin and as a parasiticide. The root is made into a decoction and used for kidney and bladder difficulties, and for bruising and other skin problems. At one time in China, it was fashionable to make sachets from Sichuan peppercorns and present them as a token of affection.

CULINARY USES

Sichuan peppercorns are indispensable in everyday Chinese cooking, used in marinades and many other dishes. Before using Sichuan peppercorns you have to crush and heat them to release their aromatic oils. They will burn very easily, so keep the heat low and the oil not too hot.

SPICY SALT AND PEPPER

This is a standard dip for a variety of dishes such as Sichuan Pepper Chicken. It is also known as Prickly Ash, or just plain Pepper-Salt when a little ground black pepper is used instead of the five-spice powder, making it less spicy.

Makes about 6 tablespoons dipping salt
Preparation and cooking time 10–12 minutes

1 heaped tablespoon whole Sichuan peppercorns
4 tablespoons salt
2 teaspoons five-spice powder

1 Heat the Sichuan peppercorns in a preheated wok or pan over medium heat. Stir constantly for about 1 minute or until fragrant.

2 Using a pestle and mortar, pound the peppercorns to a fine powder. If you do not possess a pestle and mortar, a food processor or blender will do. It is sometimes possible to obtain ready-ground Sichuan pepper, but it will not have as strong an aroma as freshly ground.

3 Reheat the wok or pan again over medium heat and pour in the salt. Stir continuously for 3–4 minutes or until the salt starts to turn golden brown. Mix in the five-spice powder and the ground Sichuan pepper. Blend well for about 1 minute and remove to cool.

4 When the mixture has cooled down, store it in a jar with an air-tight lid. It will keep for a very long time if kept dry – you need less than 1 teaspoon for each serving.

胡椒

BLACK AND WHITE PEPPER

(HUJIAO) *Piper nigrum*

As the Chinese name *hujiao* implies, pepper is of foreign origin, probably from the East Indies. Black and white pepper are both used as a condiment in Chinese cooking, but not so extensively as in the West.

HOW IT GROWS

Pepper is the fruit of a perennial vine with large leaves and white flowers. The berries are first green, then red and finally black after being dried in the sun. White peppercorns are ripe berries which have been soaked in water to remove the coating, then dried in the sun. Since the Middle Ages, moderately successful attempts have been made to cultivate the pepper plant on Hainan Island, Taiwan and other sub-tropical areas of China.

APPEARANCE AND TASTE

Neither black nor white peppercorns are generally found whole on the market in China: they are usually sold in powdered form. The black variety, though aromatic, is less pungent than the white.

BUYING AND STORING

Most common in China is ground white pepper, known as *baihu jiaofen* (white foreign pepper powder), which is usually shortened to *hufen* (foreign powder). Freshly ground pepper always tastes stronger and is more aromatic than ready-ground.

MEDICINAL USES

Carminative, warming, and eliminative properties are ascribed to pepper, and it is administered in cases of cholera, dysentery and vomiting. When I had a cold as a child in China my nanny would cook me a large bowl of vermicelli in steaming hot vegetable soup with masses of ground white pepper. My eyes would stream with tears, but I always felt much better afterwards.

CULINARY USES

As well as being a condiment in Chinese cooking, pepper is said to negate fish, meat and mushroom poisoning. There is very little use for black pepper but ground white pepper is widely used, both in marinating and cooking, for its fragrance and hotness.

HOT AND SOUR SOUP

This very popular soup in Chinese restaurants should never contain chillies – the hotness comes from very liberal use of ground white pepper!

Serves 4
Preparation time 10 minutes, plus mushroom soaking time
Cooking time 5 minutes

3–4 dried Chinese mushrooms, soaked
115g (4oz) pork or chicken meat (raw or cooked)
50g (2oz) sliced bamboo shoots, rinsed and drained
1 cake fresh bean curd (tofu, see p 196)
900ml (1½ pint) good stock (p 71)
1 tablespoon rice wine
1 tablespoon light soy
1 tablespoon rice vinegar
1 teaspoon ground white pepper
1 egg, lightly beaten
1 tablespoon cornflour paste
1 teaspoon salt
Pinch of MSG (optional)
Finely chopped spring onions to garnish

1 Squeeze dry the soaked mushrooms and discard any hard stalks. Thinly shred the mushrooms, meat, bamboo shoots and bean curd.

2 Bring the stock to a rolling boil. Stir in the mushrooms, meat, bamboo shoots and bean curd. Bring back to the boil and add the wine, soy, vinegar and pepper. Bring back to the boil once more and pour the beaten egg very slowly into the soup, stirring at the same time.

3 Gently stir in the cornflour paste to thicken the soup. Add the salt and MSG, if using, and serve hot garnished with the spring onions.

Hot and Sour Soup

五香粉
FIVE-SPICE POWDER
(WUXIANG FEN)

This is the Chinese bouquet garni: a variable mixture of five (or seven or eight) different spices. As mentioned in the Introduction, the number five plays an important part in Chinese everyday life, not least in food and cooking. It is reasonable to assume that the five basic spices used originally for this concoction were based on the proper yin-yang balance of flavours and exemplified the five basic flavours in Chinese cooking (sweet, sour, bitter, hot and salty).

MANUFACTURE

The basic five spices are: star anise, cinnamon/cassia bark, fennel seeds, Sichuan peppercorn and cloves. But if you read the small print on packages, manufacturers often include two or three additional spices, such as coriander seeds, dried orange peel, ginger and cardamom. The spices are pulverized into fine powder, then blended together.

APPEARANCE AND TASTE

The colour varies from brand to brand, ranging from brown to amber, and the grains vary too, from very fine to fairly coarse. The mixture is highly aromatic: the predominant smell is of star anise, the smell that greets you when you enter an Oriental store. The taste is well balanced between sweet, bitter and hot. It should not be too strong-tasting – it should smell more strongly than it tastes.

BUYING AND STORING

Several brands are available on the market, usually in plastic bags (which are inexpensive) and in small jars or containers (not such good value for money and you cannot tell if you like the smell or not). Always store five-spice powder in an air-tight container, away from heat, light and moisture, where it will keep for many months. So long as the smell remains strong and pungent it is good to use.

CULINARY USES

It is a myth that almost every single Chinese dish contains five-spice powder. Yes, it is an important element in Chinese cooking, but we only use it in a small number of dishes, and then only sparingly. Traditionally, five-spice is added to long-cooked dishes, such as red-cooked (stewed), steamed and braised dishes. It is also used in marinades for barbecues, deep-fried and roasted dishes.

Spice trader in northern China

SMOKED FISH

The fish in this recipe is not actually smoked at all. It acquires its smoky flavour by being marinated and braised in a spicy sauce, then deep-fried and marinated in the sauce again.

Serves 8–10 as a starter
Preparation time 10–15 minutes plus marinating and cooling time
Cooking time 15 minutes

450g (1lb) firm white fish fillet (cod, haddock etc)
About 300ml (½ pint) good stock (p 71)
Oil for deep-frying

For the marinade:
1 tablespoon five-spice powder
2–3 tablespoons sugar
3 tablespoons dark soy
3 tablespoons rice wine
2 spring onions, finely chopped
1 tablespoon finely chopped fresh ginger

1 Do not remove the skin of the fish, as it keeps the fish from breaking into small pieces. Marinate for at least 30 minutes.

2 Place the fish with the marinade in a saucepan, add stock and bring to the boil. Simmer gently for 10 minutes or so. Remove the fish and drain, reserving the sauce.

3 Heat the oil to 190°C/375°F and deep-fry the fish for 4–5 minutes or until golden and crisp. Remove and immerse in the sauce. Leave to cool for at least 2–3 hours before taking the fish out to dry.

4 Cut the fish into small slices and serve cold.

Note: Strain the sauce and when cold, store in the refrigerator where it will keep for 4–5 days. It can be re-used again and again, each time topped up with more seasoning.

Crispy Roasted Belly Pork

This was one of the late Kenneth Lo's favourites from my repertoire. He would make sure he was in class whenever I demonstrated this dish at his cookery school – he loved it, particularly the crispy skin.

Serves 10–12 as a starter or 6–8 as a main course
Preparation time 10 minutes plus marinating time
Cooking time about 1 hour 10 minutes

1kg (2lb 4oz) belly of pork, with rind on
1 tablespoon salt
1 tablespoon five-spice powder
Lettuce leaves

For the dip:
3–4 tablespoons light soy
1 tablespoon chilli sauce (optional)

1 Ideally, the pork should be in one piece, like the pork you see hanging in the windows of some Cantonese restaurants. But if you prefer, the meat can be cut into large pieces for cooking. Pat dry the skin with kitchen paper and make sure that it is free from hairs. Rub the meat and skin all over with the salt and five-spice powder, then leave to stand for at least 1 hour – the longer, the better.

2 Heat the oven to 240°C/475°F/gas mark 9. Place the pork, skin side up, on a rack in a baking tin and roast for 20–25 minutes. Reduce the heat to 200°C/400°F/gas mark 6 and cook for a further 45–50 minutes or until all the skin has turned to crackling.

3 To serve: chop the meat into small bite-size pieces, place them on a bed of lettuce leaves and serve hot or cold with the dip.

Note: Any leftovers can be used in other dishes.

Crispy Roasted Belly Pork

VEGETABLES

白菜

CHINESE CABBAGE

(BAICAI) *Brassica pekinensis*

One of the best-known vegetables in the brassica family, Chinese cabbage, commonly known as Chinese leaf or celery cabbage, is widely cultivated in the West all year round. It has a number of names in Chinese as well: apart from *da baicai* (big white cabbage), it is also known as *Tianjin baicai* (Tianjin cabbage), and *Shao cai* (Shao cabbage).

A corner of a cabbage field

HOW IT GROWS

Chinese cabbage is a cool-weather crop which prefers short days, so it is normally planted between August and December. It takes between 80 and 100 days to reach maturity. A late crop is planted in the spring to provide a continual supply for the market.

APPEARANCE AND TASTE

There are two different species of Chinese leaves widely available in the West. One is long and slender – about 30cm (12in) long, and 7cm (3in) in diameter – with pale green leaves and a long white stem; it forms a fairly tight and compact head when mature. The other one is short and stout – about 20–25cm (8–10in) long, and about 10–12.5cm (4–5in) in diameter – with curlier, pale yellow leaves. It is called *huangyabai* (yellow-sprouting-white) by most Chinese. Both have a delicate sweet taste with a mild cabbage flavour, which blends with and enhances the flavours of other foods with which it is cooked. The texture is always succulent, whether quickly stir-fried or slowly braised.

BUYING AND STORING

Traditionally, Chinese cabbage was a winter vegetable but nowadays it is available all year round, since it is grown all over the world. It keeps well: it stays in good condition for more than ten days if kept in the salad compartment of the refrigerator.

CULINARY USES

Chinese cabbage is a most versatile vegetable. It can be stir-fried, braised, or added to soups; it can be combined with virtually any other ingredients – vegetables, poultry, meat or seafood. It can even be eaten raw as a salad, for it has a mild, zesty pungency which ordinary lettuce lacks. Chinese cabbage is often blanched in stock and used as a base on which roasted duck or barbecued meat is served.

CHINESE SALAD WITH SPICY DRESSING

In China, almost all salads are parboiled or blanched for hygienic reasons, but this precaution is not necessary for vegetables that are grown in the West.

Serves 4–6
Preparation time 10–15 minutes

1 small head Chinese cabbage
1 small green pepper (capsicum), cored and seeded
1 small red pepper (capsicum), cored and seeded
½ teaspoon spicy salt and pepper (p 122)

For the dressing:
1–2 spring onions, finely chopped
1–2 small fresh red or green chillies, seeded and finely shredded
1 teaspoon sugar
1 tablespoon light soy
1 tablespoon rice vinegar
1 tablespoon sesame oil

Cabbage stall in a market

1 Separate the leaves of the Chinese cabbage, discarding the limp outer leaves. Wash and dry thoroughly, then cut each leaf into slices and place in a large serving bowl.

2 Thinly shred the green and red peppers (capsicums) and place on top of the Chinese leaves. Sprinkle the spicy salt and pepper evenly all over the salad, toss and mix well, then leave to stand for 5 minutes or so.

3 Mix the ingredients for the dressing and pour it all over the salad just before serving. Toss and mix it at the table, not before, otherwise the vegetables will lose their crispness.

Note: You can omit the fresh chillies, or substitute a little chilli sauce or oil.

'Lion's Head' (Pork Meatballs)

The meatballs are supposed to resemble a lion's head, and the Chinese leaves its mane. Legend has it that this dish was invented by a housewife in Yangchow specially for her aged father-in-law, who had lost all his teeth, and could only eat soft food that did not require much chewing.

Serves 4–6
Preparation time 10–15 minutes plus mushroom and shrimp soaking time
Cooking time 35–40 minutes

3–4 dried Chinese mushrooms, soaked
3 tablespoons dried shrimps, soaked
450g (1lb) minced pork, not too lean
1–2 spring onions, finely chopped
1 teaspoon finely chopped fresh ginger
2 tablespoons light soy
1½ teaspoons sugar
1 tablespoon rice wine
1 tablespoon cornflour
1 small head Chinese cabbage
3–4 tablespoons oil
½ teaspoon salt
About 300ml (½ pint) stock
Fresh coriander leaves to garnish

'Lion's Head' (Pork Meat Balls)

1 Squeeze dry the mushrooms, discard any hard stalks, and finely chop. Rinse and drain the dried shrimps and finely chop them as well.

2 Mix the chopped mushrooms and shrimps with the minced pork, spring onions, ginger, soy, sugar, wine and cornflour. Blend well and shape the mixture into four large meatballs.

3 Cut the Chinese leaf in quarters lengthways. Heat the oil in a Chinese clay-pot or casserole until hot and stir-fry the leaves for 2–3 minutes. Add the salt and a little stock and continue stirring for another minute or so. Place the meatballs on top of the cabbage, and pour over the remaining stock. Bring to the boil, then reduce the heat and simmer gently, covered, for 30–35 minutes.

4 Garnish with the coriander leaves and serve hot direct from the casserole with plain boiled rice.

Note: If you find the flavour of dried shrimps too strong, by all means use fresh peeled prawns or crab meat instead.

小白菜

BAK CHOY (CHINESE WHITE CABBAGE)

(XIAO BAICAI) *Brassica chinensis*

This is the common Chinese cabbage called *xiao baicai* (little white cabbage) in order to distinguish it from *da baicai* (big white cabbage), known as Chinese leaf. (Bak choy is simply the Cantonese pronunciation of *baicai*.) There are several species of Chinese cabbage and this is just another member of the Brassica family. As you will gather, the Chinese term *cai* (*choy* in Cantonese) has several meanings – besides being a vegetable, it is also used to mean a cooked dish or a course, as well as food in general.

HOW IT GROWS

Bak choy is a perennial vegetable. There are four distinct crops which follow the seasons: spring (planted January–March and harvested March–May); summer (planted April–August and harvested June–October); autumn (planted September–October and harvested November–December); and winter (planted November–December and harvested January–February). There is therefore not a single month when this vegetable is not available freshly cropped.

APPEARANCE AND TASTE

There are many varieties of bak choy, with slight differences in shape, size, and season. It can be 10–25cm (4–10in) long and all the varieties have long, white stems with dark green, loose leaves, rather resembling miniature Swiss chard. The white stems are succulent, while the leaves, like lettuce and spinach, are mostly composed of water, and thus lose a lot of volume when cooked. Though not quite as delicate or 'sweet' as Chinese leaf (p 128), bak choy has a mild, distinctive cabbage flavour.

BUYING AND STORING

Bak choy is widely available in the West, particularly in continental Europe, where it has been cultivated since the 1800s. Select crisp-looking, unblemished plants. Size is not necessarily an indication of tenderness – because its leafy parts are mostly water, bak choy tends to be tougher when cropped in the hotter months than in the cooler ones.

Bak choy does not keep as well as Chinese leaf: after 3–4 days the leaves start to wilt, and the green outer leaves turn yellow.

CULINARY USES

The texture, taste and versatility of bak choy have made it popular in both home and restaurant kitchens. It can stand on its own as a vegetable, or be blended with other savoury ingredients, vegetables and meat. Because of its high water content, bak choy should not be cooked for too long or it will lose its colour, texture and flavour. It should not be eaten raw, but can be salted and preserved or pickled.

STIR-FRIED 'FOUR TREASURES'

The 'four treasures' are four vegetables specially selected to achieve a harmonious balance of colours, textures and flavours.

Serves 4–6
Preparation time 15–20 minutes, plus mushroom soaking time
Cooking time 6–8 minutes

5–6 Chinese dried mushrooms, soaked
1 medium carrot
About 300g (10½oz) bak choy
225g (8oz) winter bamboo shoots, drained
3–4 tablespoons oil
1 teaspoon salt
1 teaspoon sugar
½ teaspoon sesame oil

1 Squeeze dry the mushrooms, discard any hard stalks, then cut into half if small, or quarters if large. Peel the carrot and cut it into thin slices.

2 Wash the bak choy in cold water. Separate the leaves from the stems and cut them into small pieces. Rinse the bamboo shoots in fresh water and drain, then cut into thin slices about the same size as the carrot.

3 Heat the oil in a preheated wok until hot. Stir-fry the carrot and bak choy stems for about 2 minutes, then add in the rest of the vegetables. Continue stirring for another minute or so. Add the salt and sugar and blend well. Add the sesame oil and serve hot.

Note: Do not overcook, or the vegetables will lose their crispness and colour.

Stir-Fried 'Four Treasures'

STIR-FRIED BAK CHOY

In everyday cooking, bak choy is usually cut into small pieces, with white stems and green leaves cooked separately, since the stems require a longer cooking time. Leaves and stems are then combined and served together. If you can get the smaller variety, say no more than 12.5cm (5in) long, it is best to keep it whole and blanch it briefly in lightly salted boiling water and drain well before stir-frying.

Serves 4–6
Preparation time 10–15 minutes
Cooking time 6–8 minutes

450g (1lb) small bak choy
115g (4oz) cooked ham
3 tablespoons oil
½ teaspoon salt
1 teaspoon sugar
A few drops sesame oil

Bak choy is one of the many cabbages to grow in China

1 Wash the bak choy in cold water, trim the roots and discard any discoloured outer leaves. Cut the ham into thin strips.

2 Parboil the bak choy for 1 minute in a pan of lightly salted boiling water, then rinse in cold water to preserve the bright green colour. Drain well.

3 Heat the oil in a preheated wok until hot. Stir-fry the bak choy for about 2 minutes, then add the salt and sugar. Continue stirring for another minute or so.

4 Arrange the bak choy around the edges of a round serving dish. Place the strips of ham in the centre on top of the vegetable, garnish with sesame oil and serve.

Note: For vegetarians, the ham can be omitted and another vegetable of a different colour, such as black or white mushrooms, substituted.

油菜心

CHOY SUM (FLOWERING GREEN)

(YOU CAIXIN) *Brassica chinensis v. parachinensis*

Caixin (choy sum in Cantonese) literally means 'cabbage heart' and is a variety of brassica closely related to both bak choy and mustard greens. Unlike many other brassicas, choi sum is picked to be eaten when flowering so it is a particularly beautiful vegetable to cook with. Since a variety of flowering green (not the one we eat) is also used to make rapeseed oil, the Chinese will sometimes refer to choy sum by the name of *you cai* (oil cabbage).

HOW IT GROWS

Choy sum was originally an autumn and winter crop, but has now become an all year round vegetable. There are three crops: early (planted between April and August, and taking 50–80 days to flower); middle (planted between September and October, and taking 60–90 days to flower); and late (planted between November and March, and taking 80–90 days to flower).

APPEARANCE AND TASTE

Choy sum has green leaves with pale green stems, and a sprig of bright yellow flowers in the centre. It is such a beautiful plant that for years gardeners in the West grew it as an ornamental plant, never knowing it was edible. The young flowering shoots are eaten just as the flowers begin to open. The stems are uniform in size usually with about four leaves of varying width and need not be peeled; the leaves are tender and the taste is mild.

Choy sum is one of the most attractive vegetables to buy

BUYING AND STORING

Choy sum is only available in Oriental stores, usually packed loose in a plastic bag, or tied in neat bundles, like piles of thick, leafy spinach. Choose crisp-looking, unblemished plants. If bought fresh, it will keep in the salad compartment of a refrigerator for a few days.

CULINARY USES

Choy sum is a standard green vegetable for the Chinese table, both at home and in restaurants, particularly during the cool season when it is most abundant and cheap. It is often simply blanched in stock for a couple of minutes, then served with oyster sauce; at home it is usually stir-fried, sometimes with other ingredients.

Stir-Fried Choy Sum with Crab Meat Sauce

This is a fancy dish only encountered in high-class establishments, but simple and easy to cook at home.

Serves 4–6
Preparation time 10 minutes
Cooking time 5–6 minutes

450g (1lb) choy sum
4 tablespoons oil
1 teaspoon salt
½ teaspoon sugar
4–5 tablespoons stock
1 teaspoon chopped fresh ginger
1 tablespoon chopped white part of spring onions
175g (6oz) crab meat
1 tablespoon rice wine

1 Wash and trim the roots of the choy sum. It is best to leave the vegetable whole.

2 Heat about 3 tablespoons oil in a preheated wok. Stir-fry the greens for about 1 minute, then add about two thirds of the salt and sugar with about 2 tablespoons stock. Continue stirring for 2 more minutes, then remove and arrange on an oval dish.

3 Clean the wok and heat the remaining oil. Stir-fry the ginger and spring onion whites for about 30 seconds. Add the crab meat, stir for about 1 minute, then add the remaining salt and stock with the wine. Blend well. Pour the sauce over the choy sum and serve hot.

Winter Mushrooms with Choy Sum

This very colourful dish is simple to prepare, absolutely delicious, and highly nutritious.

Serves 4
Preparation time about 10 minutes plus soaking time
Cooking time 6–8 minutes

12 small dried Chinese mushrooms, soaked
450g (1lb) choy sum
2 tablespoons oil
½ teaspoon salt
½ teaspoon sugar
1 tablespoon oyster sauce

1 Squeeze dry the mushrooms, keeping them whole but discarding any hard stalks. Reserve the soaking water.

2 Wash and trim the roots of the greens. Parboil them in lightly salted water for 2 minutes, remove, drain well and arrange on a serving platter.

3 Heat the oil and stir-fry the mushrooms for about 2 minutes. Add the salt and sugar with a little of the mushroom soaking water, and simmer for 4–5 minutes. Add the oyster sauce and pour it over the greens. Serve hot.

Stir-Fried Choy Sum with Crab Meat Sauce

芥菜

MUSTARD GREENS

(GAICAI) *Brassica juncea*

Yet another member of the cabbage family, mustard greens are robust peasant fare. They are not dissimilar to Brussels sprouts tops and spring greens. The seeds are pounded for use as spice mustard and also rapeseed oil.

Chinese mustard grown as rape

HOW IT GROWS

Like other cabbages, mustard greens are at their best during the cooler months. Traditionally they were planted between September and December and harvested between February and April, but they are now grown throughout most of the year.

APPEARANCE AND TASTE

In appearance, mustard greens resemble a cross between spring greens and Cos lettuce: they have long leaves, usually broad, ribbed and a dull green colour. They are somewhat bitter and strong tasting, but parboiling removes the bitterness, and leaves tender juicy stalks which absorb other flavours well.

BUYING AND STORING

Mustard greens are most available during the cold season, but only from Oriental stores. They are sold either loose or in plastic bags, usually labelled by their Cantonese name, *Gai choi*. They will keep for a few days in the salad drawer of the refrigerator if bought fresh.

MEDICINAL USES

The leaves, stalk and seeds of the mustard plant all have medicinal properties. They are recommended as corrective, digestive and expectorant remedies. They are also used as a stimulant application in toothache, varnish eruptions, and ulcers.

CULINARY USES

Mustard greens are always interchangeable with choy sum or bak choy as a green leaf vegetable. They are usually stir-fried, sometimes with pork (see p 135) and a strong seasoning such as fermented black beans. In China, only a little of the winter crop is used as a fresh ingredient; most mustard greens are salted and preserved.

MUSTARD GREENS SOUP

This soup is very simple to make. Non-vegetarians may like to add a little cooked pork, ham, chicken or duck, cut into small pieces. If you do not add meat, be sure to use a good stock as the base.

Serves 4
Preparation time 5 minutes
Cooking time 4–5 minutes

450g (1lb) mustard greens
2 tablespoons oil
1 teaspoon salt
1 tablespoon rice wine
600ml (1 pint) good stock
1 tablespoon light soy
½ teaspoon sesame oil
Chopped spring onions to garnish (optional)

1 Wash the greens well, separate the leaves and cut them and the stems into small pieces.

2 Heat the oil in a wok and stir-fry the greens for about 2 minutes. Add the salt and wine, followed by the stock. Bring to the boil and cook for about 2 more minutes.

3 Add the soy and sesame oil and serve hot, garnished with spring onions, if using.

Note: If you do add meat, it should go in with the stock at stage 2.

Rapeseed oil

STIR-FRIED PORK WITH MUSTARD GREENS

Chicken, beef or lamb can be substituted for the pork. Vegetarians can leave out meat altogether and perhaps use another vegetable or two, such as Chinese mushrooms, bamboo shoots or carrots.

Serves 4
Preparation time 10–15 minutes plus marinating time
Cooking time 5–6 minutes

225g (8oz) lean pork
½ teaspoon sugar
2 teaspoons light soy
1 teaspoon rice wine
2 teaspoons cornflour paste
About 300g (10½oz) mustard greens
3 tablespoons oil
2 tablespoons black bean and garlic sauce
About 2 tablespoons stock or water
Salt and pepper to taste

1 Cut the pork into thin slices or shreds. Marinate with the sugar, soy, wine and cornflour for 15–20 minutes.

2 Wash and blanch the mustard greens in lightly salted, boiling water for 1 minute. Rinse in cold water and drain, then cut in long diagonals.

3 Heat the oil in a preheated wok and stir-fry the black bean and garlic sauce over moderate heat until fragrant (about 1 minute). Add the pork and stir-fry for 2 more minutes. Add the mustard greens, blend well, add the stock or water and braise briefly. Adjust the seasoning and serve hot.

Stir-Fried Pork with Mustard Greens

芥兰

CHINESE BROCCOLI

(GAI LAN) *Brassica alboglabra*

Broccoli is one of the oldest recorded brassicas – it was eaten in Ancient Greece over two thousand years ago. Not everyone realizes that broccoli is one of the healthiest as well as the most versatile and delicious vegetables around.

A vegetable garden in Sichuan

HOW IT GROWS

Like all the cabbage family, broccoli used to be a winter vegetable, but is now grown all year round. There are usually three crops a year: early (planted between June and August, and harvested between September and December), middle (planted between August and December, and harvested between November and February), and late (planted between October and December, and harvested between January and April).

APPEARANCE AND TASTE

The Chinese name for this beautiful vegetable is 'mustard orchid'. You can easily distinguish Chinese broccoli from other green vegetables by the stoutness of its stems and leaves; the flowers are usually white rather than yellow. When compared with choy sum (see p132), Chinese broccoli is more robust both in taste and texture: it has thicker stalks and tougher leaves with a more pronounced cabbage taste.

BUYING AND STORING

Chinese broccoli is available most of the year, but it is at its best and most abundant during the cool season (October–April). Choose broccoli with a fresh, bright green colour, with more flowers in bud than in bloom, and make sure that the outer leaves and stalks are firm and in good condition. Always store it in a cool place, and use it within 2–3 days of purchase.

MEDICINAL USES

Chinese broccoli is very nutritious: one stalk provides one and a half times the daily requirement of vitamin C and half the daily requirement of vitamin A. It is also rich in calcium, iron and other minerals. Chinese broccoli can help to protect against two of the biggest killers of the Western world: cancer and heart disease.

CULINARY USES

Chinese broccoli is a versatile vegetable, quick and easy to prepare. The entire plant is eaten, including leaves and stalks – the Chinese consider the stalk the best part because of its crisp texture and subtle flavour. Thicker stalks are usually peeled and split part way in order to reduce cooking time and prevent them becoming fibrous.

Leaves of Chinese broccoli

Chinese Broccoli with Oyster Sauce

This is a classic Cantonese dish. Most restaurants do not slice up the whole stalk and stir-fry it, but blanch it in water or stock instead, which is a pity, because not only do you lose some of the vitamins but also the crunchy texture.

Serves 4–6 as a side dish
Preparation time 10 minutes
Cooking time 4–5 minutes

350g (12oz) Chinese broccoli
3–4 tablespoons oil
½ teaspoon salt
2 teaspoons coarsely chopped fresh ginger
1 teaspoon sugar
2–3 tablespoons stock or water
2 tablespoons oyster sauce

1 Wash the broccoli and cut the leaves with flowers into large sections. If the stalks are thick and the outer skin is tough, peel and cut diagonally into short chunks.

2 Heat the oil in a preheated wok with the salt (adding salt at this early stage gives the green broccoli an extra bright colour). Add the bits of ginger, stir a few times, then add the broccoli. Stir-fry for about 2 minutes. Add the sugar and stock or water, blend well and continue stirring for another minute or so. Add the oyster sauce. Mix and toss for about 30 seconds at most and serve hot.

Note: For vegetarians, use light soy instead of oyster sauce. The flavour will not be the same, however.

Sizzling Beef with Broccoli

This is a very colourful and delicious dish, one which causes quite a stir in restaurants as it is brought sizzling on its iron plate to the table. Any other meat can be substituted for the beef. The point to remember is that the food should be slightly undercooked at the last stage, and that the iron plate must be very hot indeed when serving.

Serves 4
Preparation time 10–15 minutes plus marinating time
Cooking time 5–6 minutes

300g (10oz) beef steak
225g (8oz) Chinese broccoli
1 small carrot
About 300ml (½ pint) oil
1 spring onion, cut into short sections
1.5cm (½in) ginger, sliced thinly
½ teaspoon salt
½ teaspoon sugar
1 tablespoon oyster sauce

For the marinade:
½ teaspoon bicarbonate of soda
½ teaspoon sugar
1 tablespoon light soy
2 teaspoons rice wine
2 teaspoons cornflour paste
2 teaspoons oil

1 Cut the beef across the grain into thin slices about the size of a large postage stamp. Marinate for several hours – the longer, the better.

2 Wash the broccoli. Cut the leaves (with the flowers) into large pieces. If the stalks are thick and the outer skin is tough, peel and cut them diagonally into short sections. Cut the carrot diagonally into thin slices too.

3 Heat the iron plate on the hob before you heat the oil in a preheated wok. Stir-fry the beef for 30–40 seconds or until the colour changes. Remove and drain.

4 Pour off the excess oil, leaving about 2 tablespoons in the wok. Add the spring onion, ginger and vegetables, and stir-fry for about 2 minutes. Add the salt and sugar followed by the beef, stir a few times, then add the oyster sauce and blend well.

5 To serve: either bring the food on the hot iron plate sizzling to the table, or put the food on a warm dish, bring it to the table, then pour it onto the iron plate just before serving. Be careful when the food is poured onto the iron plate: small beads of oil and gravy will spit all over the place.

Sizzling Beef with Broccoli

韭菜

CHINESE CHIVES

(JIUCAI) *Allium tuberosum v. odorum*

There are two species of Chinese chives. One has flat leaves like a leek, the other has long tubular stalks with a single bud at the tip, and is called *jiucai hua* (flowering chive). Both are indigenous to Siberia, Mongolia and the whole of China, and are very different from the common chive of the West, which is used only as a herb, whereas the Chinese chive is eaten as a vegetable, like the leek.

Flowering chives

HOW IT GROWS

Chinese chives are raised from seed or from the transplanted bulbs. Planting usually takes place in November and December, the leaves can be cut for market the following March and April, and flowering takes place in early summer (May–June). The second year's crop is the most abundant, and after the third crop, the bulbs are covered with specially made pots; subsequent crops are called *jiuhuang* (hotbed chives), which are extra delicate and delicious.

APPEARANCE AND TASTE

The non-flowering chive has long, flat green leaves, about 5mm (¼in) wide; the other variety has tubular green stems 20–25cm (8–10in) long with a cone-like bud at the tip of each. They taste stronger than spring onions with a fragrant, garlic flavour. The flowers smell like roses!

BUYING AND STORING

Chinese chives are available most of the year – even the flowering chive can be obtained throughout the winter months – and are always sold bulbless. The smaller, harder and tighter the flower head, the younger the stalk and the more tender it is likely to be; those with open flowers are considered too old to eat. The chives will keep in the refrigerator for up to a week. Store them in an air-tight box to prevent their strong garlic smell impregnating other foods.

Fresh vegetable market

MEDICINAL AND OTHER USES

The Chinese believe that chives nourish and purify the blood, that they act as a cordial, and are in every way beneficial to those who are ailing. They are also considered efficacious for dog bites, poisonous snake and insect bites, haemorrhages of every sort, and spermatorrhoea.

CULINARY USES

The Chinese often add chives to recipes calling for spring onions and garlic – they feel the chives enhance the flavour of these other alliums. In everyday home cooking, chives are simply stir-fried and served as a vegetable side dish or are cooked with meat, poultry or seafood, sometimes as a substitute for spring onions.

Flat-leaf chives growing

STIR-FRIED PRAWNS WITH CHINESE CHIVES

Try to use flowering chives if possible: not only do they look pretty, but they also have a subtle texture and flavour which the flat-leafed variety seems to lack.

Serves 4–6
Preparation time 15–20 minutes
Cooking time 5–6 minutes

225g (8oz) uncooked prawns, headless
1 teaspoon salt
½ egg white, beaten
2 teaspoons cornflour paste
225g (8oz) Chinese chives
About 300ml (½ pint) oil
A few small bits of fresh ginger
1 teaspoon sugar
1 tablespoon light soy
1 tablespoon rice wine

1 Peel and de-vein the prawns, then mix with a pinch of the salt, the egg white and cornflour paste. Wash and cut the chives into 4–5cm (1½–2in) lengths.

2 Heat the oil in a preheated wok until moderately hot. Fry the prawns for about 30–40 seconds, stirring to separate them. Remove as soon as they change colour, and drain.

3 Pour off the excess oil, leaving about 2 tablespoons in the wok. Add the ginger and chives and stir-fry for about 1–1½ minutes. Add the remaining salt and sugar, stir a few times and add the prawns with the soy and rice wine. Blend well and cook for another minute at most. Serve hot with rice or noodles.

Scrambled Eggs with Chives and Bean Curd

SCRAMBLED EGGS WITH CHIVES AND BEAN CURD

This is a very colourful and delicious dish, simple to prepare and cook.

Serves 4
Preparation time about 10 minutes
Cooking time 6–8 minutes

1 cake bean curd (tofu, p196)
4 eggs, beaten
1 teaspoon salt
About 100g (3½oz) Chinese chives, finely chopped
1 tablespoon rice wine
4 tablespoons oil
About 4–5 tablespoons stock
A few drops sesame oil

1 Cut the bean curd into 1cm (½in) small cubes. Parboil in a pan of water for 2–3 minutes to harden, remove and drain.

2 Mix the beaten eggs with a pinch of the salt, about half the chopped chives and 1 teaspoon wine.

3 Heat about 3 tablespoons oil in a preheated wok or pan. Scramble the egg mixture for about 2 minutes, remove and set aside.

4 Clean the wok and heat the remaining oil. Stir-fry the bean curd cubes for 1 minute. Add the stock, the remaining wine and salt, bring to the boil and simmer for 3–4 minutes. Now add the scrambled eggs with the remaining chives, blend well and sprinkle on the sesame oil. Serve hot.

茄子

AUBERGINE (EGGPLANT)

(QIEZI) *Solanum melongena v. esculentum*

Purple Chinese aubergine

This beautiful vegetable belongs to the tomato and pepper (capsicum) family, and is a native of tropical Asia. It was brought to China as early as the third century, probably by way of India and Thailand. The Cantonese name for aubergine is *ngai gwa* (short melon), yet all the different varieties I have come across in China are long and tubular rather than short and ovoid.

HOW IT GROWS

Aubergine is a perennial plant, and there are four crops a year: spring (planted in September and October, marketed between April and June); summer (planted in February and March, marketed between June and October); autumn (planted in March and April, marketed between July and November); and winter (planted in August, marketed between October and May).

Young aubergines growing

APPEARANCE AND TASTE

Several varieties of aubergine are grown in China; they vary in shape, size and colour. The most common type has smooth, dark purple skin with the cup-shaped leaf at the stem end. Straight or only slightly curved, it is 20–25cm (8–10in) long, and 4–5cm (1½–2in) in diameter. There are also pale green and white aubergines, but these are very rare. It is almost impossible to describe the taste of aubergine, for it has a unique texture and flavour, quite unlike any other vegetable. Some people complain of the bitter taste, but the Chinese never seem to be bothered by it.

BUYING AND STORING

Aubergines are available all year round, but are at their best from early summer to autumn. Buy only those which are uniformly smooth, firm, and unblemished. If bought in prime condition and kept in a dark, cool place, they should be good for a number of days after purchase.

MEDICINAL USES

Aubergines are regarded as cooling, and, bruised with vinegar, are used as a poultice for abscesses and cracked nipples. The stalk when burned can treat intestinal haemorrhage, piles and toothache.

A flower market in Chengdu, the capital of Sichuan province

CULINARY USES

Aubergine absorbs oil like a sponge, as well as the flavour of other ingredients cooked with it. It is sometimes worth dry-frying aubergine pieces in a hot wok without any oil at all before stir-frying them. That way the flesh of the aubergine becomes less sponge-like, and does not absorb too much oil.

Aubergine slices

Fish-Fragrant Aubergine

The name of this famous Sichuan dish has caused quite a lot of confusion in the West. It is often called 'fish-flavoured' or 'sea-spice' on restaurant menus, but the truth is that the term *yu-xiang* (fish-fragrant) indicates that the dish is cooked with seasonings normally used for a fish recipe (such as Toban Fish, see p 98).

Serves 4
Preparation time 10–15 minutes
Cooking time 8–10 minutes

450g (1lb) aubergine
Oil for deep-frying
115g (4oz) lean pork, thinly shredded (optional)
½ teaspoon finely chopped garlic
½ teaspoon finely chopped fresh ginger
2 teaspoons finely chopped spring onion whites
3–4 small dried chillies, soaked and cut into small bits
2 teaspoons chilli bean paste
½ teaspoon salt
1 teaspoon sugar
1 tablespoon light soy
1 tablespoon rice wine
1 tablespoon rice vinegar
2 teaspoons cornflour paste
2 teaspoons chopped spring onion greens
A few drops sesame oil

1 When served in a restaurant, the aubergines are peeled, but most home cooks would not bother to do so. Cut the aubergines into short, thin strips like french fries. Deep-fry the aubergine strips in hot oil for 3–4 minutes or until golden. Remove the strips and drain well.

2 Pour off the excess oil, leaving about 1 teaspoon in the wok. Stir-fry the pork shreds (if using) with the garlic, ginger, spring onion whites, chillies and chilli bean paste for about 1–1½ minutes. Add the aubergine with the salt, sugar, soy and rice wine. Blend well and braise for another minute or thereabouts.

3 Add the vinegar and thicken the sauce with the cornflour paste. Stir in the spring onion greens and sesame oil, and serve hot.

Note: This dish has the five basic flavours (sweet, sour, bitter, hot, and salty), as well as two additional flavours: aromatic and delicious.

Stuffed Aubergine

This recipe may appear rather complicated, but the end result is absolutely stunning. The same stuffing can be used for all sort of vegetables, such as green peppers (capsicums), bean curd and mushrooms.

Serves 4–6
Preparation time 15–20 minutes
Cooking time 4–5 minutes for deep-frying, 4–5 minutes for braising if required

For the stuffing:
115g (4oz) uncooked prawns, peeled and finely chopped
115g (4oz) pork, not too lean and finely chopped
1 tablespoon finely chopped spring onions
1 teaspoon finely chopped fresh ginger
½ teaspoon salt
1 tablespoon light soy
1 tablespoon rice wine
1 tablespoon cornflour

3 medium aubergines
150g (5oz) plain flour
25g (1oz) cornflour
3 tablespoons water
1 egg, beaten
Oil for deep-frying

For the dip:
Spicy Salt and Pepper (p122)
or
1 teaspoon sugar
2 tablespoons light or dark soy
4–5 tablespoons stock
2 teaspoons cornflour paste
A few drops sesame oil
Fresh coriander leaves to garnish

1 Make the stuffing by mixing all the ingredients together into a smooth paste.

2 Discard the stalks of the aubergines. Cut the unpeeled aubergines diagonally into 5mm (¼in) slices, cutting one slice right through, and leaving every second slice attached at the base, which makes a 'pocket' for stuffing.

3 Place an equal portion of stuffing between each hinged section of aubergine. Mix the flours, water and egg to make a batter, and dip each aubergine 'pocket' in the batter.

4 Heat the oil to about 180°C/350°F and deep-fry the stuffed aubergine for about 3–4 minutes until golden. Drain and serve hot with Spicy Salt and Pepper (p 122) as a starter or, alternatively, braise the fried aubergine 'pockets' with sugar, soy, and stock for 4–5 minutes, thicken the sauce with cornflour paste, and serve hot, garnished with coriander, as a very good main course dish.

Stuffed Aubergine

萝卜

CHINESE RADISH

(LUOBO) *Raphanus sativus v. longipinnatus*

Chinese white radishes, *luobo* (*lo bak* in Cantonese), are quite different from the little red radishes of the West. The plant is indigenous to China, where it has been cultivated from ancient times. It was exported to neighbouring countries, judging by the similarity of names for it (*lobac* in Vietnam and the Malay peninsula; *laphug* in Tibet; *laopang* and *lobin* in Mongolia).

HOW IT GROWS

Many varieties of *luobo* are grown in China. Although it used to be a winter vegetable, it is now grown all year round. There are three crops a year: summer, autumn, and winter/spring.

APPEARANCE AND TASTE

The hallmarks of Chinese radish are its largeness, alabaster-white colour and smooth skin. It is usually cylindrical like a carrot, only much longer and thicker: up to 35cm (14in) long and about 6.5cm (3in) in diameter. The flesh is always tender and juicy with a crisp texture and mild, sweet taste.

BUYING AND STORING

Chinese radishes are usually available all year round and in great abundance from October to April. Choose heavy, solid and unblemished roots; the flesh should be crisp and solid, not fibrous, with a pungent smell of radish. Store in the refrigerator where they should keep for 4–5 days.

MEDICINAL USES

The Chinese consider radishes to be healthy. They are supposed to stimulate the appetite, and to be effective in treating insanity, rheumatism and warts as well as safeguarding against poison. Crushed or grated radishes are applied locally as a dressing or poultice to burns, scalds and bruises.

CULINARY USES

Radishes feature in numerous Chinese dishes, both sweet and savoury. It is stir-fried as a vegetable and often braised with meats, particularly cuts which require long cooking, such as leg of pork, oxtail and shin of beef, because it will withstand long cooking without disintegrating. It is also served salted, dried and pickled, and often features at banquets in decorative garnishes. It is interesting to note, however, that radishes, are not considered a grand enough food to actually eat on such occasions.

SPARE-RIB AND RADISH SOUP

I have adapted this recipe from one that uses oxtail.

Serves 4
Preparation time 10 minutes
Cooking time 1 hour

500g (1lb 2oz) pork spare-ribs
2–3 small pieces peeled fresh ginger
About 1 litre (1¾ pints) water
2 tablespoons rice wine
1 medium carrot
300g (10½oz) Chinese radish
Salt and pepper to taste
Chopped spring onions to garnish

1 Trim any excess fat from the ribs, and chop each into 3–4 pieces. Place in a pan or pot and add the ginger, water and wine. Bring to the boil, reduce the heat and simmer, covered, for 40–45 minutes.

2 Meanwhile, peel or scrape the carrot and radish, cut them into slices or small chunks, and add them to the soup. Cook for 15–20 minutes – longer if so desired.

3 Adjust the seasoning and serve hot, garnished with spring onions.

A typical, beautifully presented banquet spread

苦瓜

BITTER MELON

(KU GUA) *Momordica charantia*

Like many Chinese melons, this is not a fruit but a vegetable, like marrow or gourd (see winter melon p 154). The Chinese term *gua* includes everything in the Cucurbitaceae family: melon, marrow, gourd, pumpkin, cucumber, squash etc. The plant originally came from Southeast Asia, and is now widely cultivated in southern China.

HOW IT GROWS

The bitter melon plant is a smaller version of the wild grapevine – one of several other names for it is 'leprosy grape' because of its warty skin. It can be grown in a warm climate almost all year round and I am told that it is grown in both North and South America purely as an ornamental vine, prized for its attractive foliage and strange fruit.

APPEARANCE AND TASTE

There are three varieties of bitter melon, ranging from 10cm (4in) to 30cm (12in) long; its shape varies from pear-shaped to oblong. All three share the same odd-looking warty skin. It is dark green, bitter and firm-fleshed when unripe, turning yellowish-green then orange, and becoming slightly bitter-sweet and soft as it ripens.

BUYING AND STORING

Bitter melon is only available in Oriental stores. It can be bought all year round but is best between May and October, before it fully ripens and splits open, revealing a striking but quite inedible interior. Buy bitter melon when it is yellowish-green and still firm, and use no longer than 3–4 days after purchase.

MEDICINAL USES

Bitter melon is cooling and strengthening, the seeds sweetening breath and invigorating the yang (male) principle. There is an old Chinese saying, often quoted to me as a child, that 'the more bitter the taste, the better the medicine'. I was never convinced.

CULINARY USES

Bitterness is one of the five basic flavours of Chinese cooking. The bitterness is due to the presence of quinine in the melon (as in vermouth and bitter lemon), which is an acquired taste. To diffuse it, blanch the melon first and season it with sugar and other strongly flavoured ingredients such as salted black beans, garlic and chillies.

STUFFED BITTER MELON

Never having acquired a taste for bitter melon myself, I have always avoided it but one of my daughters (who was only fourteen or so at the time) went to our local Chinese restaurant with a friend and ordered this dish, because she was always fascinated by its name, and they quite enjoyed the experience!

Serves 4
Preparation time 20–25 minutes plus shrimp soaking time
Cooking time 5–6 minutes

1 tablespoon dried shrimps, soaked
225g (8oz) minced pork
1 tablespoon finely chopped spring onions
1 tablespoon black bean and garlic sauce or crushed black beans with minced garlic
2 teaspoons cornflour
1 large or 2 medium bitter melons
2 tablespoons oil
Salt and pepper
1 teaspoon sugar
1 tablespoon soy
2 teaspoons rice wine
Fresh coriander leaves to garnish

1 Rinse and drain the soaked shrimps. Finely chop and mix with the minced pork, spring onions, black bean and garlic sauce and cornflour to make a stuffing.

2 Depending on the size of the bitter melon, either cut it in half or into large sections. Blanch in boiling water for about 2 minutes, remove the seeds from the melon and fill the cavity with the stuffing. Heap the stuffing high, as it will shrink during cooking.

3 Heat the oil and lightly brown the stuffed bitter melon pieces on both sides. Add the seasonings with a little stock or water, and braise gently for 3–4 minutes. Transfer to a serving dish, and pour the sauce over. Serve hot, garnished with coriander leaves.

Stuffed Bitter Melon

蓮藕

LOTUS ROOT

(LIAN OU) *Nelumbium nucifera v. speciosum*

The Chinese lotus or water lily is a most beautiful flower that has been revered throughout the East since ancient times. The lotus is closely associated with Buddhism, whose doctrine is universal redemption, and it has come to symbolize man raising himself above the material world to realize his divine potential – for though the lotus grows in mud, it emerges in full and splendid bloom.

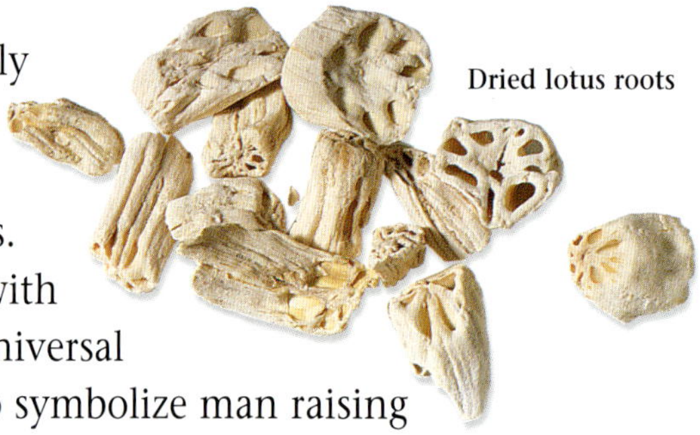

Dried lotus roots

HOW IT GROWS

The Chinese lotus grows in lakes, ponds and marshes. Planting usually takes place from February onwards, lasting several months. Blossom starts to appear in late spring/early summer, when traditionally crowds row out in small boats to admire the sumptuous red and white lotus. The seeds and roots are gathered from late summer up until the winter months.

APPEARANCE AND TASTE

In contrast to its beautiful blossom, the lotus root is rather unattractive: it looks like strings of fat sausages covered in dirt! The swollen bulbs are about 5–7.5cm (2–3in) in diameter, and 20–25cm (8–10in) long, separated by narrow constrictions. In cross-section, the air-channels of the rhizome form a lacy pattern which is most decorative. The flavour is mildly sweet, its texture tenderly crunchy.

Dried lotus seeds

MEDICINAL USES

Although the lotus grows in filthy mud, it is considered to be a symbol of purity, so is thought to rid the body of poison. Both the seed and root are thought to be nourishing, promoting strength and good health. They refresh, prevent fluxes, improve circulation and increase virility.

Lotus blossom after the rain

CULINARY USES

All parts of the lotus are edible, both raw and cooked. The leaves are usually dried and used for wrapping food (see Glutinous Rice Chicken p 29), although young leaves can be eaten as a vegetable. The seeds are eaten as a delicious sweet snack in the summer, but otherwise are sold as dried 'nuts', which can be made into a sweet paste as a filling for cakes and buns. The root is by far the most widely used part of the plant: it is eaten raw or candied as a fruit, stir-fried as a vegetable, cooked with meat, used in dried form in soup or vegetarian stew and in powder form as a starch. The blossom, or *furong*, features in the very popular *fu-yung* (egg) dishes in Chinese restaurants.

BRAISED PORK WITH LOTUS ROOT

This is a standard 'red-cooked' dish of meat with a vegetable. The meat can be pork, chicken, lamb or beef, and the vegetable can be anything from lotus root to Chinese radish, bamboo shoots, chestnuts, carrots, dried bean curd sticks or dried mushrooms. The method is the same, just remember to adjust the cooking time accordingly.

Serves 4–6
Preparation time about 10 minutes
Cooking time 45–50 minutes

Lotus paste

450g (1lb) pork, not too lean
450g (1lb) lotus root
1 tablespoon oil
2 cakes fermented bean curd, mashed
1 tablespoon chopped spring onions
2 teaspoons chopped ginger
2 tablespoons rice wine
2 tablespoons soy
25g (1oz) rock sugar or 1 tablespoon brown sugar

1 Cut the pork into 2cm (1in) cubes. Wash the lotus root well before peeling (if any surface dirt gets on the flesh, it will be very difficult to clean), then cut it diagonally into 5mm (¼in) thick slices to show the beautiful pattern within.

2 Heat the oil in a pan and lightly brown the pork and lotus root. Add the mashed bean curd with the spring onions, ginger and wine. Blend well and cook for 2–3 minutes, stirring continuously. Add enough water to cover and bring to the boil. Reduce the heat and braise gently, covered, for about 30 minutes, stirring occasionally to prevent sticking or burning.

3 Add the soy and sugar. Cook for about 10 minutes more, uncovered, stirring constantly. Serve hot with plain rice and a green vegetable dish. Any leftovers can be reheated the next day and will taste even better!

Stir-Fried Lotus Root

This was one of my childhood favourites. No one but my nanny seems ever to have cooked this dish – I have never encountered it since. I have re-created this recipe from memory with quite satisfactory results.

Serves 4 as a side dish
Preparation time 10 minutes
Cooking time 4–5 minutes

450g (1lb) lotus root
1–2 spring onions
3–4 fresh red chillies
3 tablespoons oil
½ teaspoon salt
½ teaspoon sugar
½ tablespoon light soy
A few drops sesame oil

1 Wash and clean the lotus root before peeling (though if my memory serves me, my nanny never actually peeled the lotus root, probably because we lived near a lake which was famous for producing tender and high-quality lotus roots). Cut into 1cm (½in) slices. Cut the spring onions and chillies into 5mm (¼in) pieces.

2 Heat the oil in a preheated wok and stir-fry the lotus root with the spring onions and chillies for about 2 minutes. Add the salt, sugar and soy, continue stirring for another minute or so, and sprinkle on the sesame oil. Serve hot or cold.

Note: If you do not like hot chillies, use sweet red peppers (capsicums) instead. It will look just as pretty.

Stir-Fried Lotus Root

竹笋

BAMBOO SHOOTS

(ZHUSUN) *Bambusa*

A giant grass, bamboo features heavily in Chinese life. Traditionally, the bamboo symbolizes the virtuous man, bending in the wind yet never breaking. Bamboo shoots have been eaten in China for well over a thousand years. Li Yu, the seventeenth-century gourmet-scholar, regarded bamboo as the queen of all vegetables, for it absorbs the fragrant taste of meat while retaining its own delicate flavour and crunchy texture.

Canned bamboo pyramids

HOW IT GROWS

Over 150 varieties grow in China, mostly south of the Yangtze River, ranging from the reed-like *Phyllostachys* to the giant-sized *Sinocalamus*, which grows to over 30m (100ft) tall. The best flavoured bamboo shoots are said to grow in Zhejiang province.

A dense bamboo grove

APPEARANCE AND TASTE

The tastiest shoots are those dug just before they emerge from the ground during the winter season. These are known as 'winter bamboo shoots'. They are not much bigger than a pine cone, ivory-coloured, with tender and delicious flesh. Spring shoots resemble giant asparagus spears. The even bigger summer shoots (known as 'hairy shoots' because the shells are dark brown and fuzzy) are tougher and have less flavour. 'Slender bamboo shoots', also grown in summer, are finger-sized.

Giant pandas exist almost entirely on a diet of bamboos

BUYING AND STORING

Fresh bamboo shoots are sometimes sold in Western shops. Some, particularly the large summer variety, contain a bitter poison, hydrocyanic acid, which must be eliminated by parboiling. First strip off the outer skin, then cut off and discard the tough base. Immerse the shoots in a pan of boiling water, and boil for 3–4 minutes then drain and rinse under cold water. Use ready prepared shoots within a few days of purchase.

Canned bamboo shoots

MEDICINAL AND OTHER USES

Bamboo is used in a traditional treatment for tuberculosis. The leaves are picked at dawn when still full of morning dew and the patient drinks the water thus collected. Zhuyeqing or Chu Yeh Ching (Bamboo-Leaf Green Liqueur) is a pale green liqueur made from the heady Fen spirit (alcohol content 47 percent), which is enjoyed worldwide. Bamboo is made into baskets, steamers, sieves, strainers, chopsticks, fans and hats.

CULINARY USES

Canned bamboo shoots (available in many forms) should be drained and rinsed in fresh water. Dried bamboo shoots, available in strips, should be soaked in water for 1 hour or so and rinsed in fresh water before use. They are very popular amongst Chinese vegetarians, who value their firm and crunchy texture.

Stir-fried 'Twin Winter'

I have simplified the famous Stir-fried 'Triple Winter', which uses three winter vegetables, by including only bamboo shoots and mushrooms and omitting cabbage.

Serves 4
Preparation time 10–15 minutes, plus mushroom soaking time
Cooking time 8–10 minutes

10–12 dried shiitake mushrooms
285g (10oz) sliced bamboo shoots, drained and rinsed
3 tablespoons vegetable oil
1 spring onion, cut into short sections
1 tablespoon rice wine
2 tablespoons light soy or oyster sauce
1 teaspoon sugar
2 teaspoons cornflour paste
few drops sesame oil

1 Soak the mushrooms in warm water for 35–40 minutes (or in cold water for 4–6 hours), squeeze dry, discard any hard stalks, and cut them into halves (or quarters if large). Reserve the water for later use.

2 Heat the oil in a pre-heated wok and stir-fry the mushrooms and bamboo shoots for about 1 minute.

3 Add the spring onion and the rice wine, light soy or oyster sauce and sugar with 2–3 tablespoons of the mushroom water. Bring to the boil and braise for 2 minutes, stirring continuously.

4 Thicken the sauce with the cornflour paste and sprinkle with sesame oil. Blend well and serve hot or cold.

Twice-Cooked Pork with Bamboo Shoots

This famous Sichuan-style dish is much loved in China and throughout the world. Any leftovers from a roasted joint can be used.

Serves 4
Preparation time 10–15 minutes (longer if using fresh meat)
Cooking time 8–10 minutes

275g (10oz) fresh fillet of pork or 175g (6oz) cooked pork fillet
1 small red pepper (capsicum), cored and de-seeded
3 tablespoons vegetable oil
115g (4oz) sliced bamboo shoots, drained and rinsed
1–2 spring onions, cut into short sections
½ teaspoon salt
½ teaspoon sugar
1 tablespoon rice wine
1 tablespoon yellow bean sauce
2 teaspoons chilli bean paste (toban jiang)
A few drops sesame oil

1 If you are using fresh pork you will need to cook it by simmering it, covered, in a pan of boiling water for 20–25 minutes. Turn off the heat and leave it in the water for at least 2–3 hours before taking it out to cool. Cut the pork into thin slices about the size of a large postage stamp.

2 Cut the pepper (capsicum) into pieces the same size as the bamboo shoots.

3 Heat the oil in a preheated wok and stir-fry the pepper (capsicum), shoots and spring onions for about 1 minute.

4 Add the pork slices with the salt, sugar, rice wine, yellow bean sauce and chilli bean paste. Blend well and cook for 1–2 minutes. Add the sesame oil, stir well, and serve hot.

Twice-Cooked Pork with Bamboo Shoots

绿豆芽

(MUNG) BEAN SPROUTS

(LU DOUYA) *Phaseolus aureus*

Fresh bean sprouts

Chinese cooking without bean sprouts is almost unimaginable: until the mid-sixties, practically every single dish in Chinese restaurants contained bean sprouts. It was the only fresh Chinese ingredient available in the West at the time (everything else was either canned or dried). Mung bean sprouts (as opposed to soy bean sprouts, see p 150) have become very popular in Western kitchens raw in salads, something we never eat in China, because we dislike raw vegetables.

HOW IT GROWS

Growing bean sprouts is simple. Anyone can grow them at home successfully, but since fresh bean sprouts are so cheap and so widely available, it is hardly worth it. You soak the beans in warm water overnight, rinse them in fresh water several times, place them in a large container with lots of space for the beans to sprout, and punch air-holes in the lid. Rinse the beans with tepid water two or three times the first day, then store the container in a warm, dark place. Sprouting will take three to six days, depending on the weather. Remove the sprouts from the container. Rinse them in cold water to separate them and to get rid of any bits and pieces, such as husks and beans that have not sprouted.

APPEARANCE AND TASTE

Mung beans are the tiny green beans that almost disappear in a forest of white shoots after sprouting. The shoots, or sprouts, grow to about 2.5–5cm (1–2in) long and 3mm (⅛in) wide. They have a crisp crunchy texture and a fresh, delicate and subtly sweet taste.

BUYING AND STORING

Fresh bean sprouts are available almost everywhere, usually in plastic bags stamped with a use-by date. Store in the salad compartment of the refrigerator or empty them out of the bag and store in cold water. Either way, they should keep for 2–3 days without losing their crispness or sweet flavour. Once the shoots start to go brown, they have lost their freshness and should be discarded.

Dried mung beans

CULINARY USES

Bean sprouts are more nutritious and delicious than beans, because sprouting transforms the starch into vitamins and natural sugars. In China, bean sprouts are an everyday food, seldom appearing on restaurant menus, except in a special dish known as Silver Shreds in which each shoot has its head and tail removed by hand!

STIR-FRIED BEAN SPROUTS

This is one of the simplest yet most delicious Chinese dishes. Cooked for 2–3 minutes and served hot or cold, the shoots retain their crispness, as in a raw salad but more enjoyable.

Serves 4 as a side dish
Preparation time 10 minutes
Cooking time 3 minutes

225g (8oz) fresh bean sprouts
2–3 spring onions
1–2 fresh red chillies (optional)
3 tablespoons oil
½ teaspoon salt
½ teaspoon sugar
pinch of MSG (optional)

1 Wash the bean sprouts in cold water. Discard the husks and any bits and pieces that float to the surface, rinse and drain well.

2 Cut the spring onions into short sections about the same length as the sprouts. De-seed the chillies, and cut into fine shreds the same length as the sprouts.

3 Heat the oil in a preheated wok. Stir-fry the bean sprouts with the spring onions and chillies (if using) for about 1 minute. Add the salt and sugar. Continue stirring for another minute, then add the MSG (if using), blend and serve hot or cold.

Note: Because of the high water content of sprouts, long cooking will make them soggy and they will lose their delicate flavour.

CHICKEN CHOW MEIN/FRIED NOODLES

This is the classic Chop Suey believed to have originated in San Francisco at the end of the last century. In Chinese restaurants in India a dish is puzzlinly called American Chop Suey. It just means Chop Suey with noodles.

Serves 3–4
Preparation time 20–25 minutes
Cooking time 5–6 minutes

450g (1lb) fresh or 250g (9oz) dried egg noodles
5 tablespoons oil
2 tablespoons light soy
225g (8oz) chicken meat, thinly shredded
1 small onion, finely shredded
1 green pepper (capsicum), finely shredded

Chicken Chow Mein

115g (4oz) fresh bean sprouts
1 teaspoon salt
½ teaspoon sugar
Pinch of MSG (optional)
2 teaspoons rice wine
2 spring onions, finely shredded
About 3–4 tablespoons stock or water
1 teaspoon cornflour paste
¼ teaspoon sesame oil

1 Cook the noodles in salted, boiling water for 1 minute if fresh, 2 minutes if dried. Drain and rinse in cold water. Mix with a little oil.

2 Heat about half the oil in a preheated wok. Stir-fry the noodles for 2 minutes, then add about half the soy and continue stirring for a further minute. Remove and transfer the noodles to a serving dish.

3 Clean the wok and heat the remaining oil. Stir-fry the chicken shreds with the onion for 1 minute, then add the green pepper (capsicum) and bean sprouts. Cook for 1 more minute, and add the salt, sugar, MSG (if using), rice wine, the remaining soy and spring onions. Blend all the ingredients and stir-fry for another minute.

4 Add the stock, and thicken the gravy with the cornflour paste. Garnish with sesame oil and pour over the noodles. Serve hot.

Note: This makes 'soft' fried noodles. To make 'crispy' noodles, deep-fry in hot oil at stage 2, with the soy added after the noodles have been removed from the oil.

黄豆芽

SOYA BEAN SPROUTS

(HUANG DOUYA) *Glycine hispidia*

Soya bean sprouts are one of the most nutritious and economical foods available. They are rich in minerals and unlike other vegetables, soya beans have high levels of protein and fat which make them comparable in nutritional value to meat and eggs, and give them a rich, nutty taste. Oddly enough, while mung bean sprouts are everywhere in the West, soya bean sprouts are rarely seen. The reverse is true in China – I have no explanation to offer.

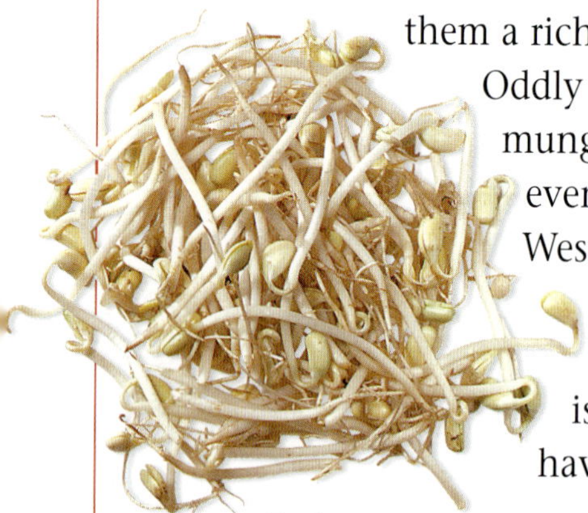

Fresh soya bean sprouts

HOW IT GROWS

There is hardly any difference between the process of sprouting mung beans and soya beans (to grow them at home, see p 148) except the latter take a couple of days longer because of the size of the beans.

APPEARANCE AND TASTE

Although mung bean and soya bean sprouts look very similar, you will have no difficulty in telling them apart. They are different sizes (soya bean sprouts are almost twice as big as mung bean sprouts, both in length and width), the colour is different (not the shoots, for the shoots of both are white, but the heads: one has a green head, the other has a yellow head), and they taste different (soya bean sprouts have a much stronger, more 'beany' flavour, but are just as sweet and tender).

A soya bean field in China

BUYING AND STORING

Soya bean sprouts are only available in the West in Oriental stores. Store in the salad compartment of your refrigerator or empty the packet into a container of cold water. Either way they should keep for 4–5 days if bought fresh. The shoots should be white – use up or discard as soon as they start to turn brown.

CULINARY USES

Partly because of their high levels of protein and fat, soya bean sprouts are the main ingredient in Vegetarian Stock (p 71), as well as a number of other delicious dishes. Please note that raw soya beans are slightly poisonous, so the sprouts must always be cooked before serving.

SOYA BEAN SPROUT SALAD

As stated earlier, fresh soya bean sprouts should not be served raw. In this 'salad', the sprouts are parboiled, then served cold with a standard dressing.

Serves 4–6
Preparation time 10–15 minutes
Cooking time 1½ minutes

450g (1lb) fresh soya bean sprouts
1 teaspoon salt
2 tablespoons light soy
1 teaspoon sugar
1 tablespoon rice vinegar
2 spring onions, thinly shredded
2 teaspoons sesame oil

1 Trim the roots off the sprouts, and wash and rinse in cold water. Discard the husks and any bits that float to the surface.

2 Blanch the sprouts in a pan of boiling salted water for just over 1 minute (definitely less than 2 minutes). Pour them into a colander and rinse in cold water until cool. Drain well.

3 Place the sprouts in a bowl or a deep dish. Add the soya, sugar and vinegar. Mix and toss, then add the spring onions and sesame oil before bringing to the table. Toss once more and serve.

Dried soya beans

ASSORTED VEGETABLE SOUP

For non-vegetarians, you can use the standard chicken/meat stock instead of vegetarian stock.

Serves 4
Preparation time 10–15 minutes, plus mushroom soaking time
Cooking time 5 minutes

4–6 Chinese dried mushrooms, soaked
1 cake bean curd (tofu, p 196)
85g (3oz) soya bean sprouts
2 medium tomatoes
60g (2oz) spinach leaves
600ml (1 pint) vegetarian stock (p71)
1 tablespoon light soy
Salt and pepper to taste
Pinch of MSG (optional)
A few drops sesame oil
Finely chopped spring onions to garnish

1 Squeeze dry the mushrooms, discard any hard stalks and cut into thin shreds. Reserve the mushroom-soaking water for the soup.

2 Cut the bean curd into thin shreds. Wash the soya bean sprouts, discarding the husks and any bits and pieces. Cut the tomatoes into small wedges, and shred the spinach leaves.

3 Bring the stock plus the mushroom-soaking water to a rolling boil. Add the mushrooms, shredded bean curd and bean sprouts with the soy. Cook for 2–3 minutes, then add the tomatoes and spinach. Cook for a further minute, adjust the seasoning (including the sesame oil) and serve hot, garnished with the spring onions.

Assorted Vegetable Soup

荸薺馬蹄

WATER CHESTNUT

(BIQI, MATI) *Eleocharis tuberosa*

Fresh water chestnuts

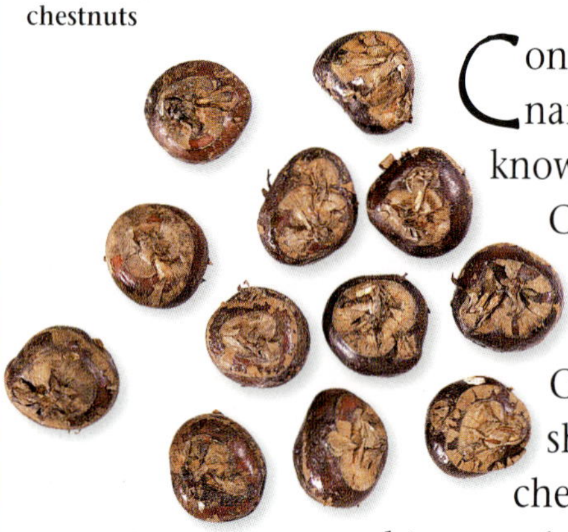

Confusingly, there are two quite different fruits bearing the same name in English. The lesser known variety (*Trapa bicornis*) is also known as water caltrop, *ling* in Chinese, and is seldom seen outside China. The other variety known as Chinese water chestnut is a big industry in China and is the ingredient used in the West. It has several names, *biqi* being the standard one. The Cantonese call it *mati*, which means horse's hoof, because of its shape and brown skin; in Fujian, it is called *dili* (ground chestnut). Chinese water chestnut is not a nut, however, but the rhizome of a sedge that is cultivated in paddy fields all over China.

HOW IT GROWS

The water chestnut is a very prolific plant: one *mu* (0.6667 hectares or 0.1647 acre) will yield some 1,500–1,750kg (3,500–4,000lb) of water chestnut. In southern China, water chestnut is usually planted in June and July, and harvested in December and January; in some cases a second crop follows three months later. Although grown in paddy fields like rice, it is harvested when the earth is dry.

APPEARANCE AND TASTE

As the Cantonese name implies, in its natural state the water chestnut resembles a horse's hoof, only more hairy and usually covered with mud. But once washed and peeled, it has snow-white flesh with a crunchy, juicy texture and pleasantly sweet taste.

BUYING AND STORING

Fresh water chestnuts have a rather short life span: 3–4 weeks after purchase, they start to shrivel and dry up. Canned water chestnuts are already peeled and cooked, and although convenient, they cannot be compared with fresh ones as much of their texture and flavour is lost in the process. Once opened, canned water chestnuts should be kept in fresh water in the refrigerator and will last up to a week if the water is changed every other day.

MEDICINAL USES

Water chestnut is cooling and ensures sweet breath. Children who have swallowed coins or other metallic substances are often given it as a purge. Bleeding from the bowels is treated with fresh water chestnut juice mixed with an equal amount of rice wine, while a preparation made from water chestnut flour is considered generally nourishing and beneficial to the digestive organs.

CULINARY USES

In China, street vendors sell peeled, raw water chestnut soaked in lightly salted water, threaded onto thin bamboo skewers, as a refreshing snack in summer, and piping hot, cooked water chestnut in winter. Sometimes it is candied (unpeeled) rather like toffee apples; a skewer of candied water chestnuts looks like a string of large red beads. In everyday cooking, water chestnut is used for its crunchy texture and mildly sweet taste and combined with soft-textured and strongly flavoured foods such as kidneys or prawns. Finely chopped and mixed with other ingredients, it appears in stuffing. It also features strongly in vegetarian dishes.

The ornate ceiling of Temple of Heaven (prayer for fine harvests)

STIR-FRIED PRAWNS WITH VEGETABLES

The vegetables in this colourful and delicate dish can be varied according to availability, so long as you retain the contrasting colours and textures. Ensure that the thickness of your vegetable slices remains constant so that they cook evenly.

Serves 4
Preparation time 30–35 minutes
Cooking time 8–10 minutes

225g (8oz) raw tiger-prawn tails, peeled
1 teaspoon salt
1 tablespoon egg white
2 teaspoons cornflour paste
60g (2oz) mange-tout
1 small carrot
75g (3oz) straw mushrooms, drained
75g (3oz) water chestnuts, drained
600ml (1 pint) vegetable oil
1–2 spring onions, cut into short sections
4–6 small pieces fresh ginger, peeled
½ teaspoon sugar
1 tablespoon light soy
2 teaspoons rice wine
A few drops sesame oil

1 Cut each prawn in half lengthways, remove and discard the black vein. Mix with a pinch of salt, the egg white and cornflour paste.

2 Top and tail the mange-tout; peel and thinly slice the carrot; cut each straw mushroom in half lengthways; slice the water chestnuts.

3 Heat the oil in a preheated wok until medium hot, stir-fry the prawns for about 1 minute or until the colour changes from grey to a pinky orange, remove with a slatted spoon and drain.

4 Pour off excess oil, leaving about 1 tablespoon in the wok; stir-fry the mange-tout and carrot for about 1 minute, then add the mushrooms and water chestnuts with the prawns, spring onions and ginger. Blend well, then add all the seasonings and continue stirring for another minute or so.

5 Sprinkle with the sesame oil and serve hot with boiled rice or noodles.

冬瓜

WINTER MELON

(DONG GUA) *Benincasa hispida*

Like bitter melon, winter melon is a marrow or gourd, not a fruit – how this mistranslation came about is a complete mystery. Another oddity is that the winter melon is in season during the summer months. One explanation is that the skin of winter melon is covered with a thin layer of a white, frost-like substance, which is why it is also known as white gourd or wax gourd. The frost-like substance is in fact a waxy exudation which helps to preserve the juicy flesh inside.

HOW IT GROWS

Winter melon grows on a single, hairy vine, rather than on a branched vine like other melons. Because of this it is easy to train on a fence or other support where it takes up less space than on the ground. There are two crops a year: early and late. The early crop is planted January–March, and harvested May–September; the late crop is planted in late July, and harvested from October onwards.

APPEARANCE AND TASTE

Winter melon is the largest vegetable on the market: it measures 25cm (10in) or more in diameter, and weights 7–25kg (15–55lb). It is oblong and has a green skin covered in a white waxy substance. The flesh is white and resembles that of the honeydew melon, but it tastes more like a slightly sweet marrow or courgette, only more delicate.

A market stall in Hong Kong

BUYING AND STORING

With the exception of very small ones, winter melons are usually sold in sections, which is a pity, because once the flesh is cut and exposed, it deteriorates very rapidly. A whole melon with its skin intact will keep for many, many months, so they are available throughout the year.

MEDICINAL USES

All of the winter melon is used medicinally. The flesh cools fevers, and is recommended as a diuretic and thirst-quencher. The pulp is a demulcent for internal and external use, as are the seeds, of which only the kernels are used. The seeds are believed to suppress hunger and prolong life, and are used to treat pimples. Incinerated seeds are prescribed for gonorrhoea!

CULINARY USES

In China, winter melon is cooked like any other marrow: the hard rind is peeled, the pulp and seeds discarded and the flesh cut into strips or slices. When cooked, it becomes almost translucent and rather delicate. It can be stir-fried by itself, or braised with meat and other vegetables, such as dried mushrooms. Another very popular way of serving winter melon is to add it to soup with ham.

STIR-FRIED MELON WITH MUSHROOMS

Use dried mushrooms here. The melon makes an interesting contrast to the strongly coloured and flavoured mushrooms.

Serves 4
Preparation time 10–15 minutes, plus mushroom soaking time
Cooking time 5–6 minutes

8–10 dried mushrooms, soaked
450g (1lb) winter melon
3 tablespoons oil
1–2 spring onions, cut into short sections
½ teaspoon salt
1 teaspoon sugar
1 tablespoon oyster sauce or light soy
½ teaspoon sesame oil

1 Squeeze dry the mushrooms and discard any hard stalks. Leave whole if small and cut into halves or quarters if big. Reserve the water.

2 Peel off the hard rind of the winter melon and discard the seeds and pulp. Cut the flesh into small, thin wedges.

3 Heat the oil in a preheated wok and stir-fry the winter melon for about 1 minute. Add the mushrooms and spring onions and cook for about 2 minutes, stirring all the time. Add the salt, sugar and a little of the mushroom soaking water. Braise for another minute or so and add the oyster sauce or soy. Blend well, sprinkle on the sesame oil and toss a couple of times more. Serve hot.

Note: For non-vegetarians, meat (pork or ham) or chicken may be added to this dish.

Winter Melon and Ham Soup

WINTER MELON AND HAM SOUP

This spectacular soup is sometimes cooked and served out of a whole winter melon, with a beautiful pattern carved on the outside of the melon. It is an elaborate dish that not only requires artistic skill, but also a giant steamer or pot to cook the melon in.

Serves 4
Preparation time 10 minutes plus shrimp soaking time
Cooking time 3–4 minutes

1 tablespoon dried shrimps, soaked
225g (8oz) winter melon
175g (6oz) ham
About 600ml (1 pint) stock (p 71)
Salt and pepper

1 Rinse and drain the shrimps. Peel off the rind of the winter melon, remove the pulp and seeds, and thinly slice the flesh. Cut the ham into small, thin slices.

2 Bring the stock to a rolling boil. Add the shrimps, melon and ham, bring back to the boil and cook for 2–3 minutes only. Adjust the seasoning and serve hot.

Pan Viet Export Banana And
Vegetables Corporation
Green

FRUITS AND NUTS

荔枝/龙眼

LYCHEE/ LONGAN

(LIZHI/LONGYAN) *Neohelium litchi v. longana*

Canned longans

Although most will have tasted lychees, or at least have heard of this delicate Chinese fruit, few will ever have heard of longans, let alone sampled them. Longans (dragons' eyes in Chinese) belong to the same family as lychees but because they are slightly smaller, they are often – and unfairly – regarded as inferior. Lychees have been cultivated in China for more than two thousand years. Up until the Tang dynasty (618–907), lychees were so precious that only the Imperial household might consume them.

The vibrant lychee skin hides a delicate flesh

HOW IT GROWS

Both lychees and longans are native to subtropical areas of southern China, those from Fujian being regarded as the best. The fruit is borne in clusters on small trees. Attempts to cultivate them in Europe in the 19th century failed because the climate was not right – they need heat and high humidity – but they have been grown successfully in parts of South Africa, from where they are exported to Britain.

APPEARANCE AND TASTE

Ripe lychees are about the size of a small plum, with a beautiful red knobbly skin. Thin and brittle, the skin soon goes brown and is easily separated from the juicy fruit inside, which is snow white in colour, sometimes with a hint of pink. It tastes something like a sweet grape, though much more scented; you do not eat the bitter-tasting brown pip.

BUYING AND STORING

Fresh lychees are available most of the year, and will keep for up to three months in the refrigerator. They are best eaten chilled. Fresh longans, which ripen later than lychees, are rarely seen in the West. Both fruits are available canned, in natural juice and in very sweet syrup.

MEDICINAL USES

Eating too many lychees is said to cause feverishness and nosebleeds, but in moderation they are thirst quenching and healthy. They are used to treat enlarged glands and tumours, while the analgesic pips are prescribed for various neuralgic disorders.

CULINARY USES

In China, lychees and longans are eaten both fresh and dried, and it is in the dried form that they are used in cooking: as a sweetmeat at feasts, and as presents for newly weds, presumably because they are believed to aid fertility. This is why young cockerel cooked with dried lychees or longans is given to pubescent youngsters.

Longans are sometimes offered as religious gifts

LYCHEE PORK

As an alternative to the ubiquitous pineapple used in the equally ubiquitous 'sweet and sour' dishes in most of the Chinese restaurants in the West, this recipe from Fujian makes a refreshing change – if possible, use lychee in natural juice rather than in syrup for this dish.

Serves 4
Preparation time 15 minutes plus marinating time
Cooking time 8–10 minutes

400g (14oz) lean pork, diced into sugar lump-sized cubes
½ teaspoon salt
¼ teaspoon five-spice powder
1 tablespoon rice wine
1 egg, lightly beaten
2 tablespoons plain flour
About 600ml (1 pint) oil
1 clove garlic, crushed
1 small green pepper (capsicum), sliced
225g (8oz) lychees, drained weight, reserve the juice or syrup
1 tablespoon light soy
2 tablespoons rice vinegar
1 tablespoon tomato paste (purée)

1 Marinate the pork with the salt, five-spice powder, and wine for 25–30 minutes.

2 Make a thin batter by blending the egg and flour, adding a little cold water if necessary. Remove the meat from the marinade and coat each cube with the batter.

3 Heat the oil to medium hot and deep-fry the pork for 4 minutes, until crisp and golden. Remove and drain. Pour off the excess oil, leaving about 1 tablespoon in the wok, lightly brown the crushed garlic, then add the green pepper (capsicum), lychees and the deep-fried pork, stir-fry for about 2 minutes, then add the soy, vinegar and the juice or syrup. Bring to the boil, thicken the sauce with tomato paste and blend. Serve hot.

Chinese Fruit Salad

CHINESE FRUIT SALAD

This novel way of serving mixed fruit is most impressive. Obviously it is not meant for an everyday meal, but for a banquet or special occasion.

Serves 6–8
Preparation time 30–35 minutes plus chilling time

225g (8oz) rock sugar (optional)
600ml (1 pint) boiling water (optional)
1 small water melon or large honeydew melon
4–5 different fresh and canned fruits, such as lychees or longans, kiwi fruit, pineapple, grapes, cherries, peaches, mango and papaya

1 If no canned fruit in syrup is used, dissolve the rock sugar in the water and leave to cool.

2 Slice about 2.5cm (1in) off the top of the melon and scoop out the flesh, discarding the seeds. Cut the flesh into small chunks. Prepare any other fresh fruit by cutting it into small chunks too.

3 Fill the melon shell with the fruit and syrup. Cover with cling film and chill in the refrigerator for 2–3 hours.

4 Serve the filled melon on a bed of crushed ice.

杏仁

ALMOND

(XINGREN) *Prunus amygdalus*

Almonds are known as the kernels of apricots, but the apricot we eat as a fruit and the fruit whose kernel we eat as a nut are two entirely different species. The apricot tree, *Prunus armeniaca*, has been grown in China for some four thousand years. I do not know of any recipes which call for apricots, which are usually dried and eaten as a snack, and are considered good for heart disorders. The fruit from which we get almonds is dusky green, leathery, and quite inedible.

Whole almonds

Almond is the kernel of a different apricot from the one we eat

HOW IT GROWS

The almond tree, *Prunus amygdalus*, was first introduced into China from Central Asia during the late Tang dynasty (9th century). It is now widely grown in northern China. The almond is the earliest fruit tree to flower: the very decorative white blossom often appears as early as January.

APPEARANCE AND TASTE

Almonds are oval with two pointed ends. They have a thin, variegated skin which can be peeled off after being soaked in water. There are two types of almonds: sweet and bitter. The latter contain prussic acid, and should never be eaten raw; their essence is distilled and used as a flavouring.

BUYING AND STORING

Almonds are sold whole or flaked, and sometimes ground or chopped. Store in a glass or plastic container. Whole and flaked almonds will keep longer than ground and chopped ones, perhaps 6–8 months after purchase. Discard when they start to smell rancid.

MEDICINAL USES

Many medicines contain almonds. They are prescribed for a variety of ailments, including coughs, flatulence and heartburn.

CULINARY USES

From a gastronomic point of view, almonds are not an important ingredient in Chinese cookery. The very popular Chicken with Almonds served in some Chinese restaurants in the West is quite unknown in China. Almonds tend to be used for sweets and cakes rather than savoury dishes.

Dried apricots from this market in Xinjiang, northwest China are eaten as snacks

Almond Shortbread

This is another favourite of mine from China. I missed it dreadfully when I first came to England – then I discovered Scottish shortbread which is good but does not taste the same. The only recipe I can unearth is meant for commercial use. I have reduced the ingredients by at least 99 percent, otherwise you would end up with enough almond cookies (shortbread) to last you the rest of your life!

Makes 24 cookies
Preparation time 25–30 minutes
Cooking time 25 minutes

285g (10oz) plain flour
50g (2oz) caster sugar
50g (2oz) lard
½ teaspoon baking powder
1 tablespoon finely chopped almonds
1 egg, beaten
Dry flour for dusting
Beaten egg for glazing

1 Sift the flour into a mixing bowl, add the sugar, lard, baking powder, almond and egg. Work gently into a smooth, firm dough.

2 Roll the dough out into a long sausage, then cut it into 24 equal portions. Roll each portion into a small ball and flatten it with the palm of your hand.

3 Place the flattened pieces on a greased baking tray. Brush with the beaten egg to glaze. Bake on the middle rack in a preheated, moderately hot oven (220°C/425°F/gas mark 7) for 20–25 minutes. Let the cookies cool before serving.

Eight-Treasure Rice Pudding

Traditionally served at New Year celebrations, this pudding reminds me of English Christmas pudding. It is much lighter, though, and, dare I say it, more delectable. It was one of my childhood favourites – and still is, even though I no longer have a sweet tooth. It is not necessary to have eight different kinds of fruit and nut, as the other ingredients can be counted as treasures too.

Serves 6–8
Preparation time 20–25 minutes
Cooking time about 1 hour

225g (8oz) glutinous rice
300ml (½ pint) water
2 tablespoons sugar
115g (4oz) lard
20 split almonds
30 raisins
15 dried red dates (jujubes), pitted
10 candied cherries
10 pieces candied angelica, chopped
225g (8oz) sweet red bean paste

For the syrup:
50g (2oz) sugar
150ml (¼ pint) water
2 tablespoons cornflour paste

1 Place the glutinous rice in a saucepan, add the water and bring to the boil. Reduce the heat and cook, covered, for 10–15 minutes. Add the sugar and about half of the lard to the rice. Mix well.

2 Smear a 850ml (1½ pint) capacity mould or pudding basin with the remaining lard, and cover the bottom and sides with a thin layer of the rice mixture. Gently press into the rice the fruit and nuts, attractively arranged in neat rows. These will show through when the pudding is turned out.

3 Cover the fruit and nuts with another layer of rice, much thicker this time. Fill the centre with the red bean paste, and cover with the remaining rice. Press gently to flatten the top. Cover with greaseproof paper or aluminium foil.

4 Steam the pudding for 1 hour. A few minutes before serving, make the syrup by dissolving the sugar in boiling water, and thickening with the cornflour paste over low heat.

5 To serve: invert the pudding onto a warmed plate. Pour the syrup over and serve hot.

Eight-Treasure Rice Pudding

红枣

RED DATE (JUJUBE)

(HONGZAO) *Zizyphus vulgaris v. jujuba*

Chinese dates (*Zizyphus vulgaris*) are grown all over China, and have been cultivated since ancient times. The variety we are concerned with is the wild 'red date', known as Chinese jujube. Believed to be a native of eastern India and Malaysia, the jujube was introduced to China over a thousand years ago.

Dried red dates

HOW IT GROWS

The jujube plant is a thorny shrub that grows in the mountains. The Chinese sometimes call it 'mountain date', even though it has become rather more cultivated than wild. The thorny shrub is used to make hedges to deter intruders.

APPEARANCE AND TASTE

The jujube is small and round, about the size of an olive with a globular pit. It tastes quite sour when green and raw, but becomes mildly sweet once it has matured and dried. When dried, it has a wrinkled red skin.

BUYING AND STORING

Dried red dates are available in small plastic bags from Oriental stores. They should carry a 'best before' date – if not, don't keep them for more than a year after purchase. Store in an air-tight container in a cool, dry place.

MEDICINAL USES

Jujubes are considered cooling and anodyne. If eaten frequently, they are said to help one put on weight and build up strength. They are recommended for rheumatic problems and insomnia, whatever the cause.

CULINARY USES

Maybe because of their red colour, which is a symbol of luck and happiness, dried red dates are one of the 'eight treasures' offered to visitors during New Year celebrations. They are used extensively as a health food because of their medicinal properties.

CHICKEN AND RED DATE CASSEROLE

There are two ways of cooking this casserole: the whole chicken is either browned in hot oil or parboiled, before being slow-cooked in stock. If you find the idea of deep-frying a whole chicken too daunting, then by all means use the blanching method.

Serves 4–6
Preparation time about 10 minutes
Cooking time 2 hours

1 chicken weighing about 1.25g (2lb 12oz)
Oil for deep-frying or boiling water for blanching
About 1.2 litres (2 pints) stock
2–3 spring onions, cut into short sections
4–5 small slices fresh ginger
1 tablespoon Sichuan peppercorns
1 teaspoon salt
3 tablespoons rice wine
175g (6oz) dried red dates (jujubes)
6 tablespoons soy
Fresh coriander leaves to garnish

1 Clean and dry the chicken well. Either deep-fry the chicken in hot oil, or blanch in boiling water for 3–4 minutes. Remove and drain.

2 Place the parboiled chicken in a pot or casserole (a large Chinese sand-pot would be ideal). Add the stock, spring onions, ginger, Sichuan peppercorns, salt and rice wine. Bring to the boil, then reduce the heat and simmer gently, covered, for 1 hour.

3 Add the red dates with the soy. Turn the chicken over and continue simmering, covered, for 50–55 minutes. The chicken should be so tender that the flesh can be pulled off with chopsticks and spoons. Serve hot with the liquid as a delicious soup.

Chicken and Red Date Casserole

杧果

MANGO

(MANGGUO) *Mangifera indica*

The mango originally came from India, and is now cultivated in Hong Kong, Hainan Island and throughout the southeastern provinces of China, where the climate is subtropical. Some people claim that mangoes are the world's most delicious fruit, but there are many different varieties of mango, some of which can be quite bland.

HOW IT GROWS

The mango belongs to the same family (Anocardiaceae) as cashew and pistachio nuts. Mango trees grow to an enormous size, their branches often spreading to 30m (100ft). The tree is evergreen with long, dark green, shiny leaves, and bears fruit from spring to summer.

APPEARANCE AND TASTE

Mangoes look rather like giant, elongated peaches, starting off pale green, and gradually turning a rich, golden pink. They have a fine-textured, juicy orange flesh with a large stone and a leathery skin. The taste is acid-sweet and perfectly balanced – some say the aroma is that of a pine wood in spring.

BUYING AND STORING

Mangoes are picked just before they are ripe, then packed in straw and sent by air to the West. Once ripe, they will keep for up to 10 days at room temperature, or up to two weeks in the refrigerator.

Shredded Duck with Mango

MEDICINAL USES

Mango is an important source of vitamin A. Besides being thirst quenching, it helps one's circulation and regulates menstruation. The root bark is good for treating diarrhoea.

CULINARY USES

Other than being served as a fruit, either on its own or as part of a mixed fruit salad, mango barely features in Chinese cookery. Its occasional appearance in Chinese restaurants in the West is as a dessert.

SHREDDED DUCK WITH MANGO

Fresh fruit is seldom used in savoury dishes in Chinese cooking, so the following recipe must have originated somewhere else in southeast Asia, where fruit plays a bigger part in the diet.

Serves 4
Preparation time about 15 minutes
Cooking time 4–5 minutes

225g (8oz) cooked duck meat, boned but not skinned
1 fresh mango or 175g (6oz) canned mango slices, drained
3 tablespoons oil
1 small onion, thinly sliced
1 small red pepper (capsicum) thinly shredded
½ teaspoon salt
2 tablespoons Hoi Sin sauce
1–2 spring onions, cut into short sectionsf

1 Cut the duck meat into thin shreds. Peel the fresh mango and cut it into thin slices.

2 Heat the oil in a preheated wok or pan. Stir-fry the onion slices until opaque. Add the red pepper (capsicum) and duck meat with the salt and stir-fry for about 2 minutes.

3 Add the mango slices with the Hoi Sin sauce and spring onions, blend well. Cook for another minute. Serve hot.

花生米

PEANUT

(HUASHENG MI) *Arachis hypogaea*

Although remains of peanuts have been discovered in archaeological sites in southeast China dating from the third millennium BC, there is no written mention of them until the sixteenth century, during the Ming dynasty, when peanuts were introduced into China from South America, about the same time as the sweet potato. Today, peanuts are one of the most important crops in China, having revolutionized farming on sandy soil, thanks to the nitrogen-fixing nodules at the roots of the peanut plant which help to preserve soil fertility.

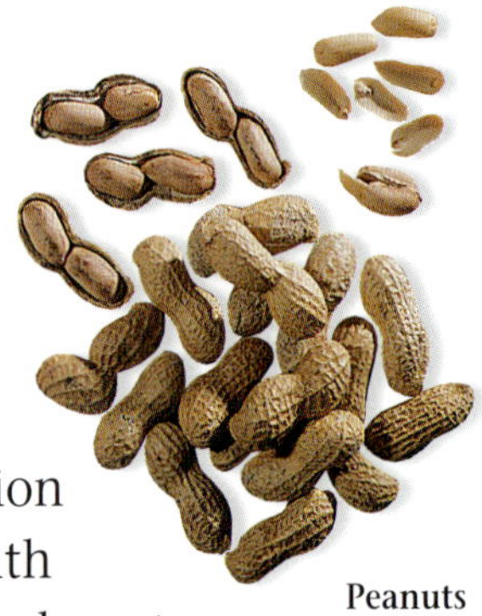

Peanuts in their shells

Peanut oil

HOW IT GROWS

Peanuts are grown in rotation with rice or wheat crops along the lower Yangtze and Yellow Rivers, the southeast coast, and the valleys of numerous inland rivers and streams. The nuts grow inside little pods which develop in clusters under the ground. This why they are also called groundnuts in English.

APPEARANCE AND TASTE

Peanut pods or shells are beige and rough to the touch, and usually contain two peanuts, although some may have three or just a single one. The peanuts themselves are oval with a slightly pointed end, and have a thin, reddish skin. Raw peanuts taste rather bland, but have a pleasant aroma.

Carefully weighing out the peanuts for sale

BUYING AND STORING

Peanuts are usually sold shelled, peeled, and roasted with salt. Occasionally it is possible to buy them still in their shells. However you buy them, bear in mind that peanuts do not keep very well: 3–4 months is the longest they will retain their freshness.

CULINARY USES

Peanuts are highly nutritious and play an important part in the everyday diet of Chinese people. As well as being a popular snack, peanuts always appear when drinks are served, alcoholic or not, whatever the time of day. They are an indispensable ingredient in the classic Kung-Po dishes of Sichuan, and they are essential for Satay sauce. They are also, of course, made into oil for cooking.

KUNG-PO CHICKEN

This is one of the most popular Sichuan dishes in Chinese restaurants. Gongbao was a court official from Guizhou, who happened to be stationed in Sichuan, and it was his cook who created this world-famous dish.

Serves 4
Preparation time 10–15 minutes
Cooking time 4–5 minutes

275–350g (10–12oz) chicken meat, boned and skinned
Pinch of salt
1 tablespoon light soy
1 teaspoon cornflour
3 tablespoons oil
4–5 dried red chillies, soaked and chopped
A few small bits of fresh ginger
2 spring onions, cut into short sections
1 small green pepper (capsicum), cut into cubes
2 tablespoons yellow bean sauce
2 teaspoons rice wine
85g (3oz) roasted peanuts
A few drops sesame oil

1 Cut the chicken into small cubes about the size of sugar lumps. Mix with the salt, soy and cornflour.

2 Heat about half the oil in a preheated wok and stir-fry the chicken cubes for about 1 minute, or until they change from pink to white. Remove.

3 Heat the remaining oil and add the red chillies, ginger, spring onions and green pepper (capsicum). Stir-fry for about 1 minute; add the yellow bean sauce and chicken. Blend well, add the rice wine, and continue stirring for another minute.

4 Add the peanuts with the sesame oil and toss a few times. Serve hot.

Chicken on Skewers with Satay Sauce

The Chinese probably learnt the Middle Eastern technique of cooking meat on skewers long ago – whether we introduced satay to Southeast Asia is open to debate. Satay sauce is said to have originated in Fujian, from where so many Chinese have emigrated, so it is possible. I recommend in all cases that you buy your satay sauce ready-made as I do.

Makes 24–26 sticks
Preparation time 25–30 minutes plus marinating time
Cooking time 10–15 minutes

450g (1lb) chicken breast meat
24–26 bamboo satay sticks
About 1 tablespoon oil
1 small onion, cut into small cubes
½ cucumber, unpeeled and cubed
4 tablespoons satay sauce

For the marinade:
1 teaspoon finely chopped garlic
1 tablespoon finely chopped spring onions
½ teaspoon finely chopped fresh ginger
½ teaspoon ground white pepper
1 teaspoon salt
1 tablespoon powdered coriander
1 tablespoon rice wine

1 Cut the chicken into 2.5cm (1in) cubes, and leave in the marinade mixture for at least 1 hour.

2 Soak the satay sticks in warm water for about 30 minutes, which will prevent them from burning during cooking.

3 Thread 3–4 cubes of chicken onto one end of each stick.

4 To cook: brush each stick of satay with a little oil and cook over a charcoal barbecue or under a hot grill for 6–8 minutes, turning frequently. Serve hot with the onion, cucumber and satay sauce.

Chicken on Skewers with Satay Sauce

栗

CHESTNUT

(LI) *Castanea vulgaris*

Several varieties of the common chestnut are grown in China, and have been cultivated throughout the country since ancient times.

Roasting chestnuts

HOW IT GROWS

The beautiful chestnut tree forms its nuts inside very prickly burs which split open when ripe to release the nuts. Chestnuts start to ripen from September – the timing depends on location and whether they are an early, late or mid-season variety.

APPEARANCE AND TASTE

Although there is some variation in flavour and sweetness of chestnuts, of greatest consideration when choosing chestnuts is whether or not they are easy to peel, which here means removing the thin brown inner skin, not the outside husk.

BUYING AND STORING

Fortunately, one can buy dried chestnuts already peeled, which saves quite a lot of bother. They will keep for a very long time, provided they are stored in a cool, dry place. Fresh chestnuts in their shells will not keep for nearly so long.

MEDICINAL USES

Chestnuts are considered to be cooling, and to be good for the breath, stomach and kidneys. They also help one endure hunger. Pulped and applied as a poultice, they are recommended for the treatment of muscular rheumatism.

Braised Chicken with Chestnuts

CULINARY USES

Chestnut is the only nut to be treated as a vegetable, since it contains more starch and less fat than other nuts. It is believed to be difficult to digest, so is not good for the sick or infants.

BRAISED CHICKEN WITH CHESTNUTS

As well as cooking them with pork, a popular way of using chestnuts is with chicken. Normally only light soy is used for cooking chicken, but in this instance, dark soy should be used to impart a deep colour and a rich flavour.

Serves 4
Preparation time 10 minutes plus soaking time
Cooking time 15 minutes

100g (4oz) dried chestnuts, soaked for 6–8 hours
450g (1lb) chicken meat, boned and skinned
¼ teaspoon salt
2 teaspoons cornflour paste
2 tablespoons oil
4 spring onions, cut into short sections, with white and green parts separate
2 tablespoons rice wine
3 tablespoons dark soy
1 tablespoon sugar
About 125ml (4fl oz) stock
½ teaspoon sesame oil

1 Drain the soaked chestnuts. Cut the chicken meat into small cubes about the same size as the chestnuts and mix with the salt and cornflour paste.

2 Heat the oil in a preheated work or pan. Stir-fry the chicken and chestnuts with the spring onion whites for about 2 minutes. Add the rice wine, soy and sugar, blend well and add the stock. Bring to the boil, reduce the heat and braise for about 8–10 minutes, stirring constantly.

3 Add the spring onion greens and sesame oil, and stir a few more times. Serve hot with plain boiled rice and a vegetable dish.

白果

Ginkgo Nut

(BAIGUO) *Salisburia adiantifolia*

The ginkgo tree, which is native to China, grows south of the Yangtze; the best examples are found in Anhui province. It is called the maidenhair tree in Japan, because the leaves are shaped like those of the maidenhair fern. It is a sort of living fossil – the last representative of a plant order important in prehistoric times.

How It Grows

The tree grows to 60–90m (20–30ft) high. In February/ March, the tree bears greenish-white buds, which open and drop off in the night, so they are rarely seen. The tree fruits prolifically. The nuts resemble lotus seed and ripen after frost.

Appearance and Taste

The Chinese name for ginkgo nut is *baiguo* (white fruit); it is also known as *yinxing* (silver apricot). The nuts are pointed at their extremities, and are marked by two or three longitudinal ridges – the three-ridged nuts produce male trees, the two-ridged female ones. Their taste is very subtle and delicate, difficult to describe. The same fruit is known in Japan as gingko biloba.

Buying and Storing

Fresh ginkgo nuts can be hard to find, but canned ones are readily available in the West. Once opened, they should be used within 2–3 days. Any leftovers should be rinsed and put in fresh water in the refrigerator, where they will keep for 4–5 days.

Medicinal Uses

Ginkgo nuts are supposed to be good for asthma, coughs, and irritability of the bladder. Eaten raw, they help to fight cancer and will counteract the negative effect of wine, namely a bad hangover! Cooked, they aid digestion.

Culinary Uses

Ginkgo nuts feature highly in vegetarian cooking in China and the Far East.

Vegetarian Casserole

This is a slightly simplified version of Buddha's Delight (p 193). The dressing is a variation on the one used for Vegetarian Noodles in Soup (p 44).

Serves 4–6
Preparation time 15–20 minutes, plus soaking time
Cooking time 4–5 minutes

25g (1oz) dried bean curd skin sticks, soaked
15g (½oz) dried black fungus ('wood ears'), soaked
25g (1oz) dried tiger lily buds, soaked
50g (2oz) dried bamboo shoots, soaked
50g (2oz) dried lotus root, soaked
115g (4oz) canned Ginkgo nuts, drained
115g (4oz) canned straw mushrooms, drained
115g (4oz) bean threads, soaked
4 tablespoons oil
1 teaspoon each of salt, sugar, light soy and sesame oil
¼ teaspoon MSG (optional)

1 Soak all the dried vegetables (except the bean threads, which only require a few minutes' soaking) separately in cold water overnight, or in warm water for about 1 hour. Drain everything well.

2 Cut the bean curd sticks into short sections, and leave everything else whole.

3 Heat the oil in a large pot or casserole. Stir-fry all the dried vegetables for about 2 minutes, then add the canned ingredients and the bean threads. Add the salt, sugar and soy and blend well. Braise for 2–3 minutes, stirring constantly. Add the MSG, if using, and the sesame oil. Toss a few times and serve hot or cold.

Vegetarian Casserole

FISH AND SHELLFISH

鯉魚

CARP AND OTHER FRESHWATER FISH

(LIYU) *Cyprinus carpio*

In China, fish is far more widely eaten than meat or poultry, partly because of its abundance which makes it less expensive. China has numerous rivers, lakes and ponds that yield a wealth of freshwater fish, the most common of which is the carp. Bream and roach, members of the same family, are common too. Also popular are mandarin fish, perch, chub, tench, dace, pike and eel. Trout have recently been introduced from the West, and of course there is freshwater shellfish: whelks, cockles, mussels, crayfish, prawns and delicious soft-shell crabs (p 176).

HABITAT

Fish farming has a long history in China – well over four thousand years, according to some records. In the countryside, ponds are used not just as reservoirs for agricultural irrigation, but also for extensive fish farming. Most farmed fish are known as grass carp, because they graze on pondgrass and are also fed cut grass.

APPEARANCE AND TASTE

The golden carp and ornamental goldfish belong to the carp family, and myth relates them to dragons. Another name for the common carp is silver carp, on account of its beautiful shiny scales. Carp can acquire a muddy taste if they live in particularly stagnant pools or the very muddy Yellow River in north China, but the firm white flesh, though quite coarse and bony, usually has a subtly sweet flavour.

A freshwater fish farm

BUYING AND STORING

In China, freshwater fish are always sold alive – carp is a very hardy creature which can survive for a long time out of water. There are two artificially bred varieties widely available in the West: the Mirror Carp, which has a few very large scales; and the Leather Carp, which has a leathery skin and no scales at all. If you buy carp which is not still alive, cook it the same day, or store it in the refrigerator for a day or two at most.

Freshwater eels are smaller than the saltwater variety

Culinary Uses

Carp is long-lived – living for up to fifty years – and can weigh as much as 20kg (44lb), so this beautiful silver-grey fish has become the symbol of great fortune. It is a must for New Year celebrations, as well as weddings, birthdays and other festivities. It is also eaten as an everyday fish because of its abundance and versatility – it can be cooked in almost any way, even eaten raw if really fresh.

Red-Cooked Carp

As I mentioned in the introduction, carp is the most common freshwater fish in China, and 'red-cooking' is the most common way of cooking it. This is a basic recipe: any kind of whole fish, ideally not too large, can be deep- or shallow-fried in hot oil, then braised in a simply prepared sauce. The sauce can be varied to give the dish a different flavour.

Serves 4–6
Preparation time 10–15 minutes plus marinating time
Cooking time 8–10 minutes

1 carp (or any fish), weighing 500–600g (1lb 2oz–1lb 5oz), cleaned
1 tablespoon light soy
1 tablespoon rice wine
Oil for deep-frying
Fresh coriander leaves to garnish

For the sauce:
1 tablespoon finely shredded fresh ginger
2–3 spring onions, thinly shredded, with white and green parts separate
1 teaspoon sugar
3 tablespoons yellow bean sauce
About 125ml (4 fl oz) stock or water
1 tablespoon cornflour paste
½ teaspoon sesame oil

1 Clean and dry the fish well. Diagonally score both sides of the fish as far as the bone at intervals of about 2.5cm (1in). Marinate with the soy and wine for 10–15 minutes.

2 Deep- or shallow-fry the fish in hot oil for about 3–4 minutes, turning once. Pour off the excess oil, and push the fish to one side of the wok. Add the ginger, spring onion whites, sugar, yellow bean sauce and the remaining marinade with the stock or water. Bring to the boil and braise the fish in this liquid with the spring onion greens for 5 minutes, turning once.

3 Thicken the sauce with the cornflour paste, make smooth and blend in the sesame oil. Serve hot, garnished with coriander leaves.

Five Willow Fish

A variation of the classic sweet and sour carp, this colourful and delicious dish from Shanghai can be adapted to accommodate almost any kind of whole fish. The 'five willow' here refers to the five shredded vegetables used in the sauce. The fish does not have to be crisply fried – it can be poached or steamed, and the sauce poured over it afterwards.

Five Willow Fish

Serves 4–6
Preparation 20–25 minutes plus mushroom soaking time
Cooking time 10–15 minutes

1 whole fish (carp, bream, perch etc), weighing about 500g (1lb 2oz), cleaned
1 teaspoon salt
Oil for deep-frying

For the sauce:
3–4 dried Chinese mushrooms, soaked
1 tablespoon thinly shredded fresh ginger
2–3 spring onions, thinly shredded
1 small carrot, thinly shredded
1 small green pepper (capsicum) thinly shredded
1–2 sticks celery, thinly shredded
2–3 fresh red chillies, de-seeded and thinly shredded
2 tablespoons light soy
2 tablespoons sugar
3 tablespoons rice vinegar
1 tablespoon rice wine
About 125ml (4fl oz) stock or water
1 tablespoon cornflour paste
½ teaspoon sesame oil

1 Clean and dry the fish well. Diagonally score both sides of the fish as far as the bone at intervals of about 2.5cm (1in). Rub the fish all over with salt, both inside and out.

2 Squeeze dry the mushrooms, discard any hard stalks, and thinly shred. Add in the green parts of the spring onion.

3 Deep- or shallow-fry the fish in hot oil for 3–4 minutes on each side. Remove the fish and place on an oval serving platter.

4 Pour off the excess oil, leaving about 1 tablespoon in the wok. Stir-fry all the vegetables and the chillies for about 2 minutes, then add the seasonings and the stock. Bring to the boil and thicken with the cornflour paste. Sprinkle on the sesame oil and pour the sauce over the fish. Serve the dish hot.

黄花魚

YELLOW FISH AND OTHER SALTWATER FISH

(HUANGYU) *Pseudosciaena crocea v. polyactis*

East China has a coastline 14,000 km (8,700 miles) long, so it is only natural that seafood should play a great part in the Chinese diet. Over one hundred different species are caught all year round, the two most abundant being the large and small yellow croaker belonging to the Sciaenidae family, known as 'yellow fish' in Chinese. There is a large variety of shellfish and delicacies like squid, abalone, sea cucumber and bird's nest, which will be dealt with separately.

HABITAT

China's coastline stretches from the Yellow Sea in the north down to the South China Sea in the south, with the East China Sea in between. The great majority of seafood in China is caught wild; yellow croakers, whose ability to make a loud drumming noise in water, are never farmed. Other popular catches include grouper, grey mullet, mackerel, sea bream, red snapper, red mullet, pomfret, sole, skate, monkfish, sea bass, sea perch, sardine and shark. There is also the Chinese shad, which is a migratory fish that swims up the rivers from the sea each spring to spawn.

APPEARANCE AND TASTE

Yellow croakers have yellow specks on their backs. The average large croaker is 30–40 cm (12–16 in) long; the small croaker is 15–25 cm (6–10 in) long. Their shape and appearance are different too: the large croaker has a long, narrow tail and smaller scales than the small croaker; the small croaker has a shorter, wider tail. They both have delicate, firm white flesh with a flaky texture.

BUYING AND STORING

Freshly frozen yellow croakers are exported to the West, and are available in most Oriental stores. Basically warm water fish, there are many related species that inhabit North American waters called hardhead, weakfish or drumfish. In Europe, you can substitute sea bass, sea bream, red mullet, grey mullet or grouper.

CULINARY USES

Yellow croakers are very versatile: they can be fried, braised, steamed or used in casseroles, and because of their abundance, croakers are also salted (p 207). The bladders of large yellow croakers are dried and sold as 'fish maw' (p 217).

Saltwater fish straight from the boat to the basket

Yellow Fish Soup

I mentioned earlier that we do not have a fish stock as such: we normally use chicken/meat stock as a base for soups of all kind. This soup is an exception, for it is made from the heads and tails of yellow fish. You may want to substitute another fish, in which case the flavour will not be quite the same.

Serves 4
Preparation time about 5 minutes
Cooking time 10–15 minutes

Heads and tails of two yellow croakers (or any other fish)
2 tablespoons oil
1 teaspoon Sichuan peppercorns
3–4 small slices peeled fresh ginger
2–3 spring onions, cut into short lengths
3 tablespoons rice wine
Salt and pepper to taste

1 Crush the heads and tails of the fish.

2 Heat the oil in a wok with the peppercorns until fragrant. Add the ginger and spring onions and stir a few times. Add the fish pieces with the wine, and continue stirring until the fish changes colour.

3 Add one rice bowl of water, cover, and bring to the boil. When you lift the lid off, you will see that the liquid has turned a cream colour. Allowing one bowl of water for each person (so four bowls of water for four servings), repeat the process, never adding more than one bowl of water at a time, and always waiting for it to boil before adding the next bowl of water. It is very important that you do not add all the water at once.

4 Adjust the seasoning and discard the fish pieces before serving as a clear soup.

Steamed Sea Bass

Qingzheng **(clear-steaming) is a cooking method in which the food (usually seafood) is steamed without much seasoning, and additional seasonings are added after the cooking process. This dish is one that is very popular in Chinese restaurants, and is often called steamed fish with ginger and spring onions.**

Serves 4–6
Preparation time 6–8 minutes
Cooking time 12–15 minutes

1 whole sea bass or grey mullet etc, weighing about 500g (1lb 2oz), cleaned
½ teaspoon salt
1 teaspoon sesame oil
2 spring onions, halved
1 tablespoon thinly shredded fresh ginger
2 tablespoons light soy
1 tablespoon rice wine
2 spring onions, thinly shredded
2 tablespoons vegetable oil
Fresh coriander leaves to garnish

1 Clean and dry the fish thoroughly. Diagonally score both sides of the fish as far as the bone at intervals of about 2.5cm (1in). Rub the salt and sesame oil over the inside and outside of the fish. Lay the fish on top of the spring onion halves on a platter, and place the shredded ginger inside and outside the fish.

2 Place the platter in a hot steamer and steam over a high heat for 12–13 minutes. Remove and discard the shredded ginger and transfer the fish to a warm serving dish. Sprinkle the soy and wine over the fish, then place the shredded spring onion on top.

3 Heat the oil in a little saucepan and pour it over the whole fish. Serve hot, garnished with the coriander leaves.

Unloading the day's catch

鱿魚

SQUID/ CUTTLEFISH

(YOUYU) *Laligo vulgaris/Sepia officinalis*

Members of the cephalopod family, squid and cuttlefish are prized seafood in China, not least because they are unusually rich in flesh for their weight, since they do not have true skeletons. Octopus, a larger member of the same family, holds less appeal for the Chinese palate, on account of its rubbery texture and flavour.

Fresh squid

HABITAT

Squid and cuttlefish are usually found at the bottom of the sea. Commercially they are caught at night with lights, which attract them to the surface.

APPEARANCE AND TASTE

Freshly caught squid are amongst the most beautiful of marine animals: firm and iridescent, they look as if they are embedded in crystal. They range from tiny creatures a few centimetres long to the giant octopus which reaches almost 18m (60ft) in length.

Octopuses are bulbous, cuttlefish shield-shaped, while squid are more like torpedoes, with a fin on either side. They have eight arms and two tentacles, all of which can be eaten, and taste quite delicious.

BUYING AND STORING

Because of pollution and overfishing in the Mediterranean in recent years, it is increasingly frozen squid from further afield which is sold in Europe. Fortunately it keeps its flavour after freezing, and is even tenderized by the process.

CULINARY USES

Squid and cuttlefish, both fresh and dried, are regarded as a delicacy in China. To prepare a fresh squid, take hold of the head and pull it out with the contents of the mantle cavity. Clean out all the remaining guts, including the ink, which is never used in Chinese cooking. Make a slit and pull out the transparent backbone. Remove the slimy skin and wash the body. Cut off and discard the eyes and beak. Dried squid should be soaked in warm water for 30 minutes, then washed clean in cold water before use.

SQUID-FLOWER SALAD

This is a warm salad. The Chinese cookery term *qiang* is very difficult to translate – it involves blanching or parboiling in water, then marinating with a highly flavoured sauce made of soy, wine, fresh ginger and vinegar etc. It can also mean to fry very briefly in hot oil, before mixing with a sauce.

Squid laid out to dry

Serves 4–6
Preparation time 25–30 minutes
Cooking time 1 minute

450g (1lb) squid or cuttlefish
Lettuce leaves

Salad dressing:
1 tablespoon mustard powder mixed with 1 tablespoon water
1 tablespoon finely chopped fresh ginger
2 tablespoons finely chopped spring onions
2 tablespoons light soy
1 tablespoon rice wine
2 tablespoons rice vinegar
1 teaspoon sugar
¼ teaspoon ground black pepper
1 tablespoon sesame oil

1 Clean the squid or cuttlefish by discarding its head, the transparent backbone and the ink bag. Peel off the thin skin, then wash and dry well. (This part should have been done if you have frozen rather than fresh squid or cuttlefish.)

2 Open up the squid and score the inside of the flesh in a criss-cross pattern. Cut into diamond-shaped pieces about the size of a large postage stamp.

3 Blanch in a pan of boiling water for 25–30 seconds only (each piece will curl up and the criss-cross pattern will open out to resemble ears of corn – hence the name 'flower'). Remove quickly and drain. Place on a bed of lettuce leaves on a serving plate.

4 Mix the sauce and pour it all over the squid flowers. Toss well and serve.

Stir-Fried Two-Colour Squid Flowers

This exquisite dish combines pieces of fresh white squid, dried brown squid, black mushrooms, red and green peppers (capsicums) and a full-flavoured sauce. Garlic and Sichuan pepper give the dish a tantalizing aroma.

Serves 4
Preparation time 35–40 minutes plus soaking time
Cooking time 5–6 minutes

3–4 dried Chinese mushrooms, soaked
175g (6oz) dried squid, soaked
225g (8oz) fresh squid, cleaned
½ green pepper (capsicum)(
½ red pepper (capsicum)
600ml (1 pint) oil
2 cloves garlic, thinly sliced
1 tablespoon chopped spring onions
1 tablespoon rice wine
1 tablespoon light soy
½ teaspoon salt
½ teaspoon ground Sichuan peppercorns
50ml (2fl oz) stock
2 teaspoons cornflour paste
A few drops sesame oil

1 Squeeze dry the mushrooms, discard the hard stalks if any, and cut each one into 4–6 diamond-shaped pieces.

2 Soak the dried squid in water for 30 minutes. Drain and score the underside in a criss-cross pattern, then cut into diamond-shaped pieces about the size of a large postage stamp. Prepare the fresh squid as for the salad recipe above.

3 Cut the green and red peppers (capsicums) into small diamond-shaped pieces keeping them the same size as the prepared mushrooms (ie smaller than the squid pieces).

4 Heat the oil in a preheated wok. Stir-fry the dried and fresh squid for about 1 minute, or until each piece rolls up into a small ball. Remove with a strainer and drain.

5 Pour off the excess oil, leaving about 1 tablespoon in the wok. Stir-fry the garlic, spring onions, mushrooms and green and red peppers (capsicums) for about 1 minute, then add the par-cooked squid flowers with the seasonings (wine, soy, salt and pepper). Blend well and add the stock. Stir until it starts to bubble, then thicken the gravy with the cornflour paste and sprinkle on the sesame oil. Serve hot.

Stir-Fried Two-Colour Squid Flowers

青蟹

SOFT-SHELL CRAB

(QINGXIE) *Carcinus maenas*

A member of the crustacean family, the crab is related to the lobster, crayfish and prawn. The Chinese name for freshwater crab is *qingxie* (green crab), a term which the French apply to the shore crab. 'Soft-shells' is the American name for fresh-water crabs collected after they have shed their old shells and before their new ones have hardened. In China, we have three types of 'green crab': inland river crab, delta river crab, and lake crab. There is little difference between them – they all belong to the same species.

HABITAT

Freshwater crabs, which usually inhabit the shallow water at river mouths, swim upstream to spawn in spring and autumn. Young crabs shed their shells five or six times before they reach their final size. Once fully grown, they move further upstream to inland rivers and lakes.

APPEARANCE AND TASTE

Adult freshwater crabs seldom measure much more than 5–7.5cm (2–3in) across the shell, and never grow to anything like the size of saltwater crabs. They have a faint greenish tint to their body, and they do not turn orange after cooking. There is not much flesh in the shell, but since you can eat the entire crab – shells, legs, claws, the lot – it has always been a very popular dish in restaurants.

First bend of the Yangtze River, a great source of freshwater fish

BUYING AND STORING

Frozen soft-shells from the lakes of North America are available all year round. Freshwater crabs from China, unfrozen and still alive, are available only during the height of the season, which is in the autumn (September–November). Freshwater crabs from China will stay alive out of water for several weeks if stored in a cool, damp place.

CULINARY USES

Although crabs are eaten almost all year round, for the true gourmet nothing can compare with eating crabs when they're at the height of their season during the Autumn Festival. Ideally one would be in a garden of chrysanthemums, drinking rice wine under a beautiful full moon in the company of fellow gourmet-scholars. Such occasions often inspired poets and artists to produce great works of art.

Live 'green crabs' neatly bundled together for sale

Soft-Shell Crab with Spicy Salt and Pepper

SOFT-SHELL CRAB WITH SPICY SALT AND PEPPER

This appears to be the only way soft-shell crabs are served in Chinese restaurants in the West, and most delicious it is too. It is not at all difficult to cook at home, but you must use soft-shell freshwater crabs: hard-shell saltwater crabs are no substitute.

Serves 4
Preparation time 10–15 minutes
Cooking time 6–8 minutes

4 soft-shell crabs
½ teaspoon spicy salt and pepper (p 122)
1 tablespoon rice wine
1 egg, beaten
1 tablespoon plain flour
Oil for deep-frying
Lettuce leaves
1 tablespoon chopped spring onions
2 teaspoons chopped fresh red chillies

1 Clean and dry the crabs well. Marinate with the spicy salt and pepper and wine for 10 minutes, then coat with the beaten egg and flour.

2 Deep-fry the crabs in hot oil for 4–5 minutes until golden. Remove and drain. Arrange on a bed of lettuce leaves on a serving plate.

3 Soak the spring onions and chillies in the hot oil (with the heat turned off) for 2–3 minutes. Remove with a strainer and sprinkle over the crabs. Serve hot.

FU-YUNG CRAB

As mentioned briefly on p 144, in most Chinese restaurants a fu-yung dish means an omelette or scrambled eggs. *Furong* (*fu-yung* is the Cantonese pronunciation) is the name for lotus blossom, which has a velvety texture and resembles creamy-textured egg whites that have been lightly scrambled.

Serves 4–6
Preparation time 10–15 minutes
Cooking time 8–10 minutes

6–8 freshwater crabs
1 tablespoon oil
1 tablespoon finely chopped spring onions
1 teaspoon finely chopped fresh ginger
1 tablespoon rice wine
½ teaspoon salt
½ teaspoon sugar
Pinch of ground white pepper
6 egg whites, beaten
About 125ml (4fl oz) chicken stock
Pinch of MSG (or salt)

1 Poach or steam the crabs for 3–4 minutes. Pull the legs off and open the shells from underneath. Remove the meat and reserve the shells.

2 Heat the oil and stir-fry the spring onions and ginger until fragrant. Add the crab meat with the wine, salt, sugar and pepper. Stir for about 1 minute, then fill the empty shells with the crab meat.

3 Steam the filled crab shells vigorously for 5 minutes. Remove and place on a warm serving dish.

4 Blend the egg white with the stock and MSG or salt, and bring to the boil, stirring all the time. When it is set, pour it over the crabs and serve hot.

Note: If freshwater crabs are not available, you may use saltwater crabs instead, taking into account the difference in their size and texture.

虾

PRAWNS

(XIA) *Pandalus borealis*

Prawns are crustaceans, like lobsters (which the Chinese call 'dragon prawns') and crabs. I shall adopt the British practice of calling small prawns shrimp, and medium to large ones prawns. You will probably have heard of a Chinese dish known as Drunken Prawns, in which live prawns are soaked in alcohol until they are 'drunk' and then eaten raw. I am afraid that not only have I seen it, but I have actually tasted it.

Fishing boats at dusk in the Gulf of Bohai, north China

HABITAT

As well as an especially long coastline, China has so many rivers, streams, lakes and ponds that fresh prawns are nearly always available and are consumed within hours of being netted. I have vivid memories of catching shrimps in a mountain stream in southern China and eating them still alive!

APPEARANCE AND TASTE

Prawns have the sweetest flavour of all shellfish. All sizes are available; the colours range from grey to light brown, but once cooked, they all turn bright pink or orange. The larger ones are called king prawns, the next, tiger prawns, and the smaller ones are just called prawns.

BUYING AND STORING

Except for stuffed recipes, ready-cooked prawns are not really suitable for Chinese cooking. You must use unpeeled, raw ones which are usually sold frozen.

PREPARATION

First defrost the prawns thoroughly (unless you are lucky enough to have fresh ones) by leaving them on the bottom shelf of the refrigerator overnight, or sitting them in running cold water for a couple of hours. Soaking them in hot water or using the microwave will part- cook the prawns. You must always de-vein prawns, particularly if they are from badly polluted waters, by holding the peeled prawn by the tail, making a shallow cut along the centre of its back, then pulling out and discarding the dark brown vein from the shallow cut.

CULINARY USES

There are numerous prawn recipes in China. Bear in mind that whatever the size of the prawn, over-cooking renders the delicate flesh tough and dry. Unpeeled prawns should be lightly poached or deep-fried (never boiled), then quickly braised with sauce. Peeled ones are first coated with egg white and cornflour, then quickly stir-fried, so they retain their delicate flavour and moisture.

BRAISED PRAWNS SICHUAN STYLE

This is one of the most popular dishes in Chinese restaurants all over the world. The spicy sauce can be replaced by sweet and sour sauce – the cooking method is the same. Use giant prawns about 10–15cm (4–6in) long, ideally with the heads still attached. Not only do they look most impressive when cooked, you can also pull off the head and suck out the brain, which, though it sounds highly unappealing, has a most delicious taste, much appreciated by connoisseurs.

Serves 4
Preparation time 10 minutes
Cooking time 6–8 minutes

Braised Prawns Sichuan Style

300g (10oz) uncooked and unpeeled king prawns, with heads still attached
Oil for deep-frying
1½ tablespoons chilli bean paste (toban jiang)
1 teaspoon finely chopped fresh ginger
1 teaspoon finely chopped garlic
1 tablespoon rice wine
1 tablespoon light soy
½ teaspoon sugar
About 115ml (4fl oz) stock (see p 71)
1 teaspoon rice vinegar
1 tablespoon chopped spring onion
Coriander leaves to garnish (optional)

1 Using a pair of kitchen shears, cut each prawn along its back to expose the dark brown vein, but leave the shell otherwise intact. Remove the vein and rinse with cold water. Dry the prawns well by patting with kitchen towel.

2 Heat the oil and deep-fry the prawns for about 2 minutes, or until they are bright orange all over. Remove and drain.

3 Pour off the excess oil, leaving about 1 teaspoonful in the wok. Stir-fry the bean paste for about 1 minute over low heat, then add the prawns with the ginger, garlic, rice wine, soy, sugar and stock. Increase the heat and bring to the boil. Braise for 3–4 minutes, stirring constantly.

4 Stir in the vinegar. When most of the liquid has evaporated, add the spring onions. Serve hot, garnished with the coriander leaves, if using.

STIR-FRIED PRAWNS WITH MANGE-TOUT (SNOW PEAS)

The Chinese name for this dish, Yuan Yang Prawns, refers to mandarin ducks, also known as love birds, because they are always seen together – they symbolize affection and happiness in China. This is a very colourful, delicious dish, a perfect marriage of pink shellfish and green vegetable, quite simple to prepare. Ideally the prawns should be about 4cm (1½in) long without their heads – the same length as the mange-tout.

Serves 4–6
Preparation time 25–30 minutes
Cooking time 10 minutes

450g (1lb) uncooked prawns, headless
Pinch of salt
½ egg white, lightly beaten
1 tablespoon cornflour paste
About 575ml (1 pint) vegetable oil
175g (6oz) mange-tout (snow peas), topped and tailed
½ teaspoon salt
1 teaspoon sugar
1 tablespoon finely chopped spring onions
1 teaspoon finely chopped fresh ginger
1 tablespoon light soy
1 tablespoon rice wine
2 teaspoons chilli bean paste (toban jiang)
1 tablespoon tomato paste or sauce
Sesame oil to garnish (optional)

1 Peel and de-vein the prawns, then mix with the pinch of salt, egg white and cornflour paste.

2 Heat 2 tablespoons oil in a preheated wok. Stir-fry the mange-tout (snow peas) for about 1 minute, add the salt and sugar, and continue stirring for another minute. Remove and place in the centre of a serving platter.

3 Clean the wok and heat the remaining oil. Stir in the prawns and blanch them for about 1 minute. Remove and drain.

4 Pour off the excess oil, leaving about 1 teaspoon in the wok. Add the prawns with the spring onion and ginger, stir-fry for 20–30 seconds, then add the soy and wine. Stir for another minute. Place half the prawns at one end of the platter.

5 Add the chilli bean paste and tomato sauce to the remaining prawns, blend well and garnish with the sesame oil, if using. Place these prawns at the other end of the platter. Serve hot.

Preserved and Processed Foods

虾片

PRAWN CRACKERS

(XIAPIAN)

Made from fresh prawn meat blended with starch and seasoned with salt and sugar, these highly popular crispy crackers are also known as shrimp chips. They are ideal for serving with drinks before a meal or at parties, and most Chinese restaurants offer them while you wait for your order. They are a great favourite with children of all ages.

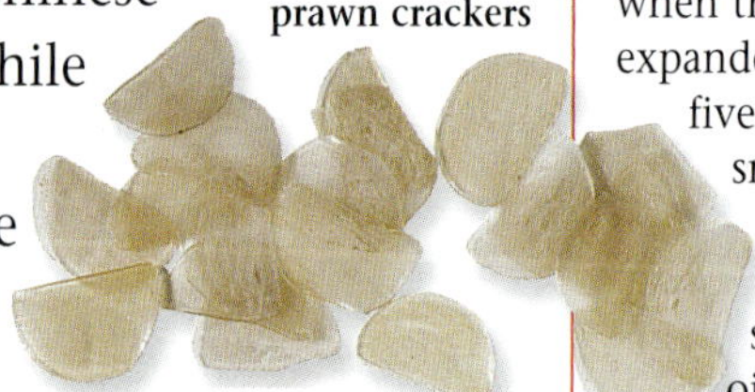

Uncooked prawn crackers

APPEARANCE AND TASTE

Rather unappetizing-looking in their raw state, when cooked, the grey discs will puff up to delicious crisp, white crackers.

BUYING AND STORING

Ready cooked prawn crackers, similar to Western potato crisps, are stocked by most supermarkets and grocers and should be consumed on the day of opening. The uncooked variety are sold from Oriental stores in cellophane bags in cardboard packets.

CULINARY USES

The best way to cook crackers is to deep-fry them, using a light vegetable oil such as sunflower or groundnut. Heat the the oil in a wok till it smokes, then turn the heat down a bit and fry a handful of crackers (6–8) at a time. They puff up rather dramatically in a matter of seconds, and when they have fully expanded, they are four to five times larger and snow-white. Remove immediately with a strainer or sieve, shake off the excess oil and drain on kitchen paper. After you have cooked the first two or three batches, heat the oil again to the required temperature. If the cooked crackers are not to be served within the hour, they should be stored in an air-tight container to retain their crispness. Soggy prawn crackers can be made crisp again by being left in a low oven for 5–6 minutes.

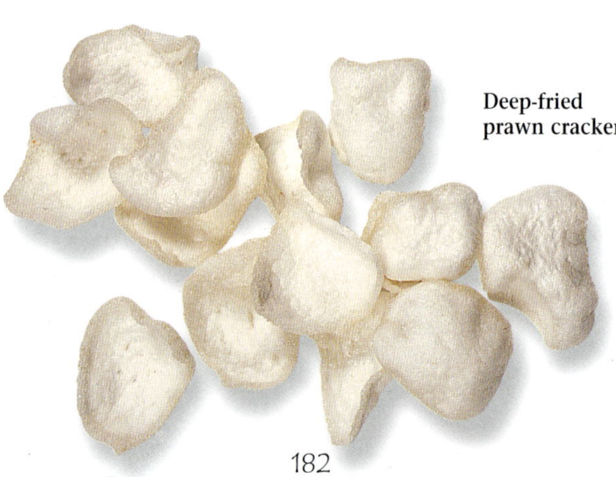

Deep-fried prawn crackers

Freshly caught prawns

SHRIMP SOY SAUCE; SHRIMP ROE

Other shrimp by-products are shrimp soy sauce, and shrimp roe. Since neither is usually available in the West, there is not much point going into detail about them. Suffice to say that the first one is a shrimp-flavoured soy, not quite so salty as fish sauce, but stronger than oyster sauce, and shrimp roe is usually used as a seasoning for mild tasting ingredients such as bean-curd or bamboo shoots and is also used in noodle making (see page 43). The shrimp noodles are usually sold in dried form and do not taste 'fishy' but have a delicate subtle flavour much appreciated by the Chinese.

醬菜 腌菜

PICKLES

(JIANG CAI, YAN CAI)

Preserved food has a long history in China. The Chinese probably preserve their food in more ways and in greater quantity than any other nation. Means by which food is preserved include smoking, salting, drying, pickling, and soaking in soy, and there is no kind of food which is exempt: fish, poultry, meat, eggs, vegetables, fruit, grains – the Chinese preserve them all.

MANUFACTURE

Before refrigeration and speedy transportation, fresh vegetables had to be preserved for unproductive seasons and for export to far-off provinces. There are four basic ways of preserving food, and these methods are still used throughout much of China.

STORAGE IN DUGOUTS OR PITS

In the autumn months, fresh vegetables are packed in layers (one type per layer) in trenches on the south side of a wall. Layers of earth are placed between each layer of food, and the top layer is covered with earth and straw. Thus stored, the vegetables will last the whole winter, and will be as fresh and crispy as those eaten in summer.

JIANG CAI

These are vegetables pickled in soy-based hydrolysate. Many very perishable vegetables are converted into *jiang cai* by semi-drying them and then dropping them into fermenting or fermented soy solution.

DESICCATION

Vegetables, salted or plain, sometimes previously steamed (to kill living tissues), are dried by the sun or another source of heat.

PICKLING

Immersion in brine or a similar liquid will preserve many vegetables for a considerable span of time – some remain edible for decades. The method for making pickles and *jiang cai* (soy-conserves) is similar. The main difference is that pickling requires a clear brine solution, while making *jiang cai* calls for a darker soy-based solution.

Large ceramic jars for pickling

BUYING AND STORING

Jiang cai and many dried, preserved and pickled foods are available in the West, some in packets, some in jars and some in tins. The choice is huge – it is impossible to list them all in this book. I have a book published in China which describes in detail how to make three hundred different types of pickles!

PICKLED VEGETABLES

As mentioned above, there are two basic brines for pickling: clear and dark. Dark pickles usually consist of just one vegetable without any chillies, while clear ones are a mixture of vegetables, as in this recipe.

Serves 10–12
Preparation time 10–15 minutes plus pickling time

For the brine:
1.5 litres (2¼ pints) water, boiled and cooled
50g (2oz) salt
1 tablespoon Sichuan peppercorns
50g (2oz) sugar
50ml (2fl oz) Chinese spirit
125g (4oz) fresh ginger, peeled and sliced
4–6 whole red chillies

Use 4–6 of the following:
Carrot, cabbage (white or green), cauliflower, celery, cucumber, garlic, cloves, leek, onion, radish or turnip

1 Make the brine by placing the cold boiled water in a large, clean earthenware or glass jar. Add the salt, pepper, sugar, spirit, ginger and chillies.

2 Do not wash any of the vegetables but peel or wipe them clean, then trim and cut into small slices or pieces. Place them in the brine and seal the jar, making sure it is air-tight. Place the jar in a cool, dark place and leave for 5–6 days before using.

3 Always use a clean pair of chopsticks or tongs to pick out the vegetables, not allowing any grease or unboiled water to get into the jar. You can replenish the vegetables, adding a little more salt each time. If a white scum appears on the surface, add a little more sugar and spirit. The longer the vegetables are left in the solution, the better they taste.

Pickled Vegetables

榨菜

PRESERVED VEGETABLES

(ZHACAI)

Once called Sichuan Preserved Vegetable after the province where it was made, this highly popular mustard pickle is now produced in all parts of China. I was surprised to discover that this world-famous pickle was first marketed as recently as 1898, which makes it the centenary year as I write.

MANUFACTURE

The vegetable used is the tuber of the mustard greens (*Brassica juncea*), described in detail on p 134. Selected tubers are dried in the sun, then pickled in brine, and after being trimmed and cleaned, they are pressed to get rid of excess liquid (hence the Chinese name *zhacai*: pressed vegetable), before being blended with chilli and spices, and stored in sealed containers to mature.

APPEARANCE AND TASTE

Preserved vegetables are not attractive and are nothing like the picture on the label. They have a dark green, knobbly exterior covered with tiny specks of red chilli; the interior is smooth with a wonderfully crunchy texture. They are very hot and salty so you may want to wash off some of the salt and chillies before eating.

BUYING AND STORING

Preserved vegetables are widely available in tins from Oriental stores in the West. Some are ready-shredded, so save you lots of bother. Once opened, store in an air-tight container in the refrigerator where the pickle will keep almost indefinitely. Just remember that, like strong cheese, the smell can permeate other food stuffs, so keep the preserved vegetables away from anything delicate.

CULINARY USES

Preserved vegetables are most versatile. They can be eaten raw as a relish, stir-fried, steamed and used in soups. They add extra flavour and an interesting texture to any mild-tasting food.

MINCED MEAT OR SEAFOOD WRAPPED IN LETTUCE

The original version of this Shanghai dish calls for quail or pigeon. Chinese restaurants generally use chicken or pork, while seafood (a mixture of prawns, squid and scallops) seems to be quite popular too. Whatever main ingredient you use, the combination of the other ingredients turns this dish into a most exciting experience.

Serves 4–6
Preparation time 15–20 minutes, plus soaking and marinating time
Cooking time 4 minutes

225g (8oz) chicken or pork or seafood
Salt and pepper to taste
½ teaspoon sugar
1 teaspoon light soy
1 teaspoon rice wine
2 teaspoons cornflour paste
3–4 dried Chinese mushrooms, soaked

A typical family-run general store selling almost every item needed in the kitchen

100g (4oz) preserved vegetables
50g (2oz) water chestnuts, drained
3 tablespoons oil
½ teaspoon finely chopped fresh ginger
1 tablespoon finely chopped spring onions
2 tablespoons oyster sauce
12 crisp lettuce leaves (Webb or Iceberg) to serve

1 Coarsely chop the meat or seafood and marinate with the salt, pepper, sugar, soy, wine and cornflour for 10–15 minutes.

2 Squeeze dry the mushrooms and discard any hard stalks. Coarsely chop the mushrooms, preserved vegetables and water chestnuts.

3 Heat the oil in a preheated wok and stir-fry the ginger and spring onions until fragrant. Add the meat or seafood and stir-fry for about 1 minute. Tip in the mushrooms, preserved vegetables and water chestnuts, and continue stirring for 2 more minutes. Pour in the oyster sauce and blend well. Serve on a warm dish.

4 To eat: place 2–3 tablespoons of the mixture onto a lettuce leaf and roll it up tightly into a parcel. Eat with your fingers and provide finger bowls and paper napkins for your guests.

Minced Meat or Seafood Wrapped in Lettuce

草菇
STRAW MUSHROOMS

(CAOGU) *Volvariella volvacea*

Straw mushrooms are native to China, and are widely cultivated in the southern provinces. They are believed to have been first discovered in the early nineteenth century: there is no record of their existence before then. They were introduced into Southeast Asia by Chinese immigrants, where they are widely grown and canned for the export market.

Threshing rice to leave behind the straw on which the mushrooms are cultivated

HOW IT GROWS

These small mushrooms are commonly grown on beds of rice straw, hence the name. They are fast growing, taking only 4–5 days to mature, and require very little attention. They should be picked twice a day, morning and evening, before the caps open up, and each batch yields at least 5–6 pickings. They thrive in a sub-tropical climate with a high rainfall.

Canned straw mushrooms

APPEARANCE AND TASTE

These small phallic mushrooms range in colour from light brown to dark grey and have a silky surface. They look much more attractive cut in half lengthways (and are much easier to pick up with chopsticks). They have a delicate, slightly sweet flavour, and an interesting texture.

BUYING AND STORING

Canned straw mushrooms are widely available in Oriental stores in the West. Once opened, they should be drained and rinsed before use. Any unused mushrooms can be stored in fresh water in the refrigerator where they will keep in good condition for up to a week.

CULINARY USES

Straw mushrooms are used mostly in stir-fried dishes, and also in soups. Straw Mushroom Soy Sauce makes a very good seasoning for stews, soups and gravy. Dried straw mushrooms are sometimes available; they have a much more powerful aroma than ordinary dried Chinese mushrooms.

STIR-FRIED THREE MUSHROOMS

The Chinese title *sanxian* (three delicacies) normally refers to three types of 'meat' (chicken, pork and prawns), or seafood (prawns, scallops and squid). In the case of vegetarian dishes, it usually indicates three different kinds of mushroom, fungi being the most delicious of all vegetables. In this recipe, as well as the three kinds of mushroom, we also have black fungus for contrasting texture and mange-tout for colour.

Serves 4–6
Preparation time 10–15 minutes, plus soaking time
Cooking time 4–5 minutes

6–8 medium-sized dried Chinese mushrooms, soaked
350g (12oz) canned straw mushrooms, drained
100g (4oz) fresh button mushrooms (champignons)
8g (¼oz) dried black fungus, soaked
65g (2oz) mange-tout
3 tablespoons oil
½ teaspoon salt
½ teaspoon sugar
1 tablespoon light soy
½ teaspoon sesame oil

1 Squeeze dry the soaked mushrooms, discard any hard stalks, and cut each one in half. Cut each straw mushroom in half lengthways. Wash the button mushrooms but do not peel, and leave them whole.

2 Rinse the soaked black fungus, discarding any hard roots, and cut any large pieces into smaller ones. Wash, top and tail the mange-tout.

3 Heat the oil in a preheated wok. Stir-fry the three mushrooms for 1 minute, then add the black fungus and mange-tout, and stir-fry for about 2 minutes. Add the salt and sugar, stir for 30 seconds or so, then add the soy. Blend well and cook for 1 more minute. Sprinkle on the sesame oil and serve hot.

Chinese Leaf and Straw Mushrooms in White Sauce

I learnt this very delicate Shangdong dish from my friend Kam-po But, chef of Ken Lo's restaurant, Memories of China, in London. It is quite simple to prepare, and always tastes delicious.

Serves 4–6
Preparation time 10 minutes
Cooking time 4–5 minutes

450g (1lb) Chinese leaf
350g (12oz) canned straw mushrooms, drained
4 tablespoons oil
1 teaspoon salt
1 teaspoon sugar
125ml (4fl oz) milk
Pinch of MSG (optional)
1 tablespoon cornflour paste

1 Cut the Chinese leaf and straw mushrooms in half lengthways.

2 Heat half the oil and stir-fry the Chinese leaf for about 1 minute. Add half the salt and sugar, continue stirring for 2 more minutes, then arrange neatly on one side of a serving platter.

3 Clean the wok and heat the remaining oil. Stir-fry the straw mushrooms with the remaining salt and sugar for 2 minutes. Remove and place next to the Chinese leaf.

4 Heat the milk and MSG. Thicken with the cornflour paste, stir until smooth and pour evenly over the Chinese leaf and straw mushrooms. Serve hot.

Chinese Leaf and Straw Mushrooms in White Sauce

香菇 DRIED MUSHROOMS

(XIANG GU) *Lentinus edodes*

Chinese dried mushrooms are made from fresh black mushrooms cultivated in mountain forests all over southern China. According to a manual on agriculture published in 1313, black mushrooms were first artificially grown by farmers in Zheijiang province during the Song dynasty, over eight hundred years ago. The Japanese variety, known as shiitake mushrooms, go back only three hundred years, though Japan is now the largest producer in the world.

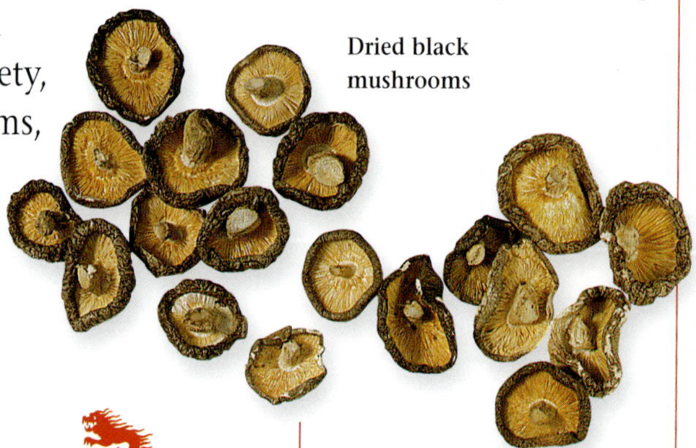

Dried black mushrooms

HOW IT GROWS

The process of growing fresh black mushrooms takes over three years. The trees in which the mushrooms will grow are cut down during August and September and the trunks are covered with branches to stop them drying out in the sun. A year later, a series of shallow cuts are made along the trunks, and the fungi grow naturally in the cuts. Harvesting takes place three years later in the autumn and winter, and usually lasts until spring. A new crop appears 4–6 years after the first crop.

APPEARANCE AND TASTE

There are three types of Chinese dried mushrooms, each with a different name and a price to match. There is *xiang gu* (fragrant mushroom); *dong gu* (winter mushroom), which costs more than ordinary dried mushrooms; and *huagu* (flower mushroom), which can be very expensive. The colour varies from black to brown, and the caps range in diameter from less than 2.5cm (1in) to over 5cm (2in). The cheaper mushrooms have rather thin, flat caps, the more expensive ones have thick, round caps, and the flower mushrooms have a cracked cap like tortoiseshell, hence the name. They all taste fragrant and have a fleshy texture, particularly the thicker ones.

BUYING AND STORING

Usually sold in bags, dried mushrooms can keep for many years if stored in a dark, dry place. Canned fresh shiitake mushrooms are available, but they do not have the same aroma, nor the same flavour or texture.

Young mushroom-sellers

CULINARY USES

Dried black mushrooms are the most important mushrooms used in Chinese cooking. They should be soaked in cold water, covered, for 1–2 hours or overnight. Soaking in hot water takes less time, but you lose much of their characteristic fragrance. Cook them with fish, poultry, meat and vegetables; they can be stir-fried, steamed, braised, or used in soups.

CHICKEN WITH BAMBOO SHOOTS AND MUSHROOMS

One of the most popular dishes in Chinese restaurants in the West, lesser establishments use fresh mushrooms for this dish, which have quite a different flavour. Worse still, most Chinese restaurants in India use canned button mushrooms (*champignons*) from China, known there as Chinese mushrooms, which completely alter the flavour of the dish.

Serves 4
Preparation time 10–15 minutes plus soaking time
Cooking time 4–5 minutes

6–8 dried Chinese mushrooms, soaked
225g (8oz) chicken breast fillet
1 teaspoon salt
1 teaspoon egg white, beaten
2 teaspoons cornflour paste
About 300ml (½ pint) oil
1 spring onion, cut into short sections
A few small pieces fresh ginger
175g (6oz) sliced bamboo shoots, drained and rinsed
½ teaspoons sugar
2 teaspoons rice wine
1 tablespoon soy or oyster sauce
Pinch of MSG (optional)
Few drops sesame oil

1 Squeeze dry the mushrooms and discard any hard stalks before cutting them into halves (or quarters if large).

2 Cut the chicken breast into thin slices, about the size of a postage stamp, and mix with a pinch of the salt, the egg white and cornflour, in that order.

3 Heat the oil in a preheated wok until medium hot. Stir-fry the chicken slices for about 30 seconds or until the colour changes from pink to white, remove quickly with a strainer and drain.

4 Pour off the excess oil, leaving about 1 tablespoon in the wok. Stir-fry the spring onion and ginger for a few seconds until fragrant, then add the mushrooms and bamboo shoots. Stir-fry for 1–1½ minutes, add the remaining salt and sugar and continue stirring for another minute. Add the blanched chicken slices, stir a few times, then add the wine and soy or oyster sauce. Blend well and stir-fry for another minute. Add the MSG, if using, and the sesame oil. Toss to amalgamate, and serve hot.

BRAISED MUSHROOMS WITH BEAN CURD

This is a good example of yin-yang harmony: black mushrooms with white bean curd, the strongly flavoured and the bland, and two contrasting textures. The result is a delicate and delicious dish. It is very refreshing, so a suitable last course at the end of a big, rich meal.

Serves 4–6
Preparation time 10 minutes, plus soaking time
Cooking time 4 minutes

8–12 medium-sized dried Chinese mushrooms, soaked
2 cakes bean curd (tofu p 196)
3 tablespoons oil
1 teaspoon salt
1 teaspoon sugar
2 tablespoons rice wine
½ teaspoon sesame oil
2 teaspoons cornflour paste
1 tablespoon light soy

1 Squeeze dry the soaked mushrooms and discard any hard stalks (reserving the soaking water). Cut each square of bean curd into 16 slices.

2 Heat the oil and stir-fry the mushrooms for about 1 minute. Add about 150ml

(¼ pint) of the mushroom soaking water, bring to the boil and add the bean curd slices and the salt, sugar and wine. Stir very gently, blending everything well. Braise for about 2 minutes, then add the sesame oil, making sure that there is enough liquid to prevent the bean curd sticking to the bottom of the wok.

3 Mix the cornflour paste with the soy and pour it over the bean curd and mushrooms to form a clear, light glaze. Serve immediately.

木耳

DRIED BLACK FUNGUS

(MUER) *Auricularia auricula*

There are several names in English for dried black fungus: wood ear, tree ear and cloud ear. The first two are literal translations of *muer*; 'cloud ear' stems from the fact that the province of Yunnan (literally, South of the Cloud) has a reputation for producing high-quality black fungus, and the Cantonese call all dried black fungi *wanyee* (cloud ear), meaning 'wood ear of Yunnan', irrespective of its origin. It is generally agreed in China that the best black fungus actually comes from Hubei province.

Black fungus growing on bark

HOW IT GROWS

Black fungus has been cultivated in China for a very long time – detailed instructions are given in a sixth-century agricultural encyclopaedia. The process involves cutting down trees such as mulberry, elm and willow, soaking the trunks in water for 5–6 months, piling the trunks in damp, shady woods, and dousing them with rice-washing water several times a day. Fungus may appear the following spring, lasts until early autumn, and continues to appear for 6–7 years.

APPEARANCE AND TASTE

There are more than ten different varieties of black fungus grown throughout China. Only two types seem to be available in the West, of which the most common is the small, shrivelled-up, irregular-shaped one. Dull black, soaking enlarges it greatly and makes it shiny. The other type is known as White-Backed Wood Ear. It is much bigger and thicker with a slightly fuzzy looking, pale coloured back. It is much tougher than the smaller black fungus, which has a pleasant crunchy texture and a mild, subtle flavour.

BUYING AND STORING

Both types are available in plastic bags in Oriental stores. Very light in weight, once soaked, they can weigh up to twenty times more. If you store black fungus in a dry, dark place, it will keep forever. After soaking, it should be kept in the refrigerator in fresh water, where it will stay good for 4–5 days.

MEDICINAL USES

Dried black fungus is rich in protein, calcium, phosphorus, iron and carbohydrates. It can cure haemorrhoids and prevent other haemorrhages. Regular intake of dried black fungus inhibits clotting of the blood, thus minimizing the risk of heart attacks.

CULINARY USES

In China, black fungus is valued for its texture and colour. It forms an essential part of some very popular dishes, such as Hot and Sour Soup (p 123), Mu-Shu Pork (p 37), Stir-fried Liver (see next recipe), and many vegetarian dishes.

Common dried black fungus

STIR-FRIED LIVER

People who do not normally like liver always enjoy this dish when I demonstrate it in my cookery classes. The secret is not to overcook the liver but to retain its delicate texture by quick stir-frying so you have the contrast of crunchy fungus and tender smooth liver.

Serves 4
Preparation time 10–15 minutes plus soaking time
Cooking time 3–4 minutes

25g (1oz) dried black fungus, soaked
225–300g (8–10oz) pigs' liver
3–4 tablespoons oil
About 600ml (1 pint) boiling water
1 tablespoon light soy
1 teaspoon cornflour
2 spring onions, cut into short sections
½ teaspoon salt
Few drops sesame oil

1 Rinse and drain the black fungus, discard any hard roots, and cut the larger pieces into smaller ones.

2 Discarding any white membranes, cut the liver into small slices about 3mm (⅛in) thick. Place in a large bowl.

3 Heat the oil in a preheated wok. While waiting for it to heat up, quickly pour the boiling water over the liver, stirring to keep each piece separate. Drain away the water and mix the liver with the soy and cornflour.

4 Add the liver to the wok with the spring onions. Stir-fry for a few seconds, then add the fungus with the salt. Stir-fry for 1 minute, blend in the sesame oil and serve hot.

BRAISED SLICED FISH IN WINE

The original recipe calls for a flavouring called *hongzao* (red fermented rice wine sediment), which is rarely seen in the West. A combination of rice wine and distilled spirit, widely used by chefs in the West, seems to work well instead.

Serves 4
Preparation time 10–15 minutes plus soaking time
Cooking time 4–5 minutes

15g (½oz) dried black fungus, soaked
450g (1lb) lemon sole or plaice fillet
Pinch of salt
½ egg white, beaten
1 tablespoon cornflour paste
Oil for deep-frying

For the sauce:
1 tablespoon oil
1 teaspoon finely chopped garlic
1 teaspoon salt
2 teaspoons sugar
2 tablespoons rice wine
1 tablespoon Chinese spirit
About 100ml (4fl oz) stock
Pinch of MSG (optional)
½ teaspoon sesame oil
2 teaspoons cornflour paste

1 Rinse and drain the black fungus, discard any hard roots, then cut the larger pieces of fungus into smaller ones so that they are all roughly even in size.

2 Trim off the soft bones along the edges of the fish. Cut the fish into matchbox-size slices and mix with the salt, egg white and cornflour paste.

3 Heat the oil in a preheated wok until it is medium hot. Add the fish piece by piece, stirring very gently to separate and to make sure it does not stick to the bottom of the wok. Cook all together for about 1 minute, remove with a strainer and drain.

4 To make the sauce, wipe clean the wok. Heat the tablespoon of fresh oil and stir-fry the fungus with the garlic for about 1 minute. Add the salt, sugar, wine, spirit and stock. Bring to the boil, then add the fish slices. Blend well and braise for about 2 minutes. Add the MSG (if using) and the sesame oil, and thicken the sauce with the cornflour paste. Serve hot.

Braised Sliced Fish in Wine

銀耳
DRIED WHITE FUNGUS

(YINER) *Tremella fuciformis*

Besides being known as *bai muer* (white wood ear), white fungus is also called *yiner* (silver ear) in Chinese, because of its rarity, the high price it fetches on the market, and its supposed medicinal value.

HOW IT GROWS

White fungus was first discovered in 1832 in Sichuan, where it grew wild on high mountain peaks clouded in mist. Artificial cultivation began in Sichuan in 1894, and white fungus is now cultivated in several mountainous provinces, the best variety coming from Sichuan and Fujian. There is hardly any difference in the methods used to cultivate black and white fungus – both are grown on felled tree trunks. What is different is the environment in which they are grown and the trees used. White fungus does not grow nearly so prolifically as black fungus.

APPEARANCE AND TASTE

If black fungus looks like an individual ear, white fungus resembles a little round ball with curly ears, not unlike a white chrysanthemum or carnation. Its texture and taste are very similar to that of black fungus, though some think white fungus has a sweeter flavour.

BUYING AND STORING

White fungus is always neatly packed in a box with a transparent cover to show off the goods inside. It is not widely available, but you should be able to find it in larger Oriental stores. If stored in a cool, dark, dry place, it should keep for many years.

MEDICINAL USES

White fungus is considered to be an important yin tonic, good for insomnia, lung disease, liver disease, poor appetite, coughs and chronic constipation.

CULINARY USES

Whereas black fungus is used in everyday cooking, white fungus is regarded as a tonic food, so is served only at banquets or on grand occasions, when it is eaten on its own as either a sweet or savoury 'soup' between courses. It also features in a special vegetarian dish which is not meant for everyday consumption.

SILVER WOOD EAR SOUP

This is a very nutritious dish served at banquets as a soup between courses – either between starter and main course, or main course and dessert. The flavour comes from the good quality chicken or meat stock, without which the soup would be very bland.

Serves 4–6
Preparation time 10–15 minutes, plus soaking time
Cooking time 5 minutes

25g (1oz) dried white fungus, soaked
100g (4oz) fresh bean sprouts
50g (2oz) peas
750g (1¼ pints) good stock
Pinch of MSG (optional)
Salt to taste

1 Wash the fungus, drain, and tear into small pieces, discarding any pithy stalks.

2 Wash and rinse the bean sprouts. Do not bother to top and tail each sprout, just get rid of any small bits and husks. Defrost the peas if using frozen ones.

3 Bring the stock to the boil, cook the fungus in it for 1 minute, then add the bean sprouts and peas. Bring back to the boil and season with MSG and salt. Serve hot.

Silver Wood Ear Soup

金針 黃花

TIGER LILY BUDS

(JINZHEN, HUANGHUA)

Lilium tigrinum v. lancifolium

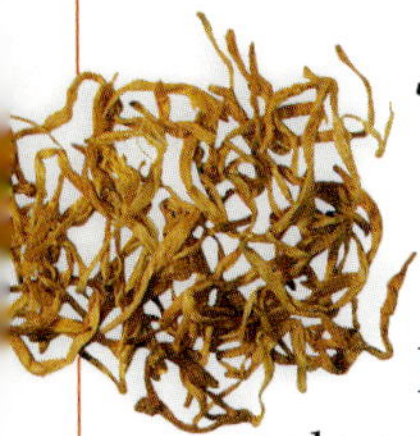

These are dried, unopened tiger lilies. The Chinese names of Golden Needles and Yellow Flowers refer to the golden orange colour of the lilies. They are traditionally used with black fungus for the contrast in colour, texture and flavour.

HOW IT GROWS

Lilies started their life in the wild but are now cultivated. Native to Asia, tiger lilies are grown all over the world as they tolerate almost any soil, and do not need the regular care and attention that even the hardiest vegetable requires. The plants produce an enormous number of buds yet the flowers last only one day, so the Chinese, who never waste anything edible, have learnt to dry the buds for food.

APPEARANCE AND TASTE

The buds dry to a dark brown blushed with gold and are about 7.5–10cm (3–4in) long and 3mm (⅛in) wide (slightly broader at the top). They have a crunchy texture and a mild, sweet taste.

BUYING AND STORING

Dried tiger lily buds are usually sold in a large tangle, bagged in cellophane, and available from most Oriental stores. They will keep forever if stored in an air-tight container, away from strong light, heat and moisture.

MEDICINAL USES

Tiger lily buds are used in concoctions to relieve nervousness, cure insomnia and also to soothe coughs.

Buddha's Delight

CULINARY USES

Like all dried ingredients, tiger lily buds have to be soaked in warm water for 30 minutes, then rinsed in fresh water. The hard ends of the stems need to be snipped off before the buds are used. They add an interesting element to several classic dishes, particularly in vegetarian cooking.

BUDDHA'S DELIGHT

The original recipe calls for eighteen different vegetable ingredients to represent the eighteen Buddhas. It is more common nowadays to use only six or eight items, a mixture of dried and fresh vegetables.

Serves 4–6
Preparation time 15–20 minutes, plus soaking time
Cooking time 6–8 minutes

50g (2oz) dried tiger lily buds, soaked
50g (2oz) dried Chinese mushrooms, soaked
25g (1oz) dried white fungus, soaked
175g (6oz) braised gluten, drained
50g (2oz) deep-fried bean curd (tofu, p 196)
100g (4oz) baby corn cobs
1 medium carrot
50g (2oz) mange-tout
4 tablespoons oil
½ teaspoon salt
½ teaspoon sugar
2 tablespoons soy
1 tablespoon rice wine
3–4 tablespoons vegetarian stock (p 71) or mushroom-soaking water
Pinch of MSG (optional)
½ teaspoon sesame oil

1 Wash all the ingredients that have been soaked. Cut the gluten and bean curd into chunks. Cut the baby corn cobs in half if large, leave them whole if small. Thinly slice the carrot, and top and tail the mange-tout.

2 Heat the oil in a casserole or Chinese sand-pot. Stir-fry the carrot and baby corn cobs for about 1 minute, then add all the dried vegetables with the gluten and bean curd. Continue stirring for 2 minutes. Add the mange-tout, salt and sugar, blend well, and add the soy, wine and stock. Bring to the boil and braise for 2–3 minutes, then add the MSG, if using, and the sesame oil. Serve hot.

腌蛋

PRESERVED EGGS

(YAN DAN)

According to Chinese legend, when the world began the universe was egg-shaped, the yolk being the earth, and the white the heavens. Then Pan-ku, the primal man, separated them and the bright and clear element, yang, became heaven, and dark and murky yin became earth.

To the Chinese, eggs represent fertility. The smooth, round shape of the egg symbolizes good luck and happiness. When a child is born the proud parents often give eggs dyed red as gifts to friends and relatives, for red represents luck and joy.

CULINARY USES

Paradoxically, the Chinese word for egg, *dan*, has impolite connotations. To call someone a 'bad egg', far from being a mild reproof, is a terrible insult. This may be the reason why most restaurants in China take great care to give their egg dishes fancy names, such as Mu-shu Pork and Fu-yung. Although both ducks and hens eggs are preserved in China, far more ducks eggs are used for this purpose, simply because they are larger than hens eggs, their shells are thicker and more robust and, most importantly, ducks eggs are oilier and have a stronger flavour.

SALTED EGGS

Traditionally, salted eggs are eaten during the Dragon Boat Festival (see page 28). At other times, salted eggs are served as part of a meal – especially with rice congee (see page 26) for breakfast. Because of the symbolism surrounding eggs, they are used to make certain festive cakes, birthday and wedding cakes, for instance, and Moon Cakes which are eaten during the mid-Autumn Festival. It is possible to make salted eggs at home as it is a fairly simple process. I used to watch my grandmother and nanny making them in China, and I have now unearthed a recipe. It is not worth preserving fewer than 50 or so eggs.

50 ducks eggs
2.25kg (5lb) earth
450g (1lb) salt
Water
Rice husks (you can improvise with straw, grass, or indeed any grain husk)

1 Blend the earth with the salt and enough water to form a smooth paste.

2 Coat the eggs in the paste and then roll them in the husks until they are completely covered.

3 Pack the eggs in a large urn, seal tightly and store in a cool, dark place. They should be ready in 30–40 days.

ONE THOUSAND-YEAR-OLD EGGS

This method of preserving eggs appears in written records dating back to 1633 but it is believed that the Chinese were preserving eggs long before then. The basic method of preparation is similar to that of Salted Eggs with the substitution of wood ash and slaked lime for mud. The eggs are mature and ready for consumption after about 40 days and should be consumed within 2–3 months. One thousand-year-old eggs are usually served just as they come. Just soak the eggs in water to soften the outer coating, then remove the shell and cut each egg into segments. Garnish with soy and sesame oil and serve as an hors d'oeuvre, or use them to make the dish opposite.

One thousand-year-old eggs

Egg seller in the market in Shanghai

Stir-Fried Pine-Flower Eggs

'Pine-flower' is another name for 'one thousand-year-old eggs'. It is an extremely simple dish and one of my favourites.

Serves 4
Preparation time 10 minutes
Cooking time 6–8 minutes

2–3 one thousand-year-old eggs
2 tablespoons vegetable oil
250g (8oz) lean pork, coarsely chopped
1 tablespoon light soy
1 teaspoon dark soy
½ teaspoon sesame oil
Chopped spring onion or parsley to garnish (optional)

1 Remove the coating and the shell of the eggs. Chop the eggs coarsely (if you chop them finely, they may disintegrate).

2 Heat the oil in a preheated wok and stir-fry the pork for 2–3 minutes or until the colour of the meat changes from pink to pale white. Add the chopped eggs and the soy and blend well. Continue stirring for 3–4 minutes more, sprinkle on the sesame oil and serve hot, garnished with the spring onion or parsley.

Drunken Eggs

Drunken Eggs

Here is a method of preserving eggs that you can try at home. They can be stored in the preserving jar for several months.

12 ducks or hens eggs
1 tablespoon salt
1 teaspoon Sichuan peppercorns
About 685ml (24fl oz) distilled or boiled water
150ml (5fl oz) Chinese spirit, such as Mou-tai, or brandy, whisky, rum or vodka

1 Soft boil the eggs (3–4 minutes for hens, 4–5 minutes for ducks). Take care with the timing as the yolks must be neither too soft nor too hard.

2 Dissolve the salt in the distilled or boiled water. (It is very important that the water be bacteria free, because egg shells are porous.) Add the Sichuan peppercorns, then allow the water to cool down before adding the spirit. (Please note that Chinese spirit is 30 percent stronger than Western liquor so adjust the measurements of Western spirit accordingly.)

3 Gently tap the shells of the eggs to crack them, but do not peel. Submerge the eggs in the spirit in a jar or bottle, making sure that every egg is covered by the liquid. Add more spirit if necessary. Seal the jar or bottle well – it must be absolutely air-tight – then leave to stand in a cool, dark place for 7–8 days.

4 To serve, remove the eggs from the liquid, peel off the shell and cut each egg in half or quarters. They are an ideal snack.

Note: The liquid can be re-used

豆腐

BEAN CURD (TOFU)

(DOUFU)

Cakes of bean curd cut from a block

It is believed that bean curd was eaten as early as the eleventh century BC, but we have no written records to confirm this. We do have proof that bean curd was sold at market during the Tang dynasty (618–907), and that it was regarded as a cheap substitute for meat. One possible reason why there was no mention of bean curd any earlier is that the better-off considered it food for the poor, so not worth mentioning in official records.

Right up until the seventeenth century, bean curd was eaten exclusively by the poor until the Qing Emperor Kung Xi (1662–1722) discovered it while visiting Suzhou in Jiangsu province when he ventured out incognito to mingle with the people in the streets. When he returned to Peking, the Emperor ordered the chefs of the Palace kitchen to produce bean curd dishes. Overnight, humble bean curd became nobleman's fare and it is now popular worldwide.

Bean curd is a by-product of soy beans

MANUFACTURE

Bean curd (tofu) is made from soy beans. The plant *(Glycine max.)* is a legume that has been in cultivation in China for thousands of years. Given the resourcefulness of the Chinese, it is not surprising that bean by-products feature strongly in the Chinese diet: soy (sauce) is one, and bean curd is another. Bean curd is one of China's most important innovations in processed food, and is regarded as the country's national dish because of its long-standing popularity, high nutritional value, and the fact that it was invented by the Chinese! Making bean curd is fairly simple, though a little time-consuming: it involves soaking the dried beans (which may be black, yellow, white or green), peeling off the skins, pulverizing the beans with water, filtering out the water-soluble element, boiling the liquid suspension briefly, then adding gypsum which causes the liquid to curdle.

APPEARANCE AND TASTE

Fresh, firm-textured bean curd is off-white in colour. It is entirely tasteless before it is seasoned, and will absorb the flavour of any ingredient with which it is cooked. Japanese 'silky' tofu is not really suitable for Chinese cooking, as it falls apart to the touch.

The Grand Canal in Jiangsu

Bean curd bubbling with other delicacies in a hot-pot, a popular winter dish in northern China

Buying and Storing

Various kinds of fresh bean curd are widely available from Oriental and health food stores, as well as from some supermarkets. Fresh bean curd is usually sold in cakes of about 7.5cm (3in) square and 2.5cm (1in) thick. Bean curd will keep for several days if submerged in water in a container and stored in the refrigerator.

Medicinal Uses

The nutritional benefits of bean curd cannot be exaggerated. It is a good source of vegetable protein, and contains the eight essential amino acids and vitamins A and B. It is free of cholesterol and polysaturates, so ideal for combating heart disease and high blood pressure. It is also extremely easy to digest, so is very good for invalids as well as infants and the elderly.

Culinary Uses

Bean curd can be cooked with any other ingredient and by any method. It can even be eaten raw, with seasonings, of course. I have a book written by the famous Sichuan chef Zhang Desheng, which contains two hundred individual bean curd recipes – not just a series of variations as on some restaurant menus – and he claims that the recipes in his book represent only part of his repertoire! No wonder bean curd is known as the national dish of China. As well as fresh bean curd, there are a number of different kinds of processed bean curd which are covered elsewhere in the book since their uses in Chinese cooking are quite distinct; and of course there is Fermented Bean Curd on p 102.

Sichuan Spicy Bean Curd

Although this Sichuan dish is popular throughout the world, very few people understand its Chinese name, *Ma Po Doufu*, let alone its origin. *Ma po* in Chinese means 'pock-marked wife', referring to the woman who was married to a chef in Chengdu, and who created this dish over a hundred years ago for her husband's modest restaurant. Its reputation spread far and wide, so much so that the couple opened a much grander establishment to accommodate their ever-increasing number of customers.

Serves 4
Preparation time 10–15 minutes
Cooking time 6–8 minutes

2 cakes fresh bean curd
3 tablespoons oil
115g (4oz) coarsely chopped beef (or pork)
Pinch of salt
½ teaspoon chopped garlic
2 teaspoons salted black beans, soaked
1 tablespoon chilli bean paste (toban jiang)
3–4 tablespoons stock
1 leek or 3 spring onions, cut into short sections
1 tablespoon rice wine
2 teaspoons light soy
2 teaspoons cornflour paste
½ teaspoon sesame oil
¼ teaspoon ground Sichuan peppercorns

1 Cut the bean curd into 1cm (½in) square cubes and drop into a pan of boiling water for 2–3 minutes to blanch and harden. Remove and drain.

2 Heat the oil in a preheated wok. Stir-fry the meat for about 1 minute or until the colour changes, and add the salt and garlic. Stir a few times before adding the salted black beans, crushing them with the cooking spoon against the surface of the wok. Add the chilli bean paste, and blend with the meat and crushed black beans. Add the stock, the cubes of blanched bean curd and the leek or spring onions. Bring to the boil and braise gently for 3–4 minutes.

3 Add the wine and soy, thicken the sauce with the cornflour, and garnish with the sesame oil and pepper. Serve hot.

FISH AND BEAN CURD CASSEROLE

Another of my personal favourites, this delicious dish is Chinese health food at its best – low in calories, and very high in protein.

Serves 4–6
Preparation time 15–20 minutes
Cooking time 10–15 minutes

2 cakes fresh bean curd (tofu, p 196)
450g (1lb) firm white fish steak (cod, haddock, monkfish, halibut etc)
1 egg, beaten
2 tablespoons plain flour mixed with 1 tablespoon water
4–5 small dried Chinese mushrooms, soaked
Oil for deep-frying
1 small carrot, thinly sliced
25g (1oz) mange-tout, topped and tailed
½ teaspoon salt
½ teaspoon sugar
1 tablespoon rice wine
2 tablespoons light soy
4–5 small slices fresh ginger
2 spring onions, cut into short sections
About 300ml (½ pint) stock
4–6 lettuce or Chinese leaves
Fresh coriander leaves to garnish

1 Cut each cake of bean curd into 16 small pieces. Cut the fish into small chunks, and make a smooth batter with the egg and flour paste. Squeeze dry the mushrooms and discard any hard stalks.

2 Heat the oil in a preheated wok and deep-fry the bean curd pieces for 2–3 minutes. Remove and drain. Coat each piece of fish with the egg and flour batter, drop into the oil one by one, and deep-fry for 2–3 minutes, or until golden. Remove and drain.

Bean curd sold from a street store

3 Pour off the excess oil, leaving about 1 tablespoon in the wok. Stir-fry the carrot, mange-tout and mushrooms for about 1 minute, then add the bean curd and fish pieces with the seasonings. Blend well and add the stock. Bring to the boil.

4 Line a casserole or Chinese sand-pot with the lettuce or Chinese leaf, transfer the entire contents of the wok to the casserole and bring back to the boil. Reduce the heat and braise, covered, for 5–6 minutes. Serve hot, garnished with fresh coriander leaves.

STIR-FRIED PRAWNS WITH BEAN CURD

This is a wonderfully delicate dish – dare I declare it to be another favourite of mine? You may become a little bit tired of my favourites, but you must understand that I just love seafood, and after I left China, I was deprived of fresh bean curd for more than ten years, so any dish that contains bean curd, particularly with seafood, I just cannot resist.

Serves 4
Preparation time 10–15 minutes
Cooking time 8–10 minutes

115–170g (4–6oz) peeled prawns, preferably uncooked
1 teaspoon salt
1 tablespoon egg white, beaten
2 teaspoons cornflour paste
2 cakes bean curd (tofu p 196)
About 600ml (1 pint) oil
25g (1oz) cooked pork, sliced
25g (1oz) sliced bamboo shoots, drained and rinsed
25g (1oz) green peas
1 tablespoon rice wine
½ teaspoon chopped fresh ginger
2 tablespoons chopped spring onions
3–4 tablespoons stock
2 tablespoons soy or oyster sauce
½ teaspoon sesame oil

1 Clean the prawns well, and mix with a pinch of salt, the egg white and cornflour paste. Cut each cake of bean curd into 16 pieces.

2 Heat the oil in a preheated wok until moderately hot. Stir-fry the prawns for about 30 seconds, or until the colour changes. As soon as it does so, quickly scoop out the prawns and drain.

3 Wait for the oil to get really hot, then deep-fry the bean curd pieces for 2–3 minutes or until golden. Remove and drain.

4 Pour off excess oil, leaving about 1 tablespoon in the wok. Stir-fry the pork, peas and bamboo shoots for 1 minute, then add the prawns, bean curd, and the remaining salt and wine. Blend well and add the ginger, spring onions and stock. Bring to the boil and braise for about 2 minutes. Add the soy or oyster sauce and sesame oil. Toss and serve hot.

Stuffed Bean Curd

A Cantonese speciality, stuffed bean curd dishes are very popular with the Hakka people, which suggests that this method of cooking originated in the Yangtze River Delta. There are a number of variations on the stuffing, some very simple and some quite elaborate. I've chosen one which is halfway between, but good results are easily achieved at home.

Serves 4–6
Preparation time 15–20 minutes
Cooking time 15–20 minutes

4 cakes fresh bean curd (tofu, p 196)
600ml (1 pint) salted boiling water
Lettuce or Chinese leaf
3 tablespoons oil
4–6 tablespoons stock
2 tablespoons oyster sauce
2 spring onions, chopped

For the stuffing:
2–3 soaked Chinese mushrooms, finely chopped
115g (4oz) minced pork
115g (4oz) minced prawns
¼ teaspoon salt
1 egg white, beaten
1 tablespoon rice wine
1 tablespoon light soy
2 teaspoons cornflour paste

1 Cut each cake of bean curd into 4 triangular pieces. Parboil in the salted boiling water for 2–3 minutes to harden, then remove and drain.

2 Blanch the lettuce or Chinese leaf in the same water, and remove and drain. Place on a serving plate.

3 Make the stuffing by blending all the ingredients together. Cut a slit in each bean curd triangle and fill with the stuffing.

4 Heat the oil and fry the stuffed bean curd for about 2 minutes on each side or until golden on both sides. Add the stock and oyster sauce, bring to the boil and braise for 8–10 minutes, turning once or twice. When the sauce is almost completely absorbed, garnish with spring onions and serve hot on a bed of lettuce or Chinese leaf.

油炸豆腐

DEEP-FRIED BEAN CURD

(YOUZHA DOUFU)

Youzha doufu is fresh bean curd cut into small cubes, or large squares or triangles, then deep-fried in vegetable oil.

APPEARANCE AND TASTE

The outer surface is golden-brown, the inside white and porous, as the curd puffs up during cooking. This gives the fried bean curd an interesting texture: slightly crispy outside, and soft inside.

Deep-frying bean curd

BUYING AND STORING

Deep-fried bean curd is available in small packets from Oriental stores. The packets normally carry a 'use by' date, and will keep much longer than uncooked, fresh bean curd. It can be stored in the freezer for up to a year or more.

CULINARY USES

Use fried bean curd in soups, stews, casseroles or braised dishes, or stuff the triangles with minced pork, chicken, fish or prawns. In order to remove excess oil, soak it in boiling water for a few minutes, then drain before using.

DEEP-FRIED BEAN CURD AND FUNGUS SOUP

This delicious soup is simplicity itself. Use good stock if possible or add a dash of MSG. Remember that most commercially made stock cubes already containing MSG.

Serves 4
Preparation time 10 minutes, plus soaking time
Cooking time 4–5 minutes

50g (2oz) deep-fried bean curd
15g (½oz) dried black fungus, soaked
50g (2oz) fresh white mushrooms
600ml (1 pint) good stock or water
2 tablespoons light soy
1 spring onion, finely chopped
½ teaspoon sesame oil

1 Cut each piece of deep-fried bean curd in half. Rinse clean the soaked fungus, discarding any hard stems, and cut into small pieces. Wash but do not peel the fresh mushrooms, and thinly slice.

2 Bring the stock or water to the boil, add the vegetables and bring back to the boil. Add the soy and cook for about 2 minutes. Garnish with the spring onion and sesame oil. Serve hot.

Deep-Fried Bean Curd and Fungus Soup

豆腐干

PRESSED BEAN CURD

(DOUFU GAN)

Doufu gan is fresh bean curd which has been pressed until almost all the liquid has been squeezed out (the Chinese name means 'dry bean curd') and the bean curd has been reduced by about a third or more. It is then seasoned with soy and a little five-spice, or star anise or cinnamon.

APPEARANCE AND TASTE

It is dark brown with a texture rather like processed soft cheese.

BUYING AND STORING

Pressed bean curd is usually sold in sealed plastic bags containing 6–8 squares. It is not that easy to find in Britain; I believe it is much more widely available in the USA. It will keep for a week or more in the refrigerator, and of course it can be frozen, in which state it will remain good for many, many months, if not years.

CULINARY USES

Pressed bean curd is often thinly shredded or sliced for cooking. It lends an interesting texture and flavour to both vegetarian and non-vegetarian dishes and is a hallmark of substantial yet unfussy food.

DICED PORK WITH PRESSED BEAN CURD AND BAMBOO SHOOTS

After the Second World War, I was a weekly border at an American missionary school in Nanchang for a year, and the food there was fairly meagre. Fortunately, I was able to go home every weekend for some slap-up meals, and I would take back to the school a supply of dishes my nanny had specially prepared for me to keep me going during the week. One of my favourites was this diced pork and vegetable concoction. I searched high and low for the recipe, but to no avail, so I have re-created this from memory. I hope you will enjoy it as much as I do.

Serves 4–6
Preparation time 15 minutes, plus mushroom soaking time
Cooking time 4–5 minutes

115g (4oz) lean pork
4–6 dried Chinese mushrooms, soaked
2 cakes pressed bean curd
50g (2oz) winter bamboo shoots
50g (2oz) Preserved Vegetables (p 184)
3 tablespoons oil
½ teaspoon salt
½ teaspoon sugar
1 tablespoon chopped spring onions
1 tablespoon light soy

1 Cut the pork into 1cm (½in) cubes. Squeeze dry the mushrooms, discarding any hard stalks, and cut into small cubes about the same size as the pork. Cut the pressed bean curd and bamboo shoots into similar sized cubes. Coarsely chop the preserved vegetables.

2 Heat the oil and stir-fry the pork cubes for about 1 minute until they change colour. Add all the vegetables, blend well and add the salt, sugar and spring onions. Stir-fry for about 2 minutes, add the soy and cook for another minute. Serve hot or cold.

A simple meal eaten outdoors on the Tibetan plateau

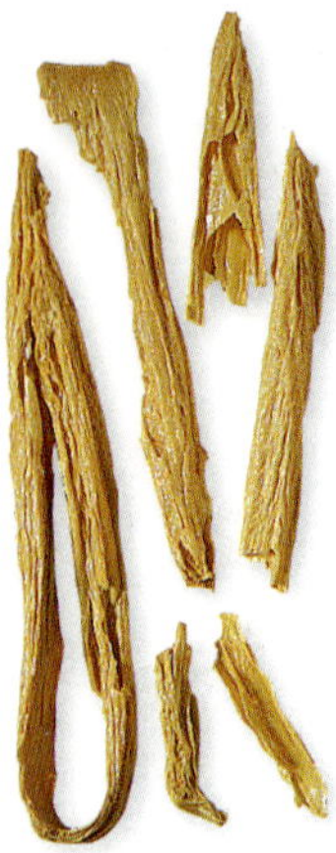

腐竹腐皮

DRIED BEAN CURD SKINS

(FUZHU, FUPI)

Dried bean curd sticks

Dried bean curd skins are made from dried soya bean milk. There are two different kinds: one is a thin flat sheet, the other is rolled into a stick. Both need soaking before use, and sticks take much longer – several hours or overnight.

Dried bean curd skins

MANUFACTURE

As a child, I used to be fascinated watching bean curd skins being made. Soya bean milk is gently brought to the boil in a large pot. When a thin layer of skin has formed on the surface, it is skimmed off with a thin stick, and hung up to dry – this is the flat sheet form. To make bean curd sticks, the skin is rolled into a stick while still soft and wet, then dried. It was always made to look very easy, but I am sure it requires great skill to peel off the skin from boiling milk with one swoop, at the same time keeping an eye on the fire, which has to stay at a constantly low heat.

APPEARANCE AND TASTE

Dried bean curd skin is yellowish and rather wrinkled. Like bean curd itself, the dried skin is tasteless, but it is excellent at absorbing other flavours when cooked with strong-tasting ingredients.

BUYING AND STORING

Both sheets and sticks are sold in packets, and are available from Oriental stores. Because dried bean curd is very brittle, it often breaks into small bits, so choose your packets carefully. It will keep forever if stored in a cool, dry, dark place.

A Buddhist monastery on the banks of the Yangtze River

CULINARY USES

Dried soyabean sticks are a tasty source of protein in the type of vegetarian diet followed by Buddhists. They are also often cooked with meat in casseroles and stews. The sheets are often used in soups, stir-fried dishes, and to wrap other ingredients.

BEAN CURD SKIN AND ASPARAGUS SOUP

This most delicious soup is extremely easy to make, provided you use good stock. However, if you do not happen to have any stock to hand, plain water with a dash of MSG will work wonders.

Serves 4
Preparation time 6–8 minutes plus soaking time
Cooking time 4–5 minutes

15g (½oz) dried bean curd skin, soaked
115g (4oz) fresh asparagus
600ml (1 pint) stock (p 71)
½ teaspoon salt
1 tablespoon light soy
½ teaspoon sesame oil
Salt and pepper to taste

1 Remove the soaked bean curd skins from the water, and cut into small pieces. Cut the asparagus diagonally into small pieces.

2 Bring the stock to the boil with the salt and add the bean curd skins and asparagus. Bring back to the boil and simmer for 2 minutes. Add the soy and sesame oil, adjust the seasoning and serve hot.

Vegetarian Bean Curd Skin Roll

This is the ubiquitous spring roll with a difference: instead of skins made from wheaten flour, sheets of dried bean curd are used for wrapping the filling, which is almost the same as for ordinary spring rolls.

Makes 12 rolls
Preparation time 45–50 minutes plus cooling time
Cooking time 8 minutes

6 dried Chinese mushrooms, soaked
115g (4oz) sliced bamboo shoots, drained and rinsed
1 cake pressed bean curd (tofu, p 201)
1 medium carrot
225g (8oz) fresh bean sprouts
3 tablespoons oil
½ teaspoon salt
½ teaspoon sugar
2–3 spring onions, thinly shredded
1 tablespoon light soy
Pinch of MSG (optional)
12 sheets soft bean curd skins
1 tablespoon flour paste
Oil for deep-frying

1 Squeeze the mushrooms dry, discarding any hard stalks, and thinly shred them. Thinly shred the bamboo shoots, pressed bean curd and carrot. Wash the bean sprouts, discarding any bits and husks, and drain.

2 Heat the oil and stir-fry all the vegetables for about 1 minute. Add the salt and sugar, continue stirring for another minute, then add the spring onions and soy. Blend well and add the MSG. Remove, drain off excess liquid, and leave to cool.

3 Peeling off one bean curd skin at a time, place about 2 tablespoons of the filling in the centre of each sheet, and fold to make a neat parcel (see p 38 for details). Use the flour paste along the edges to seal the flap firmly.

4 To cook: deep-fry the rolls in batches for 3–4 minutes until golden. Bean curd rolls will not become as crispy as spring rolls, but will still taste most delicious. No dipping sauce should be necessary.

冻粉

AGAR-AGAR

(DONGFEN) *Gellidium amausii*

Not many people are aware that this is the real seaweed. Agar-agar is the gelatinous substance obtained from the seaweed known as *shihua cai* (rock-flower vegetable); another name for agar-agar is *yang cai* (ocean vegetable). Agar-agar should not be confused with isinglass, which is made from the swim bladder of fish, so is not suitable for vegetarians.

MANUFACTURE

The making of agar-agar from seaweed is not simple. It involves first washing the seaweed in fresh water; then drying it in the sun for about 20 days, during which time it is doused with water four times a day and turned over every 4–5 days; crushing the seaweed with water and drying it in the sun for another ten days; boiling the crushed seaweed with more water until it has completely dissolved; turning off the heat and leaving it for six hours to cool in the pot and set; then cutting the jelly into thin strips and drying it in the sun for 10–15 days. Agar-agar is the end product.

APPEARANCE AND TASTE

Agar-agar looks like transparent strips of flat noodles. It weighs almost nothing and is completely tasteless!

BUYING AND STORING

Agar-agar is sold in small bundles packed in cellophane. The Japanese name for it is *kanten*, and it takes the form of flat sheets – both are available from Oriental stores. Agar-agar will keep forever if stored in a cool, dry place.

CULINARY USES

After being soaked in warm water until soft, agar-agar can be served with a dressing as an hors d'oeuvre – it has a very pleasant texture. When dissolved in boiling water, it sets solid like jelly, so it is often used as a gelatine.

Collecting seaweed in North-east China to make agar-agar

AGAR-AGAR WITH SHREDDED CHICKEN

This is a more elaborate version of Shredded Chicken in Mustard Sauce on p 121 but is much simpler to prepare, needing hardly any culinary skill at all. It looks most impressive as well as being absolutely delicious to eat.

Serves 4–6
Preparation time 10–15 minutes plus soaking time

About 25g (1oz) agar-agar
2 tablespoons mustard powder
175g (6oz) cooked chicken meat (boiled or roasted)
115g (4oz) honey-roasted ham
½ cucumber
1 tablespoon light soy
1 tablespoon rice vinegar
1 teaspoon sugar
1 tablespoon sesame oil

1 Soak the agar-agar in lukewarm water to soften (about 20–25 minutes). Mix the mustard powder with cold water to make a smooth paste and let it stand for 25–30 minutes for the flavour to mellow.

2 Drain and dry the agar-agar, separate the strips and cut into matchstick-sized lengths. Thinly shred the chicken meat, ham and cucumber (unpeeled but de-seeded) into strips the same size.

3 Arrange all the ingredients neatly in separate layers on a serving plate: it is attractive to make a pyramid by piling the cucumber shreds on a bed of agar-agar then placing the chicken and ham on top.

4 Blend the mustard paste with the soy, vinegar, sugar and sesame oil to make a dressing. Pour it evenly over the salad. Bring it to the table and mix the dressing with the salad just before serving.

ALMOND FLOAT

There is no bean curd in this dish: although you may find it listed in Chinese menus with *doufu* in its title. This is because when the dissolved agar-agar sets like a white jelly, it resembles soft bean curd. It is a most refreshing dessert after a rich meal. In China it is often served as an 'intermission' course at big banquets to clear the palate, rather like sorbets in the West.

Serves 4–6
Preparation and cooking time about 20 minutes plus cooling time

About 6g (¼oz) agar-agar
300ml (½ pint) water
4 tablespoons sugar
300ml (½ pint) milk
1 teaspoon almond essence
1 small can of mixed fruit cocktail with syrup

1 Slowly dissolve the agar-agar in the water over a very low heat. You will need a lot of patience as it may take up to 10 minutes; you must ensure that the agar-agar is completely dissolved and that there are no tiny hard bits.

2 In a separate pan, dissolve the sugar with the milk and almond essence. Mix with the agar-agar solution, blend well and pour into a large serving bowl. When cool, refrigerate for 3–4 hours or overnight, to chill and set.

3 To serve: cut the curd into sugar-lump sized cubes. Pour the fruit cocktail and syrup over it, and serve in individual bowls.

Almond Float

魚松

GROUND FRIED FISH

(YU SONG)

The Chinese name for this product is in effect untranslatable: *yu* means fish, while *song* means 'dried meat floss' or 'dried ground meat'. Ground fried fish is the best we can do – it is more accurate than Chinese restaurants' practice of calling fried shredded cabbage 'seaweed'.

MANUFACTURE

The making of ground fried fish is a fairly long and complex process. The fish, which can be yellow croaker, eel, monkfish or shark, is cleaned (scaled, gutted and the head and tail cut off), steamed, skinned and boned, ground and shredded, dry-fried until semi-dry, cooled, stir-fried with seasonings, and dried for a last time.

APPEARANCE AND TASTE

Ground fried fish is golden brown. It may not look terribly attractive but it tastes wonderful.

BUYING AND STORING

There seems to be only one brand of ground fried fish widely available in the West. It is made in Taiwan, and comes in a vacuum-packed red tin with a plastic cover, so it can be re-sealed after being opened. Consume before the expiry date.

CULINARY USES

Ground fried fish is highly nutritious. It is rich in protein and contains calcium and iron, so is an ideal food for invalids, infants and the elderly. Use it as a topping for soups and congee (rice porridge), or as a dressing for salads (see below).

CRISPY SEAWEED

This very popular dish is served in Chinese restaurants all over the world – except in China itself. Its name is misleading since it is not seaweed that is used, but ordinary cabbage. To be really authentic the dish should be made with dried scallops, but for most people they are too expensive.

Serves 4–6
Preparation time about 10 minutes
Cooking time 5–6 minutes

450g (1lb) spring greens
Oil for deep-frying
1 teaspoon caster sugar
½ teaspoon salt
Pinch of MSG (optional)
1–2 tablespoons ground fried fish

1 Separate the dark green outer leaves (reserving the pale green hearts for another use), and discard any discoloured or withered ones. Clean well with a damp cloth – do not wash in water as the leaves will take too long to dry, and unless they are absolutely dry, they will not be crispy when cooked.

2 Cut out the hard stalks in the centre of each leaf, then pile them on top of each other and roll into a tight bundle. Cut into fine shreds, and spread them out to dry.

3 Heat the oil in a wok or deep-fryer to about 180°C/350°F. Deep-fry the shredded greens in batches, stirring to separate the shreds. Remove with a strainer as soon as they are crispy, before the colour turns from dark green to brown. If they are brown, you have overcooked the 'seaweed'.

4 Drain well and sprinkle the sugar and salt evenly all over. Serve garnished with ground fried fish.

Note: The 'seaweed' will stay crisp for up to 35 minutes. If it goes limp, a few minutes in a medium-hot oven will make it crisp again.

Crispy Seaweed

腌魚咸魚

SALTED FISH

(YAN YU, XIAN YU)

The Chinese preserve both freshwater and saltwater fish with salt. There are three basic methods: preserving in salt, preserving in brine (*yan yu*) and then drying, and lastly simply drying the fish with or without salt (*xian yu*), depending on the species. Almost all fish are preserved – from tiny whitebait to large yellow croakers, as well as shrimps, scallops, oysters, squid and so on.

MANUFACTURE

Since fish preserved with salt or brine is not available in the West, I will only describe the process of drying with salt, which is fairly simple and straightforward. It involves cleaning the fish, salting it (the fish is salted in layers, the amount of salt being one-third of the weight of the fish), pressing it for ten days to extract the excess liquid then washing off the salt and drying the fish.

APPEARANCE AND TASTE

No salted fish is attractive. It has a strong taste, which not everyone likes.

BUYING AND STORING

Not much salted fish is available in the West, and only a small number of Oriental stores sell it. It will keep forever, if stored in a dry and cool place.

CULINARY USES

Because of its saltiness, salted fish is often used as a seasoning in Chinese cooking – it goes particularly well with bland food. It is usually steamed with rice, or used in stews, casseroles or soups.

CASSEROLE OF ASSORTED MEATS

The original version of this protein-rich casserole calls for no fewer than ten different ingredients – a combination of seafood, poultry, meat and vegetables. I have reduced it to just eight different ingredients, because two of the items (salted duck and Chinese bacon) are not readily available in the West. The flavour of the dish has not been compromised.

Serves 4–6
Preparation time 10–15 minutes plus soaking time
Cooking time 15–20 minutes

1 small salted fish, or part of a large one, weighing about 175g (6oz)
6 medium dried Chinese mushrooms, soaked
115g (4oz) Char Siu Pork (p 80)
115g (4oz) Crispy Roast Pork (p 125)
225g (8oz) fresh chicken meat, boned and skinned
Lettuce leaves to line the casserole
50g (2oz) deep-fried bean curd
115g (4oz) sliced bamboo shoots, drained and rinsed
225g (8oz) Chinese bok choy, or the hearts of the spring greens used for Crispy Seaweed (p 206)

Fish stall in Hong Kong

About 300ml (½ pint) stock or water
2 tablespoons light soy
1 tablespoon rice wine
1 teaspoon sugar
2 spring onions, cut into short lengths
Fresh coriander leaves to garnish

1 Wash and rinse the salted fish so it is not too salty, then cut into small pieces. Squeeze dry the mushrooms, discarding any hard stalks, and cut each in half. Cut the Char Siu and Crispy Roast Pork into thin slices. Cut the chicken into small pieces.

2 Line a casserole or large sand-pot with the lettuce leaves, then place the deep-fried bean curd at the bottom. Pile all the other ingredients (except the seasonings) on top of the bean curd, which acts like a sponge, absorbing all the flavours and juices.

3 Add the stock or water with the soy, wine, sugar and spring onions. Bring to the boil, then reduce the heat and simmer, covered, for 15–20 minutes.

4 Give the contents of the casserole a final stir and serve hot, garnished with the coriander leaves.

Note: Char Siu Pork and Crispy Pork are available from Chinese restaurants and take-aways

鮑魚

ABALONE

(BAOYU) *Haliotis gigantea*

Abalone is the Californian name for this shellfish, which has been a delicacy in China since ancient times. It is also known as ormer or sea-ear in Europe, and is called mutton fish in Australia, and paua in New Zealand. Until the outbreak of the Second World War, China imported a lot of abalone from Japan, and as a child, I was always excited by the idea of it, not because of its delicious flavour, which I was too young to appreciate, but because I had seen photographs in a magazine showing Japanese women-divers fishing for abalone wearing nothing more than goggles and a G-string!

How It Grows

Abalone are to be found clinging to the rocks in warm water along the coast of China, and in many other warm-water areas around the world, particularly in the Gulf of California. China has recently started to farm abalone in the warm water off her south coast.

Appearance and Taste

A mollusc with an oval brownish shell, and a fine mother-of-pearl lining, abalone is marketed in dried or canned form in China, so the general public has no idea what fresh abalone looks like. The edible part of the abalone is the central muscle in the shell, a broad foot with which it clings to rocks; it resembles a very large scallop. It has a very delicate texture and flavour, subtly sweet, not dissimilar to cuttlefish, but much more tender.

Buying and Storing

Occasionally, abalone is available fresh, but normally one buys it canned (the Mexican brands are best, but quite expensive; restaurants generally use the cheaper Australian brands). Do not bother with dried abalone: it takes more than 24 hours to prepare.

Medicinal Uses

Abalone is very nutritious: its meat is over forty percent protein and less than one percent fat. The shell is used for curing hypertension and eye diseases.

The blue-green abalone shell has an iridescent sheen similar to that of mother of pearl

Culinary Uses

Abalone is very versatile. It can be served cold as a starter, briefly poached in soup, and stir-fried or braised with other ingredients. Canned abalone is pre-cooked, so need only be warmed through; do not overcook fresh abalone as it will become tough and rubbery.

Braised Abalone with Asparagus

Since dried abalone takes not hours but days to prepare, it is quite acceptable to buy canned abalone which comes ready prepared and pre-cooked, so you can use it straight out of the tin – this is what Chinese restaurants use.

Serves 4–6
Preparation time 20–25 minutes
Cooking time 3–4 minutes

425g (15oz) canned abalone
12 quails eggs, cooked and peeled
225g (8oz) asparagus tips
2 tablespoons oil
150ml (¼ pint) good stock
½ teaspoon salt
½ teaspoon sugar
1 tablespoon rice wine
1 tablespoon light soy
2 teaspoons cornflour paste

1 There are usually about six abalone in a can. Cut each into 4 slices crossways, reserving the juice.

2 Hard boil the quails eggs and peel. Cut the asparagus diagonally into short sections.

3 Heat the oil in a preheated wok and stir-fry the asparagus for about 1 minute. Add the stock with the juice from the abalone can, and the salt, sugar, wine and soy. Bring to the boil, then add the quails eggs and abalone slices. Bring back to the boil, and thicken the sauce with the cornflour paste. Serve at once.

Note: Since canned abalone is already cooked, you need only warm it through before serving. Overcooking will ruin the delicate texture.

Braised Abalone with Asparagus

Abalone with Oyster Sauce

If you find Braised Abalone with Asparagus too time-consuming (all that peeling of quails eggs!), then this simple stir-fried dish should appeal to you. The albalone probably taste even better, since oyster sauce lends an extra dimension to the flavours.

Serves 4–6
Preparation time 10–15 minutes plus mushroom soaking time
Cooking time 4 minutes

425g (15oz) canned abalone
6 medium-sized dried Chinese mushrooms, soaked
175g (6oz) winter bamboo shoots, drained and rinsed
3 tablespoons oil
½ teaspoon salt
½ teaspoon sugar
1 tablespoon rice wine
2 tablespoons oyster sauce
2 teaspoons cornflour paste
½ teaspoon sesame oil
Fresh coriander leaves to garnish

1 Drain the abalone, reserving the juice. Cut each abalone at a slant into 6 thin slices. Squeeze dry the mushrooms, discarding any hard stalks, and cut each in half also at a slant. Cut the bamboo shoots into diamond-shaped chunks.

2 Heat the oil in a preheated wok and stir-fry the mushrooms and bamboo shoots for 1 minute. Add the salt, sugar and about 2 tablespoons of the juice from the can. Stir for another minute, then add the abalone with the wine and oyster sauce. Blend well.

3 Thicken the sauce with the cornflour paste. Add the sesame oil, toss and serve hot, garnished with the coriander.

魚翅

SHARK'S FIN

(YUCHI)

Oddities such as shark's fin and bird's nest epitomize Chinese cooking for some Westerners. Why do the Chinese regard these rather flavourless and extremely expensive items as delicacies? It is difficult to explain. Perhaps it is because the Chinese value texture and medicinal properties so highly.

Sharks were being made into relish as far back as the Tang dynasty (618–907), and shark's fin became popular in the early part of the Song dynasty (960–1127).

Pre-prepared shark's fin

MANUFACTURE

There are at least seven or eight different species of sharks caught off China's coast, and the fins from the back, underbelly and tail are all processed for the table. The season for curing runs from spring to summer: the fins from the various parts of the body are cut off and soaked in fresh water for a day to clean off the blood, then washed, and dried in the sun. Simple, compared with the cooking preparation...

APPEARANCE AND TASTE

The colour, shape, and quality of fins differ according to the different species of shark. Whether there is any difference in taste is arguable: connoisseurs insist that there is, as well as a great difference in texture. This seems ridiculous to me – most people would agree that the fin itself is quite tasteless and the differences in texture negligible.

Grey reef shark

BUYING AND STORING

Dried shark's fin is available in most Oriental stores, usually under lock and key because of its high price. It will keep forever in its dry form.

CULINARY USES

Shark's fin is extremely nutritious. It is over eighty percent protein, and has only a trace of fat; it also contains calcium and phosphorus. But its nutritional value is not the main reason for the Chinese eating it – there are much cheaper and simpler ways of obtaining protein. The answer must surely lie in its rarity and the prestige attached to it.

PREPARATION OF SHARK'S FIN

1 Soak in cold water for 3 days to soften.

2 Simmer for 4–5 hours until the sandy skin comes off easily, and the decayed bone hidden in the meat at the top of the fin can be removed. Do not boil fast. Change the water every 15 minutes during the first hour and every 30 minutes during subsequent hours. The transparent fin will gradually reveal itself and curl from being triangular to become crescent-shaped.

3 Rinse in cold water and scrub off any remaining skin and decayed bone. Simmer the cleaned fins with two slices of fresh ginger, 2–3 spring onions and 3 tablespoons of rice wine for 45 minutes.

BRAISED SHARK'S FIN

I am including these two shark's fin recipes purely for academic interest. This is the more elaborate recipe, but it makes a more interesting soup and also has a much richer flavour, so if you've got the time, why not have a go!

Serves 4–6
Preparation time 7–8 hours plus soaking and cleaning time
Cooking time about 1 hour

350g (12oz) prepared shark's fin
600ml (1 pint) stock

1 tablespoon finely chopped spring onions
1 tablespoon finely chopped fresh ginger
3 tablespoons rice wine
450g (1lb) chicken meat, cubed
225g (8oz) duck breast meat, cubed
115g (4oz) ham, chopped
2 tablespoons oil
About 300g (10oz) seasonal green vegetable (broccoli, mange-tout (snow peas), asparagus etc)
50g (2oz) sliced bamboo shoots, drained and rinsed
50g (2oz) minced chicken breast
1 teaspoon salt
1 tablespoon dark soy
2 teaspoons cornflour paste

1 Place the prepared shark's fin in a pot. Add the stock, about half the spring onions and ginger, and 1 tablespoon of the rice wine. Bring to the boil and simmer for 1 hour. Remove the shark's fin and discard the cooking liquid.

2 Place the shark's fin with the chicken, duck, ham, the remaining spring onions and ginger, and another tablespoon of rice wine in a pot. Add enough water to cover, bring to the boil, then reduce the heat and simmer gently for 5–6 hours. Remove the shark's fin, chicken, duck and ham from the liquid and place on a serving dish. Reserve the cooking liquid.

3 Slice the greens (except for the mangetout if using). Heat the oil in a wok and stir-fry all the greens with the bamboo shoots and minced chicken for about 2 minutes. Add half the salt and 2–3 tablespoons of the cooking liquid. Keep cooking for another minute and then remove from heat and pour over the shark's fin mixture.

4 Bring about 150ml (¼ pint) of the cooking liquid to the boil. Add the remaining salt and rice wine with the soy, thicken with the cornflour paste, and pour over the shark's fin mixture. Serve hot.

SHARK'S FIN SOUP

For the classic shark's fin recipe you still cannot avoid the preparation time, but the actual cooking is a little less time-consuming.

Serves 4–6
Preparation time about 5–6 hours plus soaking and cleaning time
Cooking time 40 minutes

225g (8oz) prepared shark's fin
450g (1lb) chicken meat, skinned and boned, cut in two pieces
175g (6oz) pork
1 tablespoon rice wine
4–5 spring onions
8 small slices peeled fresh ginger
600ml (1 pint) stock (p 71)
2 tablespoons oil
115g (4oz) crab meat
½ teaspoon salt
¼ teaspoon MSG
1 teaspoon cornflour paste

1 Place the shark's fin in an earthenware bowl. Add half the chicken meat, the pork, 2 teaspoons rice wine, half the spring onions and ginger, and enough water to cover. Steam for 4–5 hours, and check to see that the water does not evaporate. Remove shark's fin and drain. Discard the cooking liquid.

2 Place the shark's fin in a fresh bowl. Add the remaining chicken and spring onions, half the remaining ginger, and about half the stock. Steam for about 30 minutes. Remove the shark's fin from the liquid and strain it, reserving the liquid.

3 Heat the oil in a preheated wok over medium heat. Stir-fry the crab meat for 1 minute, then add the remaining stock, rice wine and ginger, and the salt and MSG. Bring to the boil, then add the shark's fin with the reserved cooking liquid to the wok. Reduce the heat and simmer for about 5 minutes. Thicken the soup with the cornflour paste and serve hot.

Shark's Fin Soup

燕窩

BIRD'S NEST

(YANWO)

Untreated bird's nest

When it comes to strange food, nothing can equal bird's nest, so prized by the Chinese. In a way, one can understand eating such oddities as shark's fin, jellyfish or sea cucumber, for at least they were once alive, but a bird's nest – what a ridiculous idea! However, the nests we eat are not the ordinary kind you find in your garden. The Chinese, with a civilization over four thousand years old, should be credited with better sense than that!

Soaked and prepared bird's nest

Chinese doctor weighing precious ingredients

HOW IT GROWS

The 'nests' are in fact the pre-digested protein from seaweed, shrimps and tiny fish gathered by a kind of petrel which builds its nest with a special gelatinous spit. The birds nest in stupendous caverns along the cliffs of small islands in the South China Sea. The petrels nest in spring and when the young have fledged and gone in summer, the nests are gathered by the local people, an arduous and often dangerous task. The nests are cleaned and dried before sale.

Gathering birds' nests in Gomantong Caves, Borneo

APPEARANCE AND TASTE

Milky white or semi-transparent, bird's nest is about the size of a rice bowl and shaped like one too, though most nests for sale in the West have been processed and packaged, so they are flat like a packet of dried seaweed. Some say bird's nest has a very delicate flavour, others insist it is quite tasteless.

BUYING AND STORING

Because of its rarity and its reputed medicinal properties, bird's nest is extremely expensive, much more so than shark's fin and other Chinese delicacies. It is available from only a limited number of Oriental stores (again under lock and key, like a precious jewel). Store in a cool, dry place, where it should keep forever.

MEDICINAL USES

Bird's nest used to be reserved exclusively for the Emperor as a tonic to restore his virility, since he would have 200–300 concubines. In modern times, bird's nest is prescribed to people who suffer from kidney and blood diseases and as a general pick-me-up.

CULINARY USES

Bird's nest was considered a delicacy several hundred years before shark's fin and is a luxury food served only at special banquets. Its preparation is fairly simple, though it requires a certain amount of patience. Soak the nest in warm water for 3 hours, rinse it in cold water until clean, pick out any feathers and bits and pieces with tweezers, then rinse two to three times more.

BIRD'S NEST IN CHICKEN BROTH

This is one of those expensive delicacies served only at banquets. The preparation and cooking are not as elaborate as for shark's fin, but the cost of the raw material is much higher, which you may find a deterrent.

Serves 4–6
Preparation time 40–45 minutes plus soaking time
Cooking time 6–8 minutes

50g (2oz) prepared bird's nest, soaked
1 teaspoon baking powder or bicarbonate of soda
600ml (1 pint) good stock (p 71)
1 teaspoon ginger juice (p 29)
1 tablespoon rice wine
50g (2oz) crab meat
1 teaspoon salt
½ teaspoon MSG
1 tablespoon minced ham
Fresh coriander leaves

1 Wash clean the soaked bird's nest, removing any feathers. Dissolve the baking powder or bicarbonate of soda in a bowl of hot water, add the bird's nest, cover tightly, and let stand for 5 minutes, by which time the nest will have swelled up quite considerably. Drain and rinse under running cold water. Dry well.

2 Bring the stock to the boil. Add 1 teaspoon of ginger juice, wine, crab meat and salt, and bring back to the boil. Add the bird's nest, reduce the heat and simmer for 5–6 minutes, before adding the MSG. Serve hot, garnished with the minced ham and a handful of fresh coriander leaves.

BIRD'S NEST SOUP

When my grandmother was taken ill in the late thirties, her Chinese doctor prescribed bird's nest as part of the remedy and guess who was the lucky fellow who got to taste this extremely expensive delicacy. I was probably very spoiled.

Serves 4
Preparation time 20–25 minutes plus soaking time
Cooking time 5 minutes

50g (2oz) prepared bird's nest, soaked
1 teaspoon baking powder or bicarbonate of soda
225g (8oz) rock sugar
400ml (14fl oz) boiling water
A few candied or crystallized fruits, such as cherries, angelica, oranges or lemons, thinly shredded, to garnish

1 Wash clean the soaked bird's nest, removing any feathers. Dissolve the baking powder or soda in a bowl of hot water, add the bird's nest, cover tightly, and let stand for about 5 minutes or until the nest swells. Drain, rinse well and squeeze dry.

2 Dissolve the rock sugar in the boiling water over low heat.

3 Blanch the nest in fresh boiling water for 5 minutes. Remove and drain. Place the cooked nest in a serving bowl, pour the rock sugar syrup over and garnish with the candied fruits. Serve hot or cold.

Bird's Nest Soup

海参

SEA CUCUMBER (BÊCHE-DE-MER)

(HAISHEN) *Holothurioidea*

A member of the holothurian family, which includes sea anemones and sea urchins, sea cucumber is also known by the rather off-putting name of 'sea slug'. Another Chinese delicacy, it is my personal favourite. It may, like shark's fin and bird's nest, be a tasteless 'texture' food but the same can be said about bean curd and dried black fungus, which also have to be cooked with other ingredients. They are all worthwhile foods – the high prices demanded for some are questionable, however.

MANUFACTURE

There are about twelve different species of sea cucumber to be found along China's coastline, the majority of them caught off the southern provinces of Guangxi and Guangdong (Canton) during all but the summer months. Once the catch has been brought ashore, the sea cucumber is gently boiled in salted water for 30 minutes, then cooled and marinated with salt in a sealed urn for two weeks. It is boiled in salted water for a second time, then mixed with charcoal ashes before being put to dry in the sun in short bursts every 2–3 days. After 3–4 days in the sun, it is considered sufficiently dry.

APPEARANCE AND TASTE

This roughly sausage-shaped creature has a dark grey coating, which becomes light brown after soaking. It has a very interesting texture which absorbs the flavour of the ingredients with which it is cooked.

BUYING AND STORING

Sea cucumber is always sold in dried form, and because of the high cost, is available only from certain Oriental stores, where it is usually kept under lock and key. It should keep forever if stored in a cool, dry place.

CULINARY USES

Dried sea cucumber is more than 75 percent protein with just over one percent fat, so it is highly nutritious. Unlike shark's fin and bird's nest, which are only served at banquets or other special occasions, sea cucumber, while not an everyday dish, is eaten much more frequently. It has to be first washed and cleaned, then soaked overnight. The next day it should be boiled for 5 minutes and simmered for 4 hours, before being cut into small pieces for cooking.

JADE-PEARL SEA CUCUMBER

This is another one of those special dishes not meant for an everyday meal. It is simpler than Happy Family to prepare, but tastes less interesting. It is worth giving it a go, if only to discover the true flavour of sea cucumber.

Serves 4–6
Preparation time 25–30 minutes plus soaking time
Cooking time 15–20 minutes

1 medium-sized sea cucumber, soaked
2 tablespoons lard
1 tablespoon chopped spring onions
1 teaspoon chopped fresh ginger
600ml (1 pint) good stock
12 quails eggs
1 teaspoon salt
1 tablespoon light soy
1 tablespoon rice wine
1 teaspoon sugar
½ teaspoon MSG
1 tablespoon cornflour paste
½ teaspoon sesame oil

1 Clean the soaked sea cucumber and cut into thick slices crossways. Heat the lard and stir-fry the sea cucumber slices with the spring onions and ginger for about 1 minute. Add about 300ml (½ pint) of the stock, bring to the boil and simmer gently for 10–12 minutes.

Many foods are preserved in the salt from China's inland salt lakes

2 Hard boil the quails eggs for 5 minutes or so, and soak them in cold water for 2–3 minutes before peeling.

3 Drain off and discard the liquid in which the sea cucumber has been simmering. Add about 150ml (¼ pint) fresh stock, ½ teaspoon salt, the soy, wine, sugar and half the MSG. Bring to the boil, then reduce the heat and braise for 2–3 minutes. Thicken the sauce with half the cornflour paste, sprinkle on the sesame oil and pour the sea cucumber with the sauce into a deep serving dish.

4 Place the peeled quails eggs in a pot and add the remaining stock, salt and MSG. Bring to the boil and thicken the liquid with the remaining cornflour. Arrange the eggs around the sea cucumber and pour the sauce over them. Serve hot.

Happy Family

This is a superior version of chop suey: an assortment of meats and seafood for a grand occasion, such as a special birthday or family New Year dinners. There is no fixed list of ingredients for this dish, apart from the sea cucumber: other items are selected for contrast in colour, flavour and texture.

Serves 4–6
Preparation time 35–40 minutes, plus soaking time
Cooking time 6–8 minutes

1 small sea cucumber, soaked
50g (2oz) fish maw, soaked (see p 217)
6 medium-sized dried Chinese mushrooms, soaked
115g (4oz) squid, cleaned
1 pig's kidney
115g (4oz) Char Siu Pork (p 80)
115g (4oz) cooked chicken meat
50g (2oz) cooked ham
3–4 tablespoons oil
115g (4oz) sliced bamboo shoots, drained and rinsed
50g (2oz) mange-tout (snow peas), topped and tailed
1 teaspoon salt
1 tablespoon rice wine
2 tablespoons soy
About 300ml (½ pint) stock
1 tablespoon cornflour paste
½ teaspoon sesame oil

1 Clean the soaked sea cucumber and cut it diagonally into thin slices. Squeeze dry the soaked fish maw and cut into small pieces about the same size as the sea cucumber. Likewise, squeeze dry the mushrooms, and cut each one in half on a slant. Score the inside of the squid in a diagonal criss-cross pattern, then cut it into small pieces as described on p 174.

2 Split the kidney in half lengthways and discard the fat and white parts in the middle. Score the surface of the kidney in a criss-cross pattern, then cut it into small pieces. Cut the pork, chicken and ham into thin slices.

3 Heat the oil and stir-fry the squid and kidney for 1 minute or until the pieces curl up and the criss-cross pattern opens up. Add the other ingredients with the salt, wine and soy and blend well. Add the stock, bring to the boil and braise for 4–5 minutes. Thicken the sauce with the cornflour paste and sprinkle on the sesame oil. Serve hot.

Happy Family

海蜇

DRIED JELLYFISH

(HAIZHE) *Rhopilema esculenta*

Jellyfish are semi-transparent with gelatinous, umbrella-shaped bodies and trailing tentacles; their heads are very similar to those of cuttlefish and squid. Jellyfish is never eaten fresh but only after it has been processed. The body and head are dried separately, and I do not recall ever having eaten the head.

MANUFACTURE

After the body and head have been separated, they are cleaned and salted with bicarbonate of soda for an initial period of 24 hours. This process is repeated twice, for seven days each time, and then the jellyfish is dried for three days.

APPEARANCE AND TASTE

Like most processed foods, dried jellyfish does not look very appealing. It is entirely tasteless, but has a very interesting texture, quite crunchy and chewy.

Soaked jellyfish

The waters around Hainan island are often fished for jellyfish and other sea delicacies

BUYING AND STORING

Only the bodies of dried jellyfish are available from Oriental stores in the West. I have no idea what happens to the heads – maybe the mere sight of them would scare the average Westerner to death! As it is salted and preserved, dried jellyfish will keep indefinitely.

CULINARY USES

The main point of eating jellyfish is for its texture, so it is always served with something that offers a contrasting texture. Always eaten cold, it often features in the cold starter course.

JELLYFISH WITH MUSTARD DRESSING

As I said earlier, jellyfish is seldom served on its own but with other cold starters, or as part of a *pinpan*, an assortment of cold cuts served at banquets as hors d'oeuvres.

Serves 4–6
Preparation time 20–25 minutes plus soaking time
Cooking time 3–4 minutes

115g (4oz) dried jellyfish, soaked
About 10cm (4in) cucumber

For the dressing:
1 tablespoon sugar
1 tablespoon light soy
1 tablespoon mustard powder
2 tablespoon rice vinegar
1 teaspoon sesame oil

1 Wash the soaked jellyfish, then drain. Thinly shred into about 10cm (4in) long strips and blanch in a pan of lightly salted water for about 3 minutes. Rinse in cold water, drain well and arrange on a serving plate.

2 Cut the cucumber into 5cm (2in) thin shreds and mix with the jellyfish. Combine the dressing ingredients and pour evenly all over the jellyfish and cucumber. Toss at the table before serving.

魚 肚

FISH MAW

(YUDU)

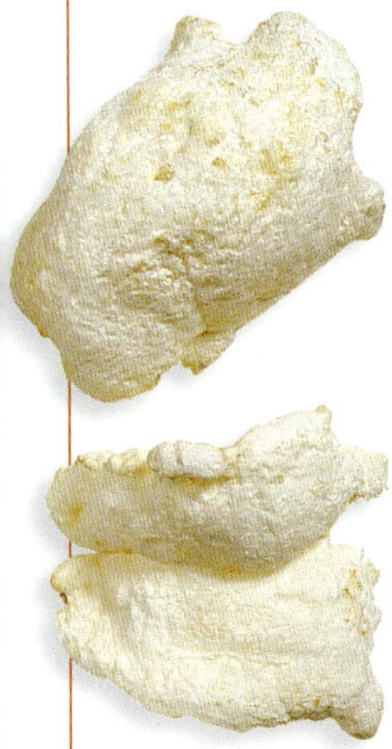

Yet another Chinese delicacy that makes the average Westerner blanch, fish maw is the bladder of certain types of fish, mainly the slate cod croaker (*Miichthys miiuy*) and the larger yellow croaker.

MANUFACTURE

I shall never forget dining at the home of a friend from Singapore, and eating Chinese hot pot with all sorts of strange-looking objects floating in it. Among the guests was a very shy English girl who had rarely encountered Chinese food before (this was back in the sixties) and who asked what the glimmering stuff was. My friend's teenage daughter replied enthusiastically: 'Fish stomach.' Whereupon the poor guest went quite green and quickly dropped the offending object, only to be reassured, 'But it is very fresh stomach.' At that point, the poor girl nearly passed out! Of course, my friend's daughter was quite wrong in saying that it was fresh, for fish maw is always sold processed: first dried in the sun for seven days, then deep-fried.

APPEARANCE AND TASTE

Deep-fried fish maw looks like giant prawn crackers – make sure you do not mistake deep-fried pork skins for fish maw, as they do look similar, and are sometimes passed off as fish maw. People who do not like the idea of eating fish stomach claim that it is tasteless, but I do not agree. I always find it delicious, especially when it is cooked with strongly flavoured food.

BUYING AND STORING

Fish maw is available from most Oriental stores and is usually sold in plastic bags. It becomes rancid after a few months.

CULINARY USES

Fish maw is used mostly in soups and stews, and in the famous hot pot. It should be soaked in hot water for 30 minutes or so, partly to soften it, partly to rid it of excess oil.

CHINESE HOT POT

Also known as 'Mongolian fire pot', a Chinese hot pot is not unlike a fondue. Stock or water is brought to the boil over a charcoal burner and everybody cooks his or her own food in it at the table; or, as in the recipe below, the prepared food is placed in the pot and cooked and seasoned then brought to the table. It is a most attractive and impressive dish with which to delight guests. The ingredients can be varied according to seasonal availability and personal preference. It is common for fish maw and sea cucumber to feature in the same dish, for colour and texture contrast, and because the flavours are complementary.

Serves 6–8
Preparation time 45–50 minutes plus soaking time
Cooking time 4–5 minutes

115g (4oz) fish maw, soaked
115g (4oz) sea cucumber, soaked
175g (6oz) uncooked prawns, peeled
175g (6oz) chicken breast
6–8 medium-sized dried Chinese mushrooms, soaked
175g (6oz) bamboo shoots, drained and rinsed
450g (1lb) Chinese leaf
115g (4oz) mange-tout (snow peas)
450g (1lb) bean threads (vermicelli), soaked
600m (1 pint) stock
1 tablespoon rice wine
1 teaspoon salt
2 tablespoons soy
1 teaspoon sesame oil

1 Squeeze dry the soaked fish maw and cut into small, thin slices. Wash the soaked sea cucumber and cut into 3.5cm (1½in) long strips. Peel and de-vein the prawns. Cut in half lengthways if large, leave whole if small. Cut the chicken into thin slices.

2 Squeeze dry the mushrooms, discarding any hard stalks, and cut each one in half. Cut the bamboo shoots and Chinese leaves into small pieces. Top and tail the mange-tout (snow peas).

3 Place the bean threads in the basin of the hot pot and arrange the fish maw, sea cucumber, prawns, chicken, mushrooms, bamboo shoots, Chinese leaves and mange-tout on top. Pour the stock over, light the charcoal and bring the hot pot to the table. When the liquid starts to boil, add the seasonings. Stir well, cook for about 3–4 minutes, and serve hot.

Chinese Hot Pot

干貝

CONPOY (DRIED SCALLOPS)

(GANBEI)

Conpoy, the Chinese cousin of Western scallops, is always sold dried, and is regarded as yet another delicacy. We have nearly reached the end of special Chinese delicacies now, so please bear with me just a little longer. Be thankful that I have spared you such items as fish lip, duck tongues, turtle skirt, bull's penis and bear's paw!

Dried scallops (left)

Soaked scallops (below)

HOW IT GROWS

In April, July and August, scallops are gathered off China's north coast from the inland sea known as Po Hai. They are cooked in their shells in boiling water, and the flesh is then removed, washed, and dried in the sun.

APPEARANCE AND TASTE

Dried scallops are a shiny, ivory colour, and unlike other dried delicacies, they actually have a strong flavour of their own.

BUYING AND STORING

For some reason, dried scallops are very, very expensive – most restaurants use ground fried fish instead for their 'Crispy Seaweed' (see p 206). They are sold in Oriental stores, usually neatly packed in boxes with transparent covers, and as you would expect with such a costly item, kept under lock and key. Should you decide to fork out half your week's wages to buy a few of these gems, use them quickly in case they deteriorate.

CULINARY USES

Dried scallops have to be soaked in boiling water for at least one hour, then broken up into small bits before being used. Here is a typical dried scallop recipe which is far removed from 'Crispy Seaweed'!

SCALLOPS AND HAM OMELETTE

This is a very special omelette: it is extremely easy to make, but tastes absolutely delicious. I'm afraid there is nothing you can substitute for the dried scallops. The ground fried fish used to garnish Crispy Seaweed just will not do here.

Serves 4
Preparation time 25–30 minutes plus soaking time
Cooking time 3–4 minutes

2 dried scallops, soaked
1 teaspoon chopped spring onion whites
½ teaspoon chopped fresh ginger
6 eggs, beaten
½ teaspoon salt
25g (1oz) ham, chopped
1 tablespoon chopped spring onions
1 tablespoon rice wine
3 tablespoons oil

1 Wash the soaked scallops, place in a bowl with the spring onion whites and chopped ginger, and add enough water to cover. Steam for about 20–25 minutes. Remove the scallops from the liquid and coarsely chop.

2 Mix the chopped scallops with the beaten eggs, salt, ham, spring onions and rice wine, and blend well.

3 Heat the oil in a preheated wok or pan. Pour in the egg mixture and shake the wok or pan. When the eggs are set, turn the omelette over and cook until golden brown. Serve hot.

Sorting scallops

发菜

Hair Moss

(FACAI) *Nostoi commune v. flageliforme*

Black hair moss belongs to the algae family, just like sea moss and seaweed, but it is found on land rather than in water.

How It Grows

Hair moss grows wild on damp rocks or hard ground at high altitude in northwest China. It flourishes during the wet autumn months, and is gathered by local people for processing. Fresh hair moss is dark green in colour, but after being cleaned and dried in the sun, it curls up and turns black.

Appearance and Taste

Ken Hom remarked at a demonstration of Chinese New Year cooking that a dish that contains hair moss looks as if someone has dropped his toupée in it. This is a very accurate description of hair moss: a mass of curly black hair. It is almost tasteless, but has an interesting texture.

Buying and Storing

Dried hair moss packed in transparent bags is available from Oriental stores. It will keep forever if stored in a cool, dry place.

Medicinal Uses

As well as being rich in protein, dried hair moss contains iron, calcium and phosphorus. It is used for curing hypertension and gynaecological problems, and is said to help wounds heal quickly after surgery.

Culinary Uses

Although hair moss is quite popular in north China, its biggest market is in Hong Kong, Macau and Southeast Asia, because its Mandarin name *facai* is pronounced in Cantonese as *fat choy*, which sounds the same as the term for 'wealth and riches'. For this reason it has became a special dish for banquets and all celebrations, particularly at Chinese New Year. Soak the moss in warm water for 1–2 hours, then rinse clean in fresh water before using.

Hair Moss with Dried Oysters

Hair Moss with Dried Oysters

The Chinese title of this dish means 'Wealth and Good Deeds'. As I mentioned, hair moss sounds like 'wealth and riches' in Cantonese, and the name for dried oysters happens to sound like 'good deeds', so this dish is a great favourite at special celebrations.

Serves 4–6
Preparation time 35–40 minutes plus soaking time
Cooking time 6 minutes

175g (6oz) dried oysters, soaked
½ teaspoon salt
1 teaspoon sugar
6 medium-sized dried Chinese mushrooms, soaked
25g (1oz) hair moss, soaked
115g (4oz) sliced bamboo shoots, drained and rinsed
1 medium carrot
3 tablespoons oil
1 clove garlic, chopped
2 spring onions, cut into short sections
A few small bits of peeled fresh ginger
1 tablespoon rice wine
2 tablespoons fermented red bean curd
1 lettuce heart

1 Wash the soaked oysters, place in a bowl with a pinch of salt and sugar, and steam for 15 minutes. Remove, reserving the liquid.

2 Squeeze dry the mushrooms, discarding any hard stalks, and cut each mushroom in half. Rinse the soaked moss, blanch in boiling water for 2–3 minute, drain and rinse again.

3 Drain and rinse the bamboo shoots. Cut the carrot into thin slices the same size as the bamboo shoots.

4 Heat the oil in a preheated wok. Stir-fry the garlic, spring onions and ginger for a few seconds or until fragrant, then add the mushrooms, bamboo shoots and carrot and stir for about 1 minute. Add the oysters and moss with the remaining salt and sugar, blend well and continue stirring for another minute. Add the wine, the fermented bean curd, the liquid in which the oysters were steamed and a little of the mushroom soaking water. Braise for 1 minute or so, and serve hot on a bed of lettuce leaves. A happy and prosperous New Year!

腊腸/香腸

CHINESE SAUSAGES

(LA CHANG/XIANG CHANG)

Liver sausages

The twelfth month of the Chinese calendar, which coincides more or less with January, is called *la yue*. This is when preparation for the New Year starts in earnest – provisions are laid in and cured meats such as bacon, sausages and duck are made in great quantities and hung up outside to dry in the winter sun.

Pork sausages

MANUFACTURE

Commercial sausages are manufactured all year round, while home-made sausages are produced only in the winter months, because of the lack of indoor drying space. In spring and autumn it is too damp outside, and in the summer it is too hot and there is always a risk of storms. The recipe for making sausages is given below. Drying outside takes a week.

APPEARANCE AND TASTE

Chinese sausages are much thinner (about 1.5cm/½in thick) than Western ones and the meat is not chopped so finely. They are more like salami. They taste quite sweet, and are fragrant as well as delicious. Red and white ones are made of pork meat, brown and white ones use pig's liver.

BUYING AND STORING

Chinese pork and liver sausages are available all year round from Oriental stores. They keep for weeks in the refrigerator, and months in the freezer.

CULINARY USES

Chinese sausages should never be eaten raw. The best way to cook them is by steaming them on top of rice. They can also be stir-fried with vegetables if thinly sliced on the diagonal.

PORK SAUSAGE; LIVER SAUSAGE

These are the strings of sausages displayed in the windows of Chinese restaurants.

Makes 24 links
Preparation time about 1 hour plus marinating and 'drying' time
Cooking time 10–12 minutes

675g (1½lb) lean pork, or liver
225g (½lb) pork fat
1 tablespoon salt
2 tablespoons sugar
1 teaspoon five-spice powder
2 tablespoons light soy
150ml (¼ pint) rice wine
About 3m (10ft) sausage casing (chipolata size)
24 pieces of string, each about 10cm (4in) long

1 Coarsely chop the pork/liver and fat. Marinate with the salt, sugar, spice, soy and wine overnight.

2 Attach the casing to the end of a funnel, and tie the other end of the casing with string. Push the meat mixture into the casing through the funnel and squeeze, distributing the meat evenly. The meat should be loosely packed.

3 Once all the meat has been stuffed into the casing, tie off the funnel end. Tie the casing at 15cm (6in) intervals and prick the sausages all over with a fine pin.

4 If you cannot hang the sausages outside to dry as in China, they can be dried indoors by electric fan.

5 To steam the sausages on top of rice, bring rice and water to the boil in a pot, then place the sausages on top of the rice. Reduce the heat to very low, and cook, covered, for 10–12 minutes. Remove, cut into thin, diagonal slices, and serve.

A Chinese 'delicatessen' where items like 'wind-dried' meats and sausagers are available

CHINESE SAUSAGES WITH CHICKEN AND RICE

Another Cantonese speciality, this is a simplified version of Chicken and Rice Wrapped in Lotus Leaves (p 29). Traditionally, this dish is cooked in individual sand-pots. Some restaurants use a section of bamboo trunk as the cooking vessel, which imparts a subtle fragrance to the rice.

Serves 4 as a snack, or 2 as a meal, with 1–2 side dishes
Preparation time 15 minutes plus soaking time
Cooking time 15–20 minutes

225g (8oz) chicken breast fillet
Pinch of salt
1 teaspoon rice wine
2 teaspoons cornflour paste
4–6 dried Chinese mushrooms, soaked
225g (8oz) long grain rice
2–3 Chinese pork sausages, cut diagonally into thin slices
1–2 spring onions, thinly shredded to garnish

For the sauce:
2 tablespoons light soy
1 tablespoon rice wine
½ teaspoon sugar
1 tablespoon finely shredded fresh ginger
½ teaspoon sesame oil

1 Cut the chicken meat into small bite-size pieces, and mix with the salt, wine and cornflour paste. Squeeze dry the mushrooms, discarding any hard stalks, and thinly shred them.

2 Wash the rice once, then place in a casserole or sand-pot with about 300ml (½ pint) water. Bring it to the boil, give it a stir, then place the chicken pieces and shredded mushrooms on top of the rice with the sliced sausage on top of the chicken. Reduce the heat to low, and cook gently, covered, for 15 minutes.

3 Heat the sauce in a small saucepan until almost boiling. Garnish the rice with the shredded spring onions and pour over the sauce. Serve hot.

DRINKS

茶

TEA

(CHA) *Camellia thea*

Oolong tea

Like rice, tea has been a part of daily life in China since time immemorial. We have written proof of a sort that tea was drunk in the sixth century BC and possibly earlier. As you will discover, the subject of tea is of great importance to the Chinese.

Jasmine tea

How It Grows

The tea plant (*Camellia sinensis* or *Thea sinensis*), which likes heavy rainfall, is a native of southwest China, but has spread eastward to cover all of southern China and even certain parts of the north where the climate is not too dry. Left alone, the plant will grow into a tree 3.2m (12ft) tall, but it is pruned to form a low bush 60–90cm (2–3ft) tall for easy picking. The leaves look something like bay leaves, and are still picked by hand, usually every 7–10 days, because the Chinese know that it is the buds that give the most delicately flavoured tea, and that removing the buds causes the plant to send off many new shoots, known as a 'flush'. The best teas come from high mountains and some so steep that monkeys are trained to pick the leaves.

Gunpowder tea

Manufacture

Once they have been gathered Chinese tea leaves are processed in three ways. For green tea such as Gunpowder tea, the fresh leaves are dried by firing immediately after picking to inactivate enzymes and prevent oxidation. For Oolong tea, the leaves are semi-fermented, producing tea halfway between green and black. For black tea, the leaves are wilted, bruised by rolling and allowed to ferment in contact with air, so that they oxidize before they dry.

Appearance and Taste

The name of the tea refers not to the colour of the tea leaves (*cha ye*) but the infusion, yet even so, the names are misleading. Black tea leaves give 'red tea' which is neither red nor black but amber or dark brown and 'green tea' is in fact a pale, yellow colour. Tea varies greatly in aroma and taste – from very delicate green tea to full-bodied strong black tea – and differs from district to district, and harvest to harvest – just like wines.

Buying and Storing

There are probably more varieties of tea in China than varieties of French wine. There are more than fifty different types of tea leaf produced in Sichuan alone and if you add the other dozen or so tea-producing provinces – some with even more varieties, some fewer – the figure is truly staggering. Just as you have wine merchants in the West, so we have tea merchants in China, and tea shops which sell several dozen varieties of tea leaf, mostly loose. Unfortunately, only a few varieties of China tea, always pre-packed, are available in the West. They are sold alongside other goods, and the choice is usually very limited.

Tea leaves, like coffee beans, must be consumed within a few months of purchase, for if you keep them too long, they will not go off, of course, but will lose their aroma and flavour. Always store tea in an air-tight container once out of the original packaging, and obviously consume within the 'use by' date.

Medicinal Uses

The Chinese have always considered tea to be beneficial. In the fourth century AD a Buddhist monk prescribed boiled tea leaves as a cure for the Emperor's headache. By the eighth century, when Lu Yu sat down to write his famous treatise on tea, *The Tea*

Tea Picking at Long Jing, Hangzhou

Classic, the Taoists claimed that it was an important ingredient in the elixir of immortality! In the words of the sixteenth-century herbalist Li Shi-zhen: 'It clears the voice, gives brilliancy to the eye, invigorates the constitution, improves the mental faculties, opens up the avenues of the body, promotes digestion, removes flatulence, and regulates body temperature.'

CULINARY USES

As well as being a beverage (which should not be drunk with meals – see below), tea leaves are sometimes used for cooking in China. Freshwater prawns from the famous West Lake in Hangzhou are cooked with green tea leaves from the equally famous, nearby Long Jing (Dragon Well); it is an exquisite dish combining two most delicate flavours. Another well-known dish is Tea-Smoked Duck from Sichuan, in which a whole duck is marinated with spices for 12 hours, then smoked with tea leaves, camphor wood sawdust and cypress tree branches. After that it is steamed for 3 hours before being deep-fried. The result is a crisp, tender and succulent dish.

THE ART OF MAKING TEA

How one makes tea is very important, particularly the type of water one uses. It is generally agreed that mountain spring water is best, river water second, and well water third. Tap water,

Tea-making in a painting from the Ming dynasty

contaminated with metal and treated with chemicals, is most unsatisfactory and one should never use metal kettles: earthenware is ideal. Tea pots and cups should also be porcelain or earthenware. Do not overboil the water, and always use freshly boiled rather than reheated water.

THE ART OF DRINKING TEA

It goes without saying that one should never add milk nor sugar to China tea, and do not let the tea leaves steep too long– it should be drunk piping hot. Some tea experts insist that the second infusion is the best, as it brings out the true flavour of the tea. At the Oriental Restaurant in London's Dorchester Hotel, the waiter 'washes' the tea leaves first and discards the water, before infusing them in fresh water.

TEA AND FOOD

There is a notion long held in the West that tea is the best thing to drink with Chinese food. What utter nonsense! Just because tea is the most popular beverage in China, that is no reason for it to accompany every meal. Tea is very popular in Britain and India too, but the British do not drink tea with their meals, neither do Indians with their curries. Tea is drunk in China throughout the day but never during meals – except by the Cantonese. You will see Chinese people apparently drinking tea with their meals in restaurants, but that is as an aperitif before the food arrives. Usually there is no charge for the tea; the tip you give to the waiting staff is sometimes called 'tea money'.

In teahouses food is consumed with tea but the tea is the important thing: teahouses don't serve proper meals. There are two types of teahouse in China. First, there is the very modest kind where no food is served except melon seeds to go with your tea – the main purpose of visiting such a place is to drink tea, meet friends, play a game of chess and so on. Some of these teahouses serve a light snack, such as spring rolls, steamed buns, noodles, wonton in soup, and cakes. The second type is almost like a restaurant, where you can eat a wide range of items known as dim sum, the Cantonese for *dian xin*, which literally translates as 'a dot on the heart', meaning: just a light snack. Dim sum are served only during the day, never in the evening, and the Cantonese refer to visiting this type of teahouse as 'drinking tea'.

Why, then, do people drink tea with their meal in Chinese restaurants in the West? The reason lies in the fact that when the first few Chinese restaurants opened in the West at the turn of the century, they were run by people who had migrated from the southern region of China (Canton and Fujian). Very few of these places employed really good chefs

Typical teahouse in Shanghai

Left to right: Green Jasmine tea; Monkey-picked *Ti-kuan-yin* (Iron Goddess of Mercy Tea) and Pu'er tea

or properly trained waiting staff, let alone a wine waiter, with the result that when you dined at a Chinese restaurant there was never anybody with a good understanding of Chinese food and wine to advise you.

When Chinese restaurants proliferated in the mid-sixties, the standard of cooking certainly improved but not the service. The 'teahouse' mentality prevailed even in so-called Peking and Sichuan restaurants, which are mostly run by Cantonese from Hong Kong, who do drink tea with their meals. I shall never forget my surprise on discovering Cantonese drinking tea with their meals when I first visited Hainan Island, for I was brought up to believe that one never drank tea with *cai* dishes (cooked food) at meal times. Chinese tea connoisseurs believe that in order to appreciate the aroma and flavour of a high-quality tea, it should be sipped on its own, maybe with melon seeds or peanuts, but definitely not with strongly flavoured and greasy food. In China, tea is usually served at the end of a meal, as a final course, partly to cleanse the palate, and partly as a gesture by the host to indicate that no more food will be served. I believe that I am one of the very few Chinese food writers to take such a stance about tea and food. The late Kenneth Lo, who was from Fujian and a teetotaller, came to agree with me and in his later works he actually suggested wines to go with some of his recipes.

The Classification of Tea

Besides the three main types of tea (green, oolong, and black), China also produces scented tea and brick tea. All these different teas are made from the leaves of the same plant: it is the processing which distinguishes them. All the tea-producing provinces make the different varieties of tea, with the exception of oolong, which is mainly from Fujian and Taiwan, and brick tea, which is made only in Yunnan province, home of the famous Pu'er tea.

It is impossible to list in this book all the teas made in China. Most are not exported, anyway, so are unavailable in the West. Below are the best known ones that are easily obtainable in Oriental stores and specialist shops.

Green Teas

Long Jing (Dragon Well)
This is generally regarded as China's finest green tea. It comes from the hillside by the famous West Lake in the scenic city of Hangzhou. It has a long history, and it was well established by the Song dynasty, so much so that the poet Su Tung-po (1036–1101) even composed a poem in praise of it. As well as having a distinctive fragrance and subtle flavour, the leaves are unique in that they are flat rather than rolled, and after infusion, the leaves all stand upright

rather than lying down. Since only small quantities of Long Jing are produced each year, the price is extremely high – the top 'before the rains' grade is on a par with gold dust.

Yun Wu (Cloud and Mist)
As its name implies, this tea comes from high mountain cliffs. The best brand is from Mount Lushan in Jiangxi, my parents' home province. Since the third century, poets and scholars have recorded their appreciation of its clarity, beautiful colour and strong flavour. It is known in the West as Pekoe.

Shui Xian (Water Nymph or Narcissus)
A delicate green tea from Fujian's Wuyi Mountains, which lie on the Jiangxi border. Fujian is famous for its red and Oolong teas (see below) – Shui Xian is its one famous green tea.

Gunpowder or Pearl Tea
Another well-known (and popular) green tea from China. It looks grainy, with leaves curled into balls, hence its alternative name of Pearl Tea. The infusion is pale, with a sharp, distinctive taste.

BLACK (RED) TEAS

Keemun Red Tea
A black *gongfu* (*kungfu*) tea from the beautiful Huangshan Mountains in Qimen county in southern Anhui. The best blend has a delicate flavour with a powerful scent. Only green teas were produced in Qimen until 1875, when a certain official from Anhui resigned his post in Fujian, returned home and started making red tea in Qimen, using the techniques he had learnt in Fujian. It is known also as Kungfu Tea because it is so labour intensive and time consuming to produce.

Wuyi Cliff Tea (Bohea Leaf)
The best red tea in China is undoubtedly Wuyi Cliff Tea, known in the West as Bohea Leaf of the Bohea Hills, an English name for the Wuyi Mountains. The Wuyi Mountains lie on the border of Fujian and Jiangxi, and as there are thirty-six cliffs with seventy-two peaks, a wide variety of tea is produced here – red, green and Oolong.

Lapsang Souchong
A large-leafed red tea from Hunan, Fujian and Taiwan, with a distinctive taste of tar and a smoky smell from the fires over which it is dried. Very popular in the West, this tea is produced largely for the export market.

Cake Tea

Pu'er Tea
This unique 'black' tea comes only from Yunnan province in southwest China. This tea is regarded as a medicine as it is an excellent digestive, helping to dissolve fats and neutralize poisons in the digestive tract. There are two types of Pu'er tea on the market: one sold loose in small packages, the other compressed into round 'cake tea' or square 'brick tea'.

OOLONG TEA

Ti-kuan-yin (The Iron Goddess of Mercy)
Generally regarded as the best example of Oolong tea, it is made in Fujian. It has an exquisite fragrance with a very full flavour, and is almost black in colour, hence the name 'iron', which also gives an indication of its strong flavour.

Taiwanese Oolong Tea
Several brands of Oolong teas are made in Taiwan by emigrants from mainland Fujian, just across the Taiwan Strait. They are deservedly popular in Southeast Asia, Europe and North America.

SCENTED TEAS

Jasmine Teas
Green or red tea leaves that are mixed with jasmine flowers and then steam-heated for 5 minutes before being dried in a spin dryer. The flowers are detectable both in the fragrance and taste. The best blends are from Fujian and Jiangxi. There are several other types of scented tea, such as rose, magnolia, chrysanthemum, and lychee but few are exported.

Brick tea

BRICK TEA

Coarse black tea leaves with stalks still attached are steamed and pressed into blocks known as 'bricks'. Made originally for easy transportation to Russia, brick tea is also popular in Tibet, where a small piece is broken off and brewed with yak butter and salt. These bricks (which at one time were used as a form of currency) can be stored for a long time without losing their strong flavour.

Jasmine (*Jasmine officinale*) in full bloom

黄酒

RICE WINE

(HUANG JIU)

Archaeologists have found drinking cups and bowls, and urns for brewing, dating back to the twenty-second century BC, which suggests that the Chinese started making and drinking wine more than four thousand years ago. In the twelfth century BC a form of barm or leaven began to be used in wine-making, which gave control over both the flavour and alcoholic content of wines made from fruits and grains. By the beginning of the Zhou dynasty (around 1028 BC), brewing was an established industry. Strict rules controlling method and quality were enforced by the bureaucrats of the day (the French *appellation controlée* law pales in comparison).

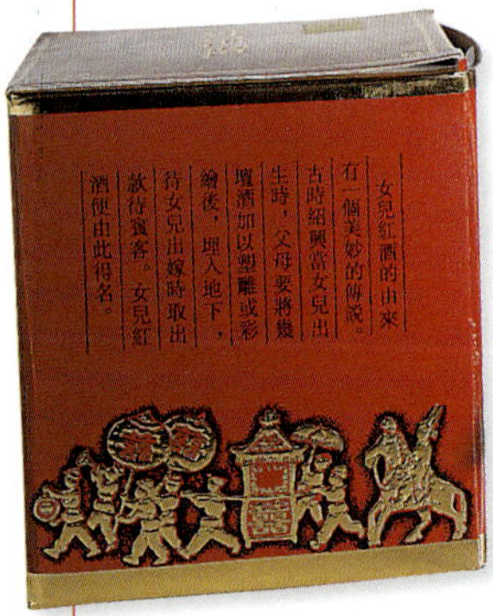

Rice wine packaging – note the traditional wedding procession depicted (left)

Matured Shao Xing wine

MANUFACTURE

Special micro-organisms start the process of alcoholic fermentation, and once you have made the starters, the brewing of rice wine is quite easy. Grains (glutinous rice, millet or ordinary rice) are soaked for about 18 days, then steamed at least once until well-cooked. They are spread out on bamboo mats to cool before being transferred to urns. The starters are dissolved in 'sweet' water (water with a low salt content) and mixed with the meal. After about 4–7 days, the meal floats to the surface, and when the liquid is filtered after 70–90 days, you have wine. It is then stored in sealed urns to mature underground for a minimum of three years before being bottled and sold.

APPEARANCE AND TASTE

Unlike Japanese sake, which is almost colourless, Chinese rice wine ranges from golden amber to dark brown in hue. It is commonly known as *huang jiu* (yellow wine) for this reason. The aroma is quite distinctive: anything from mildly fragrant to powerfully smoky, not unlike a Madeira.

Chinese rice wine is meant to be drunk warm (and not just at room temperature, but heated by standing the pot in hot water) and always with food – it is never served on its own. The warming process intensifies its aroma as well as the rich flavour. Chinese rice wine is medium-dry, and should only be sipped, as it is really quite strong: its alcoholic content can range from 16.5 percent to 18 percent.

BUYING AND STORING

The best-known rice wine, which dates back to 470 BC, is Shao Xing, named after the district south of Hangzhou in Zhejiang province where it is made. What makes Shao Xing wine so special is the water used for its brewing, which comes from a large lake. Very few Chinese rice wines are exported, and most of these are from Shao Xing. It comes in either a glass bottle or a rather attractive earthenware jar. Once opened, it should be consumed within 2–3 months, otherwise it will become insipid.

At weddings, bride and groom will share a cup of rice wine

CULINARY USES

As well as being a 'table wine' drunk with meals, rice wine features strongly in Chinese cooking (p 59). As a table wine, it is always served lukewarm in small porcelain cups, and it should be drunk with the starters – both cold and hot – but not with the main courses, which are usually served with rice.

I mentioned briefly in the Introduction the distinction between *fan* and *cai* in Chinese cooking (p 12), but I did not mention that *cai* dishes are divided into *jiu-cai* (dishes to be eaten with wine, and wine here means any alcoholic beverage, be it beer, rice wine, grape wine, or spirits) or *fan-cai* (dishes to be eaten with rice or other grains). Wine dishes are hot or cold dishes that do not contain any gravy or much sauce, for instance, cold cuts, deep-fried or quickly stir-fried food, and are usually (but not always) served in restaurants rather than homes, except on special occasions or when entertaining. Rice dishes tend to be served with a soup as a 'drink', not with tea or water.

Commercials for medicinal wine are widespread

MEDICINAL AND OTHER USES

Medicinal wines, which have had certain herbs added to the yeast or 'starters' before the fermentation process, have been popular in China since the Western Jin dynasty (265–316). But ordinary rice wine is used in China for medicinal purposes too, as a tonic for the weak, particularly for pregnant women and nursing mothers. At Chinese weddings, it is traditional for the bride and groom each to drink half a cup of wine, then to exchange cups and finish the other's wine, or to share the same cup, each drinking half. It is a sign that they are man and wife, and that they will love and respect each other forever.

Medicinal herbs are added to all sorts of wines in China

THE DIFFERENT VARIETIES OF RICE WINE

SHAO XING

The best Shao Xing wines are supposed to be over a hundred years old, but most are only 3–5 years old. I was recently presented with an 8-year-old bottle, the kind normally served at state banquets – it had a deep amber colour and tasted rather wonderful. When I visited my father in Hong Kong in 1979, he held a special dinner party in my honour as we hadn't seen each other for quite a number of years. We had a Shao Xing wine that was over forty years old, and when the seal of the urn was broken, the aroma was so powerful that it filled the whole room, and lingered in the air for the entire evening.

Of the whole range of Shao Xing wines, the following brands are commonly found in Oriental stores in the West.

Eight-year old Hua Diao from Shao Xing

Hua Diao (Carved Flower) The most famous and popular of all Shao Xing wines. The name refers to the pretty patterns carved on the urns in which wines are stored. Another name for Hua Diao is Nu Er Hong (Daughter's Red Wine), which has romantic origins. It used to be the custom to store a few urns of Hua Diao on the birth of a daughter to be given as part of her dowry and to be drunk at her wedding feast, normally 17–19 years later – a practice not dissimilar to the British tradition of laying down port for a son's coming of age.

Yuan Hong (Primary Red) Reddish amber in colour with a distinctive bouquet and flavour, this has a slightly bitter aftertaste. About 15–16 percent volume.

Jia Fan (Rice Added) Quite a popular blend because of the added glutinous rice, it tastes sweeter than Yuan Hong and has a higher alcohol content (16–17 percent volume).

Jia Fan rice wine

Shan Niang (Fine Brew) Brewed with matured Yuan Hong instead of water, then stored for at least three years before going on sale, this wine has a unique bouquet and flavour. It is soft and round, yet quite low in alcohol (13–14 percent volume) compared with other rice wines.

Xiang Xue (Fragrant Snow) Fortified with spirit distilled from *jia fan* mash (the dregs left after brewing), it is quite high in alcohol (20–24 percent volume), yet is very smooth with a powerful aroma. It is deep amber in colour and, unlike all the other rice wines, it should not be warmed before serving.

CHEN GANG (SUNKEN URN)

This is another famous 'yellow wine' from Fujian. The most plausible explanation for its name is that during the process of brewing, the empty saccules known as 'floating ants' that float to the surface have to sink and resurface three times until they finally sink to the bottom of the urn. Like Shao Xing wine, Chen Gang is fragrant and deep amber in colour, but is a little sweeter in taste.

GLUTINOUS RICE WINE

While 'yellow wine' is made from a blend of different rice grains, glutinous rice wine uses just one type: glutinous rice. Much glutinous rice wine is home made, as it is very simple to brew (glutinous rice has a high sugar content, which makes the fermentation process that much easier and quicker). It requires no time to mature. Commercially made glutinous rice wine is usually blended with herbs and other unmentionable items (snakes, lizards, tiger bone and dog's penis amongst them) as medicinal wine.

Porcelain wine pot and cups

DRINKING WINE

Hu Ssu-hui (or Hoshoi), the Imperial Dietician between 1315 and 1330, late in the Yuan dynasty, wrote in *Yinshi Chengyao (The Correct Guide to Drinks and Food)*:

Do not over-indulge yourself when drinking wine.

If you must get drunk, do not get dead drunk, or you will feel ill for the rest of your life.

Do not drink wine incessantly: it is bad for your stomach.

When drunk, do not ride a horse or jump about: you may injure yourself.

When drunk, do not have sexual intercourse. It will give you a spotty face at best, and diarrhoea and dysentery at worst.

When drunk, do not lose your temper or shout loudly.

When drunk, do not fall asleep in draughts.

Never drink wine without food.

Avoid sweet food with wine.

Do not lift heavy weights if drunk.

Do not take a bath if drunk: it will give you an eye ailment.

If you have an eye infection, avoid getting drunk and eating garlic at the same time.

Celebrate the New Year with a cup of rice wine

白酒

Distilled Spirits

(BAI JIU)

Mou-tai

Spirits distilled from various grains are mentioned in China's earliest book on wine by Zhu Yi of the Southern Song dynasty (420–479), and we know that distillation has been practised in China for more than 2,500 years. Alchemists used it to extract the essence from herbs and other plants in search of the elixir of life – the progression from fermented wine to distilled spirit was merely a matter of time but it is difficult to pinpoint exactly when it happened because one word, *jiu*, is used to mean any alcoholic beverage.

Manufacture

Distillation operates on a very basic principle: when the liquid (in this case, fermented wine) is boiled, the more volatile elements vaporize first and can be collected and converted back to liquid in a purer and more concentrated form. This is the distilled spirit. Sometimes the spirit is put through the same process for a second or third time.

Appearance and Taste

Pure spirit is colourless and the taste depends on the grains used and whether herbs or spices have been added. The alcohol content also affects the flavour of the end product. Most Chinese spirits are on average much stronger than any Western spirit, and are an acquired taste. For a people with such a sophisticated approach to food and such a highly developed cuisine, the Chinese are remarkably indiscriminate about alcoholic drinks. Most Chinese do not distinguish between fermented wine, in which the alcoholic content is low, and distilled spirits, in which it is high. We have a much wider range of distilled spirits than fermented wine in China because whereas almost all rice wines are made from rice or millet, spirits are made from a variety of grains, with some brands containing added herbs.

Buying and Storing

Very few Chinese spirits are available in the West. They are usually sold in decorative porcelain jars or glass bottles with colourful labels. Some of the descriptions in English make puzzling reading – I'll try to decipher them for you in the following pages. The high alcohol content means they keep for a long time: for perhaps a year after opening.

Medicinal Uses

Most Chinese spirits have medicinal properties, and are supposed to benefit one's health one way or another, if taken in small doses.

Culinary Uses

As well as being used as a table wine in China, Chinese spirits are sometimes used for cooking. They are also used extensively in preserving and pickling.

The Different Varieties of Chinese Spirit

Mou-tai

Mou-Tai is without doubt China's Number One spirit: it is used for toasts at state banquets and other official occasions. It comes from a village of the same name (meaning Thatched Terrace in Chinese) just south of the Sichuan border in north Guizhou province in southwest China. The special feature of this spirit is the water used, taken from a stream running through a nearby gorge. The climate is moist and warm, and a thin layer of mist hovers permanently over the fast-flowing stream. The distillery was established back in 1529, but nothing much happened to the product until 1704,

Shaanxi depiction of harvesting

when a salt merchant from Shaanxi in north China visited Mou-Tai on business and was so enchanted by the beauty of the village that he decided to settle down there. Using the technique employed in his native province for making the famous *Xifeng*, the man blended sorghum with other grains and started to distil Mou-Tai with water from the nearby stream. It soon attracted attention all over the country, and since 1915, it has enjoyed a worldwide reputation.

Mou-Tai is very strong, its alcoholic strength being 53 percent volume (106 proof), therefore it should not be trifled with.

Fen Chiew

This spirit from a village called Apricot Blossom in northern Shanxi has a history of well over fifteen hundred years. It is made from sorghum and millet, and owes its unique quality to the water of a tributary of the famous Yellow River. It has always been greatly appreciated by poets. The great Tang poet, Tu Fu (712–770), even composed a famous poem in praise of it. The last two lines of his poem about the Qing Ming festival appear on every jar of Fen Chiew:

Upon inquiring where to find a good wine shop
The shepherd points to the village of Apricot Blossom in the distance.

Chu Yeh Ching (Bamboo Leaf Green)

This is really a medicinal liqueur. It also comes from the village of Apricot Blossom and uses Fen Chiew as its base, blending it with no fewer than twelve different flavourings, including dried orange peel and bamboo leaves. Hence the name, for instead of being colourless like all other spirits, Bamboo Leaf Green has a pale green tint and tastes very refreshing despite being 47 percent volume.

Chu yeh ching

Wu Liang Ye (Five-Grain Liqueur)

This heady spirit from Sichuan has a history of over 1,200 years. It has a very powerful aroma that fills the entire room when the bottle or jar is opened. The five grains are sorghum, rice, glutinous rice (the last two in their husks), sweet corn and wheat (unhusked also). The usual alcoholic strength is 60 percent volume, but it is reduced to about 52 percent for export. I have to confess that I have rather a weakness for this particular liqueur.

Fragrant rose petals

Mei Kuei Lu (Rose Dew)

This is a quite sweet liqueur. Distilled from sorghum and other grains, it is blended with rose petals and other aromatic herbs. It is very fragrant and pleasant to drink.

Wu Chia Pi (Five-Layer Skin)

This is also made of sorghum but caramel essence is added, which gives it a slightly burnt taste not unlike a Madeira, only much stronger as it is well over 50 percent volume. It is used medicinally as well as being drunk socially.

Wu liang ye

Dong chiew

Dong Chiew (Dong Mellow Wine)

Nicknamed 'Son of Mou-Tai', because it comes from a place nearby in Guizhou and is made by a retired distiller from its more illustrious neighbour, Dong Chiew has sorghum and glutinous rice as its main ingredients. Its alcoholic strength can reach as high as 58–60 percent for the domestic market; it is reduced to around 48 percent volume for export, still quite strong by Western standards.

A few more brands make an occasional appearance in the West, but they are similar to the ones already mentioned: above 40 percent in alcoholic volume, with sorghum as the main ingredient. The taste does not, to my mind, vary that much – but then, my favourite digestif is a good French cognac.

SELECT BIBLIOGRAPHY

As can be expected, I have consulted numerous publications, both in Chinese and English, during the course of research for this book. I have listed below a selection of the major works originally written in English, and a few of the Chinese works that have been translated into the English language.

An English-Chinese Dictionary of Botany.
Scientific Publishing House, Beijing 1978

An English-Chinese Dictionary of Food Science and Technology.
Shanghai Science & Technology Publishing, Shanghai 1982

Bailey, Adrian:
The Book of Ingredients.
Michael Joseph, London 1980

Bharadwaj, Monisha:
The Indian Pantry.
Kyle Cathie, London 1996

Chang, Chung-yuan:
Creativity and Taoism.
Wildwood House, London, 1963

Chang, K. C. (ed):
Food in Chinese Culture.
Yale University Press, New Haven & London 1977

Cheng, F. T.:
Musings of a Chinese Gourmet.
Hutchinson, London 1954

China Pictorial (ed):
The Secrets of the Master Chefs of China.
Allen D. Bragdon, New York 1983

Chinese Cooking (English Edition).
Zhaohua Publishing House, Beijing 1986

Dahlen, Martha & Karen Phillips:
A Guide To Chinese Market Vegetables.
South China Morning Post, Hong Kong 1980

__________:
A Further Guide To Chinese Market Vegetables.
South China Morning Post, Hong Kong 1981

Fieldhouse, Paul:
Food & Nutrition: Customs & Culture.
Croom Helm, London 1986

Gong Dan:
Food and Drink In China.
New World Press, Beijing 1986

Harrington, Geri:
Grow Your Own Chinese Vegetables.
Collier Books, New York 1978

Hsiung, Deh-Ta:
Chinese Cookery Secrets. Elliot Right Way Books, UK 1997

__________:
Chinese Regional Cooking.
Macdonald, London 1979

__________:
Chinese Vegetarian Cooking.
The Apple Press, London 1985

__________:
The Festive Food of China.
Kyle Cathie, London 1991

__________:
The Home Book of Chinese Cookery (Revised Edition).
Faber, London & Boston 1987

Institute of the History of Natural Sciences, Chinese Academy of Sciences (ed):
Ancient China's Technology and Science.
Foreign Languages Press, Beijing 1983

Keys, John D.:
Chinese Herbs.
Charles E. Tuttle, Rutland, Vermont & Tokyo, Japan 1976

Li Shih-chen (1518-1593):
Chinese Medicinal Herbs,
Translated and Researched by F. Porter Smith MD & G. A. Stuart MD. Georgetown Press, San Francisco 1973

Liao, Sung J. (ed):
Chinese-English Terminology of Traditional Chinese Medicine.
Hunan Science and Technology Publishing, Changsha, Hunan, China 1983

Lo, Kenneth:
A Guide to Chinese Eating.
Phaidon Press, Oxford 1976

Loewe Michael:
Everyday Life in Early Imperial China.
Carousel Books, London 1973

Lu, Henry C.:
Chinese System of Food Cures.
Sterling Publishing, New York 1986

Lu Yu (733-804):
The Classic of Tea,
Translated by Francis Ross Carpenter. Little Brown, Boston & Toronto 1974

Mayes, Adrienne Ph.D.:
The Dictionary of Nutritional Health.
Thorsons Publishing, Wellingborough & New York 1986

Montagne, Prosper:
New Larousse Gastronomique,
Translated from the French by Marion Hunter MIL, and Edited by Janet Dunbar.
Hamlyn Publishing, London 1977

Shih, Sheng-han:
A Preliminary Survey of CHI MIN YAO SHU - An Agricultural Encyclopaedia of the 6th Century.
Science Press, Beijing 1982

Stobart, Tom:
The Cook's Encyclopaedia.
Macmillan, London 1982

Tropp, Barbara:
The Modern Art of Chinese Cooking.
William Morrow, New York 1982

SOME USEFUL ADDRESSES

There are a great number of Chinese and Oriental provision stores throughout the world. In the larger cities they usually centre around a district known as Chinatown, otherwise, your local Chinese restaurants should be able to tell you the name and address of their supplier.

THE BRITISH ISLES

ENGLAND

Birmingham
Wing Yip, 375 Nechells Park Road, Nechells, Birmingham B6 5NT

Janson Hong, St Martins House, 17-18 Bull Ring, Birmingham B5 5DD

Leeds
Wing Lee Hong, 6 Edward Street, Leeds LS2 7NN

Liverpool
Chung Wah, 31-32 Great George Square, Liverpool L1 5DZ

Hondo, 5-11 Upper Duke Street, Liverpool L1 9DU

London
Wing Yip, 395 Edgware Road, Cricklewood, London NW2 6LN

Wing Yip, 550 Purley Way, Croydon CR0 4RF

Loon Fung, 42-44 Gerrard Street, London W1V 7LP

Loon Moon, 9A Gerrard Street, London W1V 7LJ

See Woo Supermarket, 18-20 Lisle Street, London WC2

Hoo Hing, A406 North Circular Road, Near Hanger Lane, Park Royal, London NW10

Manchester
Wing Yip, Oldham Road, Ancoats, Manchester M8 4BA
Wing Fat, 49 Faulkner Street, Manchester M1 4EE

Newcastle
Eastern Pearl, 27-31 Fenkle Street, Newcastle-upon-Tyne NE1 5XN

Oxford
Lung Wah Chong, 41-42 Hythe Bridge Street, Oxford OX1 2EP

Portsmouth
Sun Hun Chan, 6 Tricorn Shopping Centre, Portsmouth, Hampshire PO1 4AE

SCOTLAND

Edinburgh
Pats Chung Ying, 199 Leith Walk, Edinburgh EH6 8NX

Glasgow
Hongs, 7A Bath Street, Glasgow G2 1AA

WALES

Cardiff
Global Foods, Stadium Close, Cardiff CF1 7TS

NORTHERN IRELAND

Belfast
H A S International Foods, 189 Ormeau Road, Belfast BT7 1SQ

REPUBLIC OF IRELAND

Dublin
Chinaco, 67 Bride Street (off Camden Street), Dublin 8

INDEX

All recipe names are in bold

PHOTOGRAPHIC ACKNOWLEDGEMENTS

KEY
AB – Adrian Bradshaw
DT – David Tipling
JD – Julie Dixon
KO – Kate Oldfield
LH – Laura Hodgson
MR – Martyn Rix
RP – Roger Phillips
NH – Nigel Hicks
MF – Michael Freeman

BAL – Bridgeman Art Library
HL – Hutchison Library
WWI – Woodfall Wild Images
Link – Link Picture Library
IBM – Ingrid Booze Morejohn
PB – Paddy Booze
SRG – Sally and Richard Greenhill
RGS – Royal Geographic Society

All recipe photography by Julie Dixon

1 JD
2–3 RGS (Chris Caldicott)
5 JD
7 Link (PB)
8–9 Link (IBM)
10 BAL
11 Link (PB)
12 AB
13 Link (IBM)
14 Link (PB)
15 Windrush (DT)
16 AB
17 AB
19–21 JD
22–23 Link (IBM)
24 top right, left JD; bottom right NH
25 SRG
26 top left SRG; bottom right NH
28 left JD; bottom right SRG
30 top right NH; 30 middle left JD; bottom left MF
32 left JD; bottom right HL (Michael Macintyre)
34 left, bottom right JD
35 top right JD; bottom left SRG
36 top JD; bottom right HL (N. Durrel McKenna)
38 middle GH; bottom right Windrush (DT)
40 top right HL (Trevor Page); bottom left KO
42 top right Link (PB); bottom left Link (IBM)
43 top right Link (IBM); bottom left to right JD
44 top left JD; top right SRG
46 top right, bottom left JD; bottom right BAL
48 JD
49 JD
50 JD
51 top right Windrush (DT); middle left JD; bottom left JAC
52 top right JD; middle left NH; bottom right SRG;
54 JD
55 top right AZ; middle right AZ; bottom left AZ (Dan Sams)
56–57 Link (PB)
58 JD
59 JD
60 JD
61 top right JD; middle left RGS (Peter Hibard)
62 top right HL(Christine Pemberton); middle left JD; bottom right NH
63 top right AB; middle left, bottom right JD
64 top, bottom left JD; bottom right NH
65 Link (IBM)
68 JD
69 JD
68 top right SRG (Sam Greenhill); bottom left JD
70 JD
71 Link (IBM)
72–73 AB
74 JD
75 JD
76 top right Link (PB); top left JD; bottom left AZ (Michael Jones)
78 JD
79 JD
80 top right AB; bottom left JD
82 top right Link (IBM); middle left JD; bottom middle Link (IBM)
84 top right, left JD; bottom right Link (IBM)
85 JD
86 middle Link (IBM); bottom left JD
87 middle left AB
88 top right, middle JD; bottom right MF
90 top right JD; bottom middle Link (IBM)
92 middle JD; bottom right Link (IBM)
94 JD
95 top left JD; bottom right NH
96 top left JD; bottom left SRG
97 JD
98 middle JD; bottom left MR
100 top right AZ (Rosemary Greenwood); middle left JD
101 JD
102 top right JD; centre Link (IBM)
103 JD
104 middle left JD; bottom right Link (PB)
105 NH
106–7 NH
108 middle left, bottom left JD; middle right MR
110 middle left JD; bottom left MR; bottom right AB
112 middle, bottom middle JD; bottom right AB
114 middle left JD; bottom right AZ (Maurice Nimmo)
116 JD
117 JD
118 top left JD; bottom right: AZ (Perry Joseph)
120 JD
121 top left JD; bottom left SRG
122 JD
123 JD
124 top right JD; bottom middle Windrush (DT)
126–127 AB
128 top right JD; middle left MR; bottom right AB
130 JD
131 bottom middle MR
132 bottom left JD; middle right AB
134 top right, bottom left JD; middle left AZ(Bob Gibbons)
136 top right MR; bottom right JD
138 top right, bottom right MR; bottom left JD
140 top right Link (IBM); middle left, bottom right JD; bottom left MR
142 middle JD; 142 bottom right NH
143 JD
144 middle JD; bottom middle NH
145 JD
146 top right NH; middle left, bottom right JD; bottom left Link (IBM)
148 JD
150 top middle SRG; middle left, bottom right JD
152 top left JD; bottom right Link (IBM)
154 middle JD; bottom middle SRG
156–157 NH
158 top right SRG; middle JD; bottom right MF
160 top right AZ (David Henderson); middle JD; bottom left NH
162 JD
163 JD
164 middle left JD; top right SRG
166 middle left NH; bottom middle JD
167 JD
168–169 Link (IBM)
170 left JD; middle MF; bottom right SRG
172 middle left JD; bottom right SRG
173 Windrush (DT)
174 middle left JD; top right Link (IBM)
176 middle left JD; top right Link (PB); bottom right Link (IBM)
178 bottom left JD; top right Windrush (DT)
180–181 SRG
182 middle, bottom middle JD; top right KO
183 top right Link (PB)
184 middle left JD; bottom right Windrush (DT)
186 middle NH; bottom left JD
188 middle JD; top right PB
190 left AZ (Mike Maidment); bottom middle JD
192 JD
193 JD
194 top left, right JD; bottom right SRG (Richard Greenhill)
196 top right, middle left JD; bottom right Link (PB)
197 Link (PB)
198 SRG
200 top left JD; bottom left SRG
201 middle JD; bottom left NH
202 top left, middle JD; bottom middle Link (PB)
204 top left JD; bottom right Windrush (DT)
206 JD
207 middle left JD; top right MF
208 top JD; bottom LH
210 middle JD; top right WWI (George Gornacz)
212 top left, middle JD; top right SRG; bottom left WWI (Mike Powles)
214 middle JD; bottom right NH
216 middle Link (IBM); bottom left JD
217 JD
218 middle JD; bottom right Link (IBM)
219 JD
220 top left, middle JD; bottom right Link (IBM)
222–223 SRG
224 left JD; bottom right Link (IBM)
225 top left BAL; bottom right Link (IBM)
226 JD
227 top right, middle JD; bottom right AZ (Maurice Nimmo)
228 JD
229 top left AB; top right Link (IBM); bottom right NH
230 JD
231 AB
232 top left JD; bottom right Link (IBM)
233 top NH; middle left, right, bottom JD